SKY
FULL OF
STARS

SKY FULL OF STARS

PENPALS ACROSS A CENTURY

SHEILA KENNARD & HAROLD MUSSON

Denise Tombs of Den@Zen Design created the book cover; the front is a composite picture of Étaples Cemetery and Southern Cross night sky. The photo of Étaples Cemetery is by Tony Emptage. Isla Kennard took the photo of Sheila amidst great hilarity.

Published 2017
by Sheila Kennard

ISBN 978-0-473-40772-8

© Copyright 2017
All rights reserved.

Except for the purpose of fair reviewing, no part of this publication may be reproduced or transmitted in any form or by any means, electronic or mechanical, including photocopying, recording or any information storage and retrieval system, without prior written permission from the publisher.

Printed by The Copy Press, Nelson, New Zealand. www.copypress.co.nz

*Dedicated to the family of
Harold and Con Musson,
in particular
Isla Beth Kennard
who handed me the
inspiration to create this book.*

Harold and Constance Musson – date unknown.

Contents

Introduction	ix
Who's who	xi
1916–2017	1
July 1916	7
August 1916	35
September 1916	73
October 1916	105
November 1916	133
December 1916	161
January 1917	181
February 1917	203
March 1917	229
April 1917	257
May 1917	281
June 1917	319
July 1917	351
August 1917	361
26 September 1917	367
October 1917	371
Acknowledgements	*377*
Bibliography & Resources	*378*

Introduction

Life has a funny way of making unexpected plans, and *Sky Full of Stars* is a perfect example of that. The idea for this was born on Anzac Day 2014, a promise made to my granddaughter Isla, after a rather harrowing experience at a re-enactment of life in the trenches of France during The Great War. My initial intention was to write up the letters from Harold Musson to his wife, Con, in a legible form as a gift for my husband Jim, Harold's grandson. However, Harold appeared to have different ideas for me as he crept into my psyche and, thanks to modern technology, revealed himself.

I knew that I had to do something with the letters, yet I did not want to simply produce a dry account of my findings. I wanted the letters to be used to teach, and to pass on the message that peace, and not war, is the better way forward. I viewed the letters as not just from Harold, but also from every man in the conflict writing to a loved one. For me, Harold's voice became many and I felt at times haunted by them as they asked for their stories to be told. I wanted to tell Harold this and the best way I felt was to become his penpal; in this way I could tell him of all the things that had revealed themselves to me.

Harold and Con travelled to England in 1916 from their home in Argentina, with a three-month-old baby, so that he could join the Royal Field Artillery as an officer. Con was able to live with her father in his comfortable home, known as *Westhanger,* in Surrey.

Harold often mentioned that he was not a great communicator of the written word; his letters were written on paper of varied quality, often in pencil and difficult to read. I introduced paragraphs into the manuscript, and occasionally made small changes in order for his words to make more sense. His story telling was at times muddled, his initial excitement turning to resignation as time passed. Harold also added a few words in Argentine Spanish; I have translated these in the text, although I had help with the longer passages.

I have no replies to Harold's letters, and I could only imagine the impact the war had on Con. I was able to get a sense of them both; they undoubtedly had lots of friends and acquaintances alongside their strong family ties. Harold frequently mentions names, some of them I was able to find, and they have become key players in his story. Others I know nothing about, but have left their names in as they form an essential part of Harold and Con's story. I feel they loved life and took all they could from it.

The letters make up a historic document, I have added to that with the use of footnotes as a guide for those who may want to explore further. The list of names will assist in identifying who's who. The maps are simple, created by Jim to show route marches and places of action as deciphered from Harold's diaries. Many of the photos are over a hundred years old; they are not clear yet they tell their own story. Harold also kept diaries that record his daily actions and whereabouts; in typical British fashion they normally ended up with a comment on what the weather was doing.

The journey of the letters has been amazing for me, and I now invite you to share and to glean all you need from the following pages.

Who's who

This list shows the key players in the letters, there are more names of people that I have not been able to identify.

Harold's family members:

Ethel	Harold's older sister, married to Hugh. I think that references to a child named Jack is their son.
Eric	Harold's younger brother. He married Susan; baby Peter is their son.
Aunt Janie	Harold's maternal aunt.
Aunt Bella	Harold's maternal aunt.
Uncle Fred	Harold's maternal uncle.

Con's family members:

Donald	Con's eldest brother.
Beatie	Con's twin sister.
Raymond	Con's younger brother.
Kathleen	Con's younger sister and a VAD nurse.
Helen	Con's youngest sister and a VAD nurse.

Other people mentioned in the letters that I have been able to identify:

The Captain	Neil Fraser-Tytler, captain of Harold's Battery.
Flurry	Lt. Florence Crimmin, a close friend.
John Campbell	A friend from Argentina and polo player, married to Myra.
Lucy	A friend from Argentina, possibly also a polo player.
Patsy	A friend from Argentina, possibly also a polo player.
Alice	Bindy's nanny.

> In the hospitality of war we left them
> their dead to remember us by.
>
> Archilochus 680 – 645 B.C.

The War

Guns bang,
soldiers walk around the battlefield nervously
waiting for the dreaded battle to begin.
Digging of trenches is happening.
Soldiers hiding from their enemies.
Soldier's wives hoping their husband will survive.
Bombs exploding.
Hear aeroplanes in the distance.
Dust flying everywhere,
the foul smell fills the air.
Young soldiers frozen with fear shouting, "I can't get up, I can't get up."
Shells fly over the place and metal bits kill people.
People fall to the ground gasping for breath.
Soldiers refusing to fight,
shouting of the general can be heard from miles away.
There are no trenches to be seen only dead bodies.
A few years later poppies bloom in the field as remembrance.

Lest we forget.

© Isla Kennard, 2014 (aged nine)

1916–2017

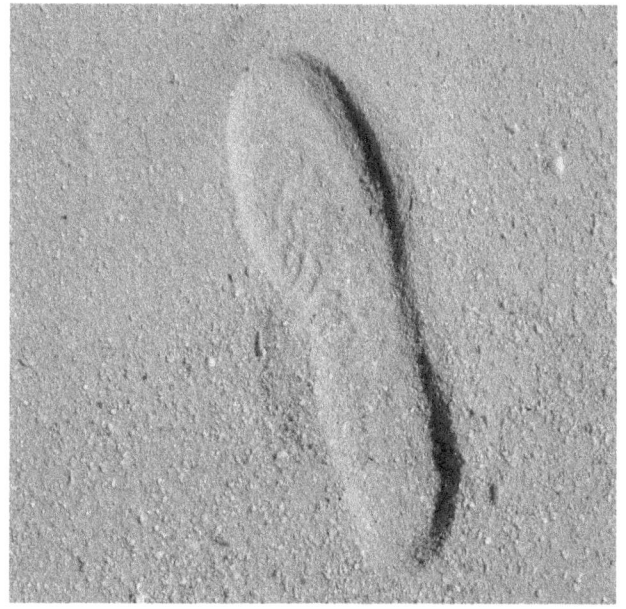

A journey through the sands of time
Starts with a single step.
Sheila Kennard

> School of Instruction
> R.H & R.F.A.*
> Lark Hill
> Salisbury
> 16 June 1916

Dearest Lassie,

Here we are, and find the place quite comfortable. We are treated as officers, and do not salute anybody except staff officers. Inglis and I are quartered in one room, which is very nice, and have a very decent batman to look after us. On arrival here we were told that no beds or blankets were given, so expected a fine nights rest, however after a talk with the batman, he procured beds, mattresses, pillows etc., so are like kings. The mess room seems good and clean which is the chief thing. Have a very comfortable smoking, writing and reading room combined, just like Eric had, only a good deal bigger. The manual work here is easy, but there are a lot of lectures etc., and one has to study up hard, which is about 2½ hours studying at night. We breakfast at 7.30 and parade at 8.30.

The camp is situated right at the top of a hill, like Stonehenge and should think that in winter it must be the devil. Today is a grand day but a strong wind, which buzzes round the corners. It is a big place, but will give you all particulars by next letter.

Re rooms, Brockman has had a good look round, and at present every corner is filled up, it is sickening but hope that there will soon be a few vacancies. Tonight I have no time to go round, as we only arrived here at 4 p.m. and am busy settling down and getting things ready for tomorrow. Durrington looks quite a nice wee place and is about a twenty-minute walk from here and I think there are plenty of taxis to take one back and forwards. Am going to get our batman to go down and find out if there are any rooms to be had.

I got an hour off after reporting myself at 9.30 so went round and saw Aunt Janie, and then we both went to Milford for a few minutes, to say adios. If we can get rooms here Aunt Janie is very keen on coming, which would be nice and I think will do her good, as she is feeling very lonely at the flat and longing to have you and Bindy back, so whenever you are in town try and get round to see her.

Have just discovered there is no post after 4.30, so this will leave by tomorrow's post at 8.30 a.m. Well sweetheart, hope you got back safely and are feeling yourself again, and that wretched sick feeling gone. You must get very

---

*   Royal Horse and Royal Field Artillery

fit and do not try to do too much. Give my love to all and will let you know as soon as possible about rooms. Am just off for a walk round the camp, so as to find my bearings.

Night night and best of love to you two dears.

Your loving
Harold

Nelson
New Zealand
2017

Dear Harold,

Life is the most mysterious thing, how could I have known what my encounter with you would become when I first opened that tatty brown envelope and untied those three bundles of letters, tied up with tartan ribbon. I had no idea that you would creep into my life, and I would become a willing voyeur. What was initially a small idea would grow into this amazing adventure that I feel I have shared with you. It is almost as though you have been an absent magician, transforming me and giving me the gift of creation. You have drip-fed me secrets, dropped them as gifts into my lap, and watched and applauded as I have unravelled them. Not only have I discovered you, but also your friends and acquaintances, and all through one year of letters to your beloved Con. My journey with you has been extraordinary, I felt the best way to share it with you was through letters, to become your penpal across a century.

    A Chinese proverb tells of the red thread, which I feel is most fitting for all the unexpected meetings I have had through your letters: -

An invisible red thread connects those
who are destined to meet,
regardless of time, place or circumstance.
The thread may stretch or tangle
but will never break.

I only got to know Con through the letters, I did not meet her. She died during my first year of marriage to your grandson, Jim, while we were living in Hong Kong. I wonder if you were there to meet her when she took her final walk, reunited once again.

    I can tell you that Jim adored her. She was known as Gwally to him and your two granddaughters, Olivia and Angela. One recurring memory for Jim is her Sunday trifle, as her age increased so did the amount of sherry that was tipped in. Other than that, I am afraid I know little of her. I got to know her through your letters; I guess that the ones she wrote to you were lost, maybe buried in mud and grime. I have been able to feel her presence in the letters you lovingly wrote, almost on a daily basis, regretting the days you missed.

However, I cannot even begin to imagine having to walk a mile in her shoes throughout that year and beyond.

I wonder what made you decide to leave your beloved ranch, *Estancia Lucero*, in Argentina and travel to England to take part in this war. Perhaps you, like so many British who lived abroad still regarded England as home, and so felt it your patriotic duty to defend your homeland. You had all your life before you, your marriage to Con was still relatively new and you had a tiny daughter.

The Great War started in 1914 and would last four years. It had been going for a couple of years before you arrived to take up arms and join the campaign on the Western Front, which mostly took place in trenches. The war was between alliances of countries, known as The Allies and The Central Powers. The Allies consisted of Great Britain, France and Russia, and were known as the Triple Entente, member countries of the British Empire fought alongside them, and America entered the arena after you did. The Central Powers were Germany and Austria-Hungary; they were joined later by The Ottoman Empire and Bulgaria. There were many factors that led to the outbreak of war, but the one deciding factor was the assassination of Archduke Ferdinand of Austria by The Black Hand organization of Serbia, and events snowballed from that point. Of course you knew all of this, you understood that those in politics and power were prepared to lose young men and women for their own cause, and so you offered yourself, brave or mad, I am not honestly sure.

I see that your letters are a catalyst for change; we need that in the world right now. Sadly your war was not the last. The world today remains a tinderbox, I wish I could tell you that humankind has settled into a peaceful existence, but I can't. But I believe that your legacy of these letters can be an instrument of change, and I am so pleased that I am able to assist you in this.

With love

Sheila

July 1916

The Borderers Polo Team – date unknown.

This team in so great a demand,
It beats others hand over hand
Though with practice rare
Their play is so fare
They deserve to be first in the land.
Ode to the Borderers – writer unknown 1913

South Western Hotel, Southampton
10 July 1916 – 6 p.m.

Dearest Con,

Just a wee note to let you know that I have got this far, and we have to be on board at 7 p.m. and arrive at Le Havre about 5 a.m., this is where we think we are going, but are not certain. Have just had a huge tea with Patsy and feel well stoked, and ought to keep the load from pitching about. The crossing ought to be smooth. There are about 200 officers on board to go across on the *Archangel*.

It was just horrid seeing you disappear on the platform and felt an awful wrench at leaving you, poor girl, you had such a rotten time, but was very glad you had dear Aunt Janie with you, and am sure you must have been. Anyhow darling we must look forward to our next meeting and keep up a brave heart; you may depend on it that I will get back as soon as possible. Bindy will be a great comfort to you.

There seems to be no chance of getting a bed on the boat, they were all booked up before we arrived, but will try and get one out of the chief steward. The place is full of troops, both coming and going.

Well darling best of luck and keep fit for me, time will soon go. Give a big hug to Bindy and hundreds to you, but only wish I had the satisfaction of giving them to you. Must be off now.

Your loving
Harold

To send:
Nail scissors
Suspenders
Housewife *(sewing kit)*
Profactor gut
Pyjamas?

11 July 1916

Dearest,

Just a wee line to let you know that so far we have arrived safely and will probably be here for 2 or 3 days. I managed to get a bunk and quite a good crossing, a slight movement but nothing very much.

We have quite comfortable billets and everything is kept in good order, flowers all over the place and what grass there is, is very well kept. There are 6 of us in one hut, rather crowded, as there are a good many of us here at present. I have just met Bowen, you remember him, (the Rabbit) and he has been out here about 10 months.

There is absolutely no news and cannot rake up any to give you. I expect Kathleen will be leaving Godalming today and come over tomorrow, hope I shall come across her.

Best of love darling, and write soon.

Your loving
Harold

British Officers' Club,
A.P.O. No. 1
B.E.F*
12 July 1916

Darling Con,
Am afraid that this notita will arrive rather soon on top of the last one, as it was only posted today. We have been having a very slack time of it here, in fact we have done nothing except eat, sleep and go for walks. Le Havre is a very slow place and nothing to do at all, so got my haircut and finished off my shopping. Tomorrow we move off, I have been posted to the 30th Division, but do not know which battery I go to, or what part of the line it is in; expect we will be four or five days getting there, and am afraid very little chance of writing to your dear self, but will do my best, as I may probably be in Rouen on Friday.

I am sorry to say that Patsy and I have been split up, and am going with 12 men I do not care very much about, so hope I will find some conucido (*acquaintance*) at the other end. Eric's man cannot have had time to apply for me, as there is no word from him. Your letters will have very little chance of finding me at present; so until I give you the correct address you had better send them to HMM R.F.A. 30th Division B.E.7.

This is quite a nice club and comfortable. It is very hot over here and looks as if we are going to have a real good rain. Even from here we can hear the guns, just like some old man beating the carpet, even here it is very hard to realise that one is anywhere near the guns, as the country is looking fine, and very much like England.

Well how are you two dears? Hope keeping very fit and revelling in sunshine.

---

* British Expeditionary Force

Give my love to all and thank your Dad for all his goodness to me, it will never be forgotten.

Your loving
Harold

Will you order a pair of field boots from Taylors as per enclosed, but I want them with more room in the feet than he gave me in the latter ones he made. Also I want the holes for the laces, not hooks, and a small steel plate in the toe and heel to keep them from wearing out, and screws in soles. Also get me a revolver pouch for a field service revolver. Am in a great hurry for these, so get them as soon as you can. I tried for them in the Army Stores but they had nothing that would suit me. Tell Taylors that I want a good strong pair, and cheap and not to finish them off as if I was going to sit about in a drawing room, and to give them a real good oiling.

    Sorry to trouble you pet, do not run up to town if you have nothing else to do. If you can get them cheaper anywhere else do so, but they must be about 18 inches long. I think it would be better to get them elsewhere, as you can send them right away, that is when I send you an address.

Grand Hotel De La Poste,
Rouen
14 July 1916

Darling Con,

Just a wee line to say that I have arrived safely so far, we were on the move all last night, and on arrival here had a fine bath, which bucked me up fine. We shift on about 4 p.m. and expect to have a good 24 hours of it on the train.

    So far I have not received any letters, as the address I gave you was too vague. As I am going to the 30th Division you might try R.F.A., 30th Division B.E.7.

    I got a revolver pouch today so do not trouble about getting one. The country around here is very fine and reminds one very much of England and looking perfect. The cathedral looks a fine old place, but I am not going into it, as it looks a very <u>dark hole</u> and might get lost.

    Patsy and I part company today, and I am very sorry about it, we did our best to get together but no luck.

    Yesterday I was censoring letters, and out of some got a great deal of amusement, some of the Tommies' remarks are very affectionate and endearing, one of them wrote to his mother and finished up by saying that if she did not write to him soon he would give her a thick ear, such a great way of laying out his affections. There were several such remarks but slightly more polite. I should not care to do much of that work, as it gets tiring.

I wonder where Kathleen has got to, and hope to come across her soon but expect she will be miles away. This is a far better, finer place than Le Havre and has a very decent hotel that is this, so if you come across remember it. There is no news, we get much less than you do.

Well dearest how are you both? Hope keeping each other in good company, with heaps of love.

Your loving
Harold

No Date

Darling Con,

So sorry I missed last night but we were on the move until 7 p.m. and had no chance of getting in a word. Up to now I have not been attached to any brigade, and am putting in a few days here until I get notice where to move to, which will be some battery in the 30th Division, or may stop on in the colours. You can address your letters to 30 D.A.C.,* No 1 section R.F.A., BE7 France. Then if I am moved on they will forward my address.

On Saturday and Sunday we had a 1½ days slack, waiting for the lorry to bring us up here. When I was lunching at Rouen I met Arthur Le Rossignol, had a few words with him, he was very fit and getting quite a good job.

Up to the present I have not received a single letter but hope to do so from now on. Expect if you have sent any they will have gone astray. Am afraid I cannot give you any news, as it is forbidden but at the present things are going well. We are living in tents and quite comfortable and am in the best of health, but longing for a letter from your dear old self to hear how you two are getting on.

It is now raining quite hard but luckily there is very little mud about here and the country is very much the same as around Salisbury Plain. I expect there will soon be a letter from Johnnie Forbes, if it comes read it, in fact read all letters before forwarding them.

Well darling, goodbye and heaps of love to you two dears.

Your loving
Harold

---

*   Divisional Artillery Column

Darling,

Just a quick line as just after my last was posted. I have had orders to join the 150th Brigade, and so tomorrow I go and report and join whichever battery in this I am told to. They are hard at it so expect that by this time tomorrow night I will have had my first experience, very likely I shall not be in it long, as we shall probably be very soon relieved. The firing is tremendous tonight, I am about 6 miles behind the lines and the air is fairly jumping.

Well darling I will write as soon as ever I can, but cannot tell when that will be.

How is Susan? Give her my best love and with a huge hug and just heaps of love to you my dear.

Your loving
Harold

15 July 1916

Darling,

Just a wee line to let you know all is well, we are right in the country and our division has just come out of action. I expect to have about 10 days in the rear at least.

We had a very tiring journey up here, about 16 hours of it, and have been kept at a loose end here for about 7 hours and are now waiting for the motor lorry to take us to our division. They have been in the thick of it.

In the country where we are now you could not believe that there ever had been a war, but the Germans were all over it at the end of 1914. There are a lot of prisoners here, who look quite cheery.

Must close now, as the lorry will soon be up.

Love you to all.

Your loving
Harold

Harold's diary entries

17 July – Posted to D/150 Moved with wagons from the Bois du Tay then came to H.Q. at Maricourt. Was heavily shelled, several wounded and killed. Went to Battery with F-Tytler, shelled on road. Maricourt

18 July – Went to forward trenches and observed our fire, saw Huns for 1st time, shelled trench and working party. Huns heavily shelled Trones Wood trenches, many killed and wounded. Trones wood

---

Faviere Trench (22nd July 1916)

Musson, the new subaltern, is a rancher from Central Argentina, a real good tough sort, and above all keen, but he could not have chosen a worse moment to arrive. It was a case of duck and dodge all the way back to the guns, and the cruelest blow was yet to come. Thirty minutes before dinner a 5.9 landed near our kitchen and the cook went "loony" from shell shock. After rushing wildly about he went to ground in a covered-in sap. No one could get him out. I tried coaxing him out by crawling in with a biscuit, a sergeant grasping my legs to pull me out in case he bit me. Eventually we had to take the roof off, and he was sent off in a passing ambulance.........................

Later in the day I went with Musson and extended the wire round the road leading from Trones to Guillemont, from where we could observe well, and had quite good sport. After experiencing an hour of concentrated shelling from my battery, a lot of Huns bolted from an isolated trench NW of Guillemont, and took cover in a wheatfield. It was no target for us Howitzers, so I phoned down and got three 18-pdr batteries to reap that field with shrapnel. It keeps one quite busy shooting three batteries at once down one phone.........................

Musson was top-hole, but being up there with him straight from England, and with some decent feelings left, made me realise what a disgusting business war is.

Lt-Col Neil Fraser-Tytler, *Field Guns in France - Pg. 94*

19 July 1916

My own darling,
I could not possibly get a letter written yesterday, that is if you call these letters, I am now in my old dugout, 10.30 p.m. and about to get into bed. I was going about an hour ago, but we suddenly had orders to loose off, and were at it for sometime.

This is a great dugout, just wide enough for my valise to lay out, and 4½ft high, am getting bags cut open so as to replace paper on the walls. There are a very fine lot of fellows in the battery, do not think I could have been luckier. The officer commanding is a great man and very good at his work.

My address is 150th Brigade, 30th Division BE7.

I came up here yesterday and am now getting quite used to all the row, which in reality is not very much. It is a really wonderful sight if we could only leave the awfulness out of it, and some nights just long to get out to *Lucero*,* and what a time of it we will have when we get there. The nights here are quite fresh and one sleeps very well. Have been very fit all the time and no indi.†

What I am longing for is a letter from your dear self, and hear how it goes for you and Bindy, and that you are on the best of terms with each other. Darling, will you get me a pair of gum boots size 11, and also occasionally send some cake or potted meat, sausages or anything you think would be good, we all share with one another and have our meals in the open.

You will be shocked to hear that I have not had a bath for 5 days and do not look like getting one for sometime to come, and usually only one wash a day. Never mind, they say that one soon gets used to it, I hope so.

Well darling, night night and just heaps of love to you and the wee one.

Ever your loving
Harold

19 July –   2 attacks by us on Maltz Horn Farm, great failure and big losses to us, otherwise calm on front.
Maricourt
Fine.

20 July –   Attack on Maltz Horn Farm, failure. Night attack by Huns, failure.
Fine

☆☆☆☆☆☆☆☆☆☆☆☆☆☆

21 July 1916

My own darling,

Your two letters of the 16th and 17th have just arrived, so before I go on with this will get into camita (*bed*) and read them. Oh it was just ripping to read your dear

---

*   Harold and Con's estancia in Argentina.
†   Harold's name for indigestion.

letters and hear your news, but it would be lovely to be with you.

My correct address is Howitzer D/150 Brigade R.F.A. B.E.7. Sorry to have sent you so many addresses but this will be the one for further notice.

Sorry I did not give you the size of my boots, quite a slip, 11 is right. Hope in the end you did not get the boots from Taylors as the last ones I got have turned out very badly and are splitting right across, so do not pay for them, and I will go and see about it on my return.

Well darling night night and best of love to you two dears.

Your loving
Harold

P.S. Have been in for 2 days and expect will be a good long time before I go out, will let you know when I do.

P.P.S. Send me some envelopes and paper.

21 July –   Captain went to Arrow Head Copse and enfiladed* Hun trench with rifle fire, 55 rounds fired.

Received on 29-7-16

22 July 1916

Darling Con,

Am just longing for the mail to come in and hear something about your dear old self. I did not get a letter yesterday, but as I got two the day before I feel thoroughly bucked.

We have had quite a warm time of it this afternoon, but they have not quite got our range and hope that they will not be able to do so. I expect it was in retaliation for what we gave them last night; they must have had a hard time of it.

We have now been transferred to the 9th Division; they push us about like a basura (*rubbish*) heap. The best tip will be not to put the division, but just put D/150 Brigade R.F.A. B.E.7. France.

That aeroplane that was brought down the other day was German, and another came down yesterday, but do not know which it was. On most clear days one sees air fights.

---

*   Enfilade - direct a volley of gunfire along the length of a target.

The post has just arrived, no letter, am afraid a lot goes astray and it is sickening. Where we are is nearly the centre of the push, if you look for the wood in the centre you will more or less know where I am. One cannot realise what havoc our shells made and what a ghastly time the Germans must have had, all the villages and woods are flat, hardly one brick on top of the other, and the trees are just chewed up stumps and where we have our dugouts is just a mass of shell holes. In fact the ground has been ploughed up for a depth of about 5ft.

The French soldiers are a fine lot of men and real good fighters, and look very fit. They join up with us and are doing very fine work. I see by the home papers that the Germans have brought up 500,000 men against us, sounds a useful mob.

23/7/16

Yours of the 17th has just come and it does buck me up to get them. You will have got my letter by now saying that I am in a first-class battery, and the men are a fine lot. I have a great deal to learn yet, and am afraid am an awful chambon (*duffer*), but must try and pick it up quickly.

I do not remember if I asked you for more envelopes, if not please send a good many, about 50, it is almost impossible to get them here and have not got one to my name.

Kathleen seems to be in luck's way and very comfortably quartered, am very glad, as she thoroughly deserves it, I expect she was very keen to be getting back to her work. Hope Eric will be able to get away, but on this part of the front there is no leave been given and not likely to be for sometime to come. I wrote to him some days ago, hope he got it.

It is great to hear Bindy is so fit and expect putting on kilos. I do long to see you both. I expect she will soon get used to the boiled egg and polish it off pretty quickly and ask for another. Glad to hear that the spot is nothing and can wait, as if we have to take it out she will stand it better later on.

The weather has turned quite fresh and dull and very hard for observation work, the wind is in the wrong direction and in favour of the Germans.

Will you write to Mrs. Felty and find out Patsy's address as I must write to him and find out where he is. I am with the guns.

I see you ask if I am taking my medicine and jelloids, the former I am taking but not the jelloids, as I do not need them, have not taken any bicarb for some time now and am trying to keep off it. The food is quite good, not much variation and not very digestible, that is for me. Bully beef is the principle diet and occasionally we get good vegetables, but never any puddings, I thought that I could not live without them but now would feel quite unhappy if one was put before me. That tin of coffee you put in was very much appreciated by my mates. Will you send a daily paper out once or twice a week, and also an occasional illustrated one.

I broke the glass on my watch the day before yesterday, I wonder if you could get me a couple and send them, think that I can put them in, ask if there is any special way of doing it.

You may be pleased to hear that there is no chance of getting a bath until we go behind the lines, and do not think that this this will be for months. There is always enough water for drinking and washing purposes but not for more, am just getting used to it.

When I was in Rouen I tried to get something for Bindy but of all the rotten mass of toys etc. I have ever seen, those took the cake, so will have to wait for another opportunity.

Well dear, I have plenty of time for writing but there is nothing to write about and this one is full of rubbish, so good afternoon to you two dears.

Your loving
Harold

22 July –   McLean went with forward guns to Bernafy Wood. 1 man wounded taking ammunition. Attack on Guillemont great failure, heavy casualties. Were the only Battery standing up officers.

23 July –   Heavy firing all day

30-7-16

24 July 1916

Darling,

It was just grand to get all your letters, one yesterday morning and two in the evening. We had a very quiet night of it, and so had a really good sleep. By Jove the officers and men in this battery are fine fellows and all of them deserve the D.C.M. *(Distinguished Service Medal)* or M.C. *(Military Cross)*. What they have been through and the good they have done is great, and where other men have hidden themselves these have gone right through with it. The second day that I was here the Captain took me with him right to the front line and we could see several of the German lookouts about 100 yards off. Since then I have not been up and not likely to for some days. The more one sees of the whole thing the more marvelous and hateful it becomes. I only hope that we shall soon make another big push and that it will be very successful, if we really did make one I think that things might move very quickly.

Up to now I have not come across anyone I know, or anyone from Argentina, in all the batteries round here there is not a soul one knows.

The boots sound quite alright but if you have not sent them do not do so until I let you know, as I can get on for a short time without them, but if you have sent them it will be quite alright. Am going to send most of my spare kit behind the lines, as if we have got to move I hear that it usually gets lost. Probably does anyhow. This diagram is the size for the photo frame, so sweetheart send it along as soon as you can, as I want it very much indeed and very soon. I will finish this letter later on, as I must now have a look around and do a little work.

Just finished about 100 letters and now will finish this short notita. I have never told you about our battery mascot. It is an old toy horse that one of the gunners picked up in one of the villages, it stands about 12 inches high and is rather a wreck, it is always put in the most open spot and when the battery is on the move it goes on one of the guns or limbers, so I hope it will always bring us good luck. If it comes out safely at the end of this war I must try and get it as a relic.

The men are all fit and cheery, but want a rest of about 3 weeks. Some of the infantry are having a very hot time of it, poor men, it is hard luck.

Well sweetheart must now close. Give my love to all and hope that you are all in the pink and not having too strenuous a time of it. How is the housekeeping going on? Hope you like it and expect it gives you something to do. What about Donald, how does he like Shawbury? I saw Jack was gazetted and expect that he will soon be coming out; I hope that he comes here.

Well a very big hug to you and Bindy and just heaps of love.
Your loving
Harold

24 July –   Jean shell Trones Wood, McLean slightly wounded. Sgt. Lynn and Brent killed, Brown and Smith wounded. Hell of a day, shell fell within 3 yards of Captain.

30-7-16

25 July 1916

Darling,

Just a wee note to wish you good afternoon and hope this finds you very fit, as it leaves me. Am just off with the Commanding Officer to shoot the guns, we go about 2 miles off, am connected up by wire.

When you are in town next will you have 20 packets of Reina Victoria sent out, as am running a bit short. Also let me know whenever the cash at the bank is running a bit short, will send you a cheque on *Cox & Co.**, expect there is quite a good credit running up there.

Wonder if Eric has got his leave yet; hope it will be a good one.

There was a German attack here last night but as far as I can make out it must have failed, anyway hope so. We are having very good weather here, not much sunshine but no rain, and not very clear.

Well sweetheart I must now close up as am just going to lunch and then off. So bye bye and just heaps of love to you two dears.

Your ever loving
Harold

25 July –   *Morning quiet. Captain and self went to Maricourt, place heavily shelled. Fine.*

☆☆☆☆☆☆☆☆☆☆☆☆☆☆☆

30-7-16

26 July 1916

Querida mia,

I have now run short of envelopes and so hope that the others will soon arrive, as I do not like writing on these wretched things. The post here is very irregular, 2 days ago I got 3 letters from you, since then there is no other, so hope that they will be here today. Am going on another jaunt this afternoon so will get this away this morning.

Have you had your photo taken or are you getting a smaller print of the old one?

I will keep writing this letter in Spanish, so the soldiers here cannot read it. You will see lots of mistakes here, I apologise. The day is a bit cold, it seems it is going to rain, but will get better in the afternoon. We are hitting the enemy day and night, and them us, I don't know when they will finish this war, but there is always hope that it will finish soon, and the sooner the better for us, and if you want when it finishes we will go to Lucero without stopping in England. The Captain of this battery is very nice and a hard worker, all the soldiers have a lot of respect for him. I don't have anything else to say. Send lots of love to everyone, kisses and hugs to your Dad and Bindy.

Your loving
Harold

---

* A bank used by army personnel.

26 July –   Went to Maricourt and shot on Dalfamont Farm, line held good but were heavily shelled and glad to get out of it.

3-8-16

27 July 1916

Darling Con,

We have been having a very quiet day of it, except for this morning when we took quite a lot of prisoners. The rest of the day we have been making a new dugout for ourselves, two of us in it and made quite a comfortable place out of it. It is 7ft x 7ft, just room for two beds, a passage down the centre, with a table at the end made out of some munitions boxes. It has got quite a good splinter-proof roof on it and looks safe, our other had next to nothing on it and very insecure, so glad to be out of it. In a few minutes I must get all my kit changed over, am having it well sunned in the meantime.

Last night had my Tommy cooker* on the go and it works very well indeed, did

---

*   A Tommy cooker was a compact, portable stove, fuelled by something referred to as solidified alcohol, which was issued to British troops (Tommies) in WW1. It was notoriously ineffective; one soldier complained that it took two hours to boil half a pint of water. – Wikipedia

not bring out any refills, so whenever you are near the shop will you please send me out a couple, expect you can get them at the place in Godalming.

It has been a most gorgeous day and am now sitting in the sun and having a lovely bask and only wish you were by my side, excepting for the place we are in and what is going on around us. The wretched Germans are using gas shells quite a lot, and so one has continually got to have one's mask near and put it on at the first alarm. They usually drive these at you during the night and the guards have to keep a very lively look out for them. You will see articles in the papers about our artillery, really one cannot realise what it is until you see it, and then it is the devil. Sorry I cannot say much about it, but after the war is over you will have some yarns. The papers on the whole have been very accurate, but there are some things that might be left out and others that might be put in. Last night there were crowds of planes up and the whole place was like a beehive, but no actual fights.

The post has come again and no notita, so hope to get a pile of them tomorrow. I expect by now the Yarrows have gone up to Scotland and hope that Aunt Janie will follow and have a good long stay and get thoroughly fit again, although if Eric will be soon over expect that she will wait to see him.

In my last I sent you the size of photo I wanted so hope that you got it and will soon send it out. Well darling will close and that this will find you in the pink, as it leaves me at the present moment. Just heaps of love to your dear self and Bindy and a great big hug.

Your loving
Harold

P.S. Sometimes you may see this battery spoken about in the papers, it is known as Palatine and was very famed in the time of Cromwell.

27 July –   Captured Longeuval. Heavy S.O.S.* and counter attack.

☆☆☆☆☆☆☆☆☆☆☆☆☆☆☆

3-8-16

28 July 1916

Querida,
We are doing well here and the weather has been very hot and is good, but we need rain although it seems there is no hope that it will rain.

---

*   Support or Suppression - Firing in response to SOS flares from forward troops.

Whenever you are in town, or if you are not going for sometime will you get the following sent out as soon as possible:

Burtons 4.5 Howitzer slide rule, and a leather case for the same, also directions for use. They cost 17s 3d including the case and can be got at Elliot Brothers, 1 Central Building, Westminster S.W.

You will be fed up with my notitas as there is nothing in them, and what there is is usually the same. I started writing this in Spanish but got too lazy to go on with it. The mail should soon be in now and so hope to have notita. Love to your dear self and Bindy.

      Your loving
      Harold

☆☆☆☆☆☆☆☆☆☆☆☆☆☆☆

3-8-16

28 July 1916

My own darling,

I wrote you such a rotten little postcard this morning that I do not feel satisfied and must try and make up for it in this. The post has again arrived and no notita, it is now 5 days. Am now putting my address again in case you have not got my last, it is D Howitzer Battery, 150th Brigade, B.E.7. France. I never could realise how rotten it would be to get nothing, but it must come alright in the end.

We have had a very slack day of it, in fact not enough to do, which makes one feel miserable. There has just been another air fight but nothing doing and they were so high up that we could not distinguish which was which; it must be exciting up there and no mistake. Some of the planes look quite transparent and as the sun glistens on them they look very fine.

The papers arrived, about 4 days old, and the Russians seem to be plugging along and doing fine work. Hope they will get no setback and be able to keep going on as they are doing.

My stable companion is a chap called MacDonald, and he comes from the same clan as my MacDonald of *The Alfalfares*, he does not know him. He is married and has a son and daughter; he is a fine man and very cheery and interesting. Before the war he was head salesman in a jeweler shop in Manchester and has one or two very interesting little yarns on the subject of tricks of the trade. The Captain has got some relatives living in Godalming, I will find out who they are and let you know. He seems to know that county very well.

They are very keen on patience here and play every evening, so will you send a couple of packs of cards out and will join in with them. We also play poker; at least we are going to, they used to play a bit in their old position during last winter. They seem to have been quite comfortable and in a way quite enjoyed themselves, especially as they have made great pals of each other. Now we talk of the day when we go behind the lines for a rest and hope it will be soon. When we get there we will have quite an easy time of it and can always get a bath and 2 or 3 times a week we roll into one of the towns and have a good time of it, but more of this when it comes off. They deserve a good rest, they have been a long time in action and had hard work and done very fine work.

I see in the papers that Rob Gould has been wounded while flying, have you heard anything about it; I hope it is not serious. Wonder if Jack Gordon will come to this part of the line, if you see him tell him to let me know where he goes. I wrote to Lucy sometime ago and so will you drop him a note and give him my address. Will finish this tomorrow, as it is nearly dinnertime and then will turn in. Must write to Flurry, in case I do not you might drop him a postcard and tell him to write.

Night night dear love and God bless you both and keep you well.

Your loving
Harold

P.S. If you have not sent the envelopes off you might as well send some notepaper with them. Envelopes here are a casualty and make no mistake. I shall have to hunt around for this one.

28 July –   Heavy shelling all day and S.O.S.

☆☆☆☆☆☆☆☆☆☆☆☆☆☆

3-8-16

29 July 1916

Darling,
Just got 4 of your letters and I cannot tell you how ripping it was to get them and all the news. Poor wee Bindy, was very sad on hearing that she had not been well but hope she is quite fit now, and will have no more trouble and she will pick up very soon. Dotu*, it is just grand to hear that another is on its way and hope it will be a wee laddie. You must take great care of your dear self and be very fit and well, I only hope that this war will be over by then, and that I shall be there to welcome him and see you through it all, as I would not stand being here.

---

*   Dotu appears to be a term of affection.

The boots arrived from Manfields this morning, that is one of them, the left. I do not know if they sent them separately but the packet came quite intact and did not look as if it had been tampered with. You might ask if it has gone astray, they will have to send a right one to match the left. Personally I think that they must have forgotten to pack it. A tin of oil also came with it. It seems rather too absurd to think that anybody should take one out.

Am sorry you are getting my letters so irregularly, but since I have been out I have only missed one day and will try not to miss any more, but one never knows.

Our new dugout is quite nice and when one is in it you can hardly hear any sound, but when there is a bombardment all the earth shakes and there is a good deal of it, as we are in a very busy spot. Have you any idea where I am? Let me know, I am afraid I cannot tell you and they are very strict on the subject on this side, and there have been one or two court martials of men who have marked letters etc. The woods all round here look as if we are in the middle of winter, except they are so jagged and torn up.

What is the general opinion of the people at home with regards to the war? Do they still believe it will be over in 3-4 months or another year? Here the opinion is very varied so cannot give you a good one, expect it is the same with you.

Thanks for sending the pyjamas and expect that they will arrive alright, but really do not require them, as I seldom get into them and very probably if anyone goes home from here I will send some of the clothes back, as they take up such a lot of room and only get damp and mouldy.

I will answer all your questions in my next letter, as this must be off very soon and must have something to write about in my next notita. I am most awfully bucked about your good news and that you are so pleased about it. I hope we will live for many long years to appreciate the little ones and make them regular little bricks. Well best of luck and only wish I could have you in my arms, and that you could fly over here and have a cup of tea and hard biscuit with me, or better that I could go over to you and have a good tea and a soft biscuit, although the army biscuits are very good and nourishing. We have good bread but I do not touch it.

Our adjutant has just come back from town and brought a lot of stores etc. with him so are going to have a good feed, this evening consisting of sardines on toast, soup, beef steak, peas, potatoes, asparagus, chocolate pudding, tinned fruit, cheese and fresh fruit, this on account of it being the Captain's birthday.

Well, goodbye and hasta mañana and two big hugs for you and Bindy.
Your loving
Harold

P.S. I missed the post, so will just add a few lines to this. The other boot has just arrived; why they sent them separately I do not know. I clean forgot that I had ordered gum boots, if they have not been sent forward, please keep them for a few days and will let you know where to send them. Must close as it is 11 p.m. and have to up at 2.45 a.m. Night night my own and will write after tomorrow is over. Just a big kiss and hug to you both.

Your loving
Harold

29 July – Went to H.Q. with Captain. Fairly quiet. Heavily shelled with gas.
30 July – Gas shell during night and had got a little ill stomach. Started 3 a.m. for Maricourt, got lost in mist. Big attack on Maurpas. Bomb store exploded and were heavily shelled.

30th July 1916

Saturday, the 29th, was my birthday, and it started well, as when shaving in my hole on the firestep, to my great surprise, Peter (Captain P.S. Fraser-Tytler, who on 3rd August 1916, was killed near Montauban) turned up with an army of signalers.......He came back to join my birthday dinner (our light cart had previously gone to Amiens to buy food and liquor suitable for the great occasion). Unfortunately just as we were starting, orders came in that I was to go immediately to Group HQ, and so five courses and a bottle of champagne had to be gulped down in quick time.

I returned to the battery at 10 p.m., with the orders for the big attack the next day, and we started making out the barrage tables for the guns. The Hun commenced a very heavy and prolonged gas-shell bombardment, and I found working on a map with a gas helmet on was a job very trying to the temper. At 3 a.m., after a mouthful of tea and bacon, both tasting vilely of gas, I started off with Musson and two signalers to try and get to the French line. It was a pitch-dark night with dense mist; often the gas hanging in the hollows necessitated wearing gas masks, so we had a difficult walk over the wilderness of shell craters, but in the end managed to find our way. At dawn the mist still hung about like a London fog, so we waited at the French brigade HQ in Faviere Wood, and were thus able to phone back early news of the French progress.

By 7.45 a.m. all the French forward wires were broken, so as the mist was lifting I sent Musson back to the guns and pushed on towards the front line with my signalers...............at 4.p.m Musson came up and relieved me, and by evening things were quiet. We had, indeed, gained a certain amount of ground, but the confusion in the dawn mist marred the complete success of the attack.

But it was a wonderful day all the same.

Lt-Col Neil Fraser-Tytler, *Field Guns in France* - Pg. 99–100

*29 July 1916**

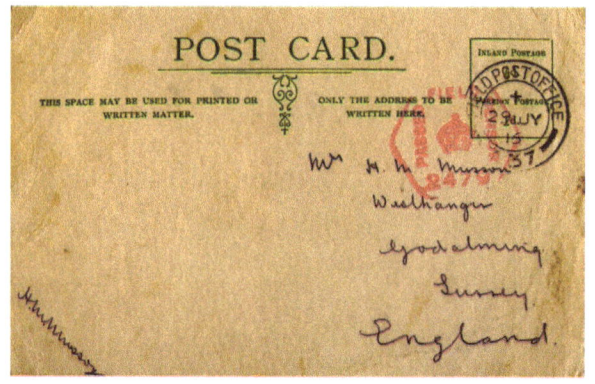

---

* Postcards were supplied as a quick means of communication – Harold sent several, the ones shown here are a composite of the best preserved ones.

11-8-16

31 July 1916

My own darling,

Here I am again and very fit and well, that only thing is that I had 4 days of indi, but am glad to say that it is on the mend again and hardly feel it all. Yesterday we had a very busy time of it, I was most of the day up in the front lines with the French, only wish that I could speak it, as it would be very useful to me. I expect you would be very amused if you could hear my tries at it, it is a mixture of English, French and Spanish, at times they can understand a certain amount, but usually hold up their hands in despair, but are very nice about it. I think a very small pocket dictionary, with as little as possible, would be very useful.

We are in great hopes of going back to rest in a few days for the very least 3 weeks, but do not know anything definite yet. It will be great as all the men require a good rest and after that I do not know where we will be shifted to. Will let to know when we get out.

Quite a lot of prisoners passed here yesterday, about 200 looking quite well and good men, excepting for about 5% of them, who looked very poor seedy men. They are putting up a very fine resistance, and will take a lot of cracking, or in their words, breaking their line.

Will you send 12 pairs of socks for the new boots as they are rather big, but just right for the winter when I can put 2 pairs of socks on, but want them well broken in by then, you know the socks I require, they are those pads to put in the bottom of boots.

I do believe we are going behind the lines tomorrow or the day after, as the new battery have just arrived to take one of the sections, and so will be sure to come in tomorrow to take the rest over. Will let you know more about it tomorrow or the day after. The men are so bucked and hope that some of them will get leave as they have been at it far above their time.

I said that I would answer all your questions in this but the post is just off and so must close, or go on until they come and drag it out of my hands. Sorry to hear that D. Newcombe has been wounded, but hope that it is nothing serious. Eileen's husband you say is leaving hospital, that sounds very cheery and I hope he will have no more setbacks; he has had a bad innings and deserves a lot of good sound rest.

Today is a most glorious day and during the early part of the morning you could hardly realise there was a war on, even now there is very little firing to what there usually is.

Your parcels arrived safely and many thanks for them, I will start on them today and have a rare old feed, I think it will be as well not to send any more for a few days, as when we are behind the lines we will most likely get well done, and then the rest will be better when we get up to the front lines again.

How did my photos turn out? I hope well and that you were pleased with them, you might send over one or two of the best proofs for me to see and will give you my opinion.

Well dearest just lumps of love and kisses to you, my own two, and will try and write to your Dad when I get more time.

Your loving
Harold

P.S. Address the same as usual.

31 July – Quiet day except for one strafe blew 2 horses to pieces and man holding them covered with flesh and blood but not hurt, wonderful escape.

Bois Des Tailles. (2nd August 1916)

One section of the battery was due to be relieved that night. An orderly bringing a message had come up with two horses and was holding them beside one of the gun-pits. I was just thinking of sending them away, when I heard a close shell coming and jumped for safety into the mess which is at the bottom of 12-inch shell crater: merely a square hole roofed with a piece of green canvas. As soon as the shell had burst I looked out just in time to see a red lump rising out of a red pool. It was the horse holder! I pulled him into one of the trench dugouts and started a party to clean him and then report damages. Extraordinary as it appeared, he was practically untouched, and he told them that he lay down with the reins in his hand when he heard the shell coming. The shell must have burst on the back of one of the horses, as there was no crater in the ground.

As soon as the shelling stopped, we began to clean up the place, finding one head, three legs and one hindquarters at distances up to a hundred yards, while the remainder of the two horses was in small fragments over the whole position. It was indeed an indescribable mess, which was soon surrounded by a dark cloud of bluebottles. The horse holder seemed quite unshaken, and, having been fitted out with clean clothes, went back on foot to the wagon line………….

On the eve of departure one realises more the foulness of the spots in which we spent so many happy hours fighting. Now all the jump and life seemed to have gone out of things, and there was nothing left but the appalling stench, the torn up ground, and the eternal cloud of flies rising in front, and giving a friendly hint to prepare to meet some fresh horror.

By the afternoon, as I had only one gun to get away, my army had dwindled down to myself, Musson, and the BSM, and three men. It was like waiting to leave school, and we were all as nervous as cats lest some disaster should happen before we escaped. Our gun team and horses came up at 10 p.m. and the relieving gun arrived soon after. Poor people! Their troubles had already begun, as their cook's cart, following behind their gun, had been scuppered on the way up. Musson and the others went off at once and I merely waited to send off the final message to "Group": "have handed over position".

Lt-Col Neil Fraser-Tytler, *Field Guns in France* – Pg. 102–104

Nelson
New Zealand
2017

Dear Harold,

I expect you are wondering what possessed me to undertake unraveling your letters to Con, especially as I knew the ending. It was not on my to-do list in anyway, I knew the letters existed, but I hadn't seen them. They were in fact with your great granddaughter Laura at the time, we thought it may be a little project for her, but like her father she never got around to it. All I knew was that you apparently had a Daimler car as this was mentioned in the letters and Jim, being a car enthusiast, had latched onto that.

My unexpected promise to myself was made on Anzac *(Australian and New Zealand Army Corps)* day, which is marked on 25th April annually. You may have been aware of this day as although it started in 1915, it was first officially marked as a holiday in 1916, and was to remember the men who braved the horrors of Gallipoli. It is an important day here in NZ, always marked by dawn ceremonies and events at cenotaphs around the country, these are monuments erected to remember the dead and have the names of those who were lost engraved on them. Such a lot happened as a result of the war that you would have no idea about, but your name is engraved in a few places. I have found it on a huge plaque in Ablain St.Nazaire French Military Cemetery also known as Notre Dame De Lorette, your old school of Oakham in Rutland and in St. Andrew's church in Buenos Aires.

Anzac Day 2014 was significant as it was 100 years since the start of your war, I went to our local service in the village hall with your great grandson Alastair, his wife Linsey and their children, Kirra, Isla and Ben – I wish you could meet them and your other two great-great grandchildren Taj and Jessica, who live in Australia and always attend the dawn Anzac service. The day holds huge importance here, as does 11th November, which is Armistice Day, and marks the ending of your war. At each ceremony there is a minute of silence as the flags are lowered, it ends with a bugler playing the Last Post. As a small girl in England I used to help my mother sell paper poppies, which people wear to mark the occasion. Poppies are still sold every year to raise money to care for those who have been scarred by war. I loved that you saw poppies on the fields, although you had no idea the significance they would play in the years ahead of you.

In the afternoon we all went to a reenactment of wartime things at a local park, people were dressed up in costumes, singing songs of the day and putting on little cameo plays. The big event was a walk through the trenches that had been created in a large shed. It started in the 1914 German trenches, apparently they were built far better than the Allied ones, where we time travelled to enter these in 1916. We saw No Man's land and the wounded pulling themselves back to the safety of the trench, we experienced a gas attack, we heard someone shot for cowardice, and we left through a Field Hospital where the wounded were treated. The sign above the entrance to this display read "Welcome to Hell." They were scenes probably so familiar to you, but not ones you would have chosen. Although it was unreal and all acted out, it was the most terrifying thing, the smoke, the noise, the filth and the dirt all so well depicted. Isla, then 9 years old, was terrified. We walked around together holding hands, clutching onto each other tightly. She wrote a poem afterwards, which she entered into a competition, and won for her age group. Yes, that is the poem that opens your book, she captured it so well and one could almost imagine that she was there. The following year she read it out at the Anzac service in the village, but more of that later.

I told her about your letters and heard myself tell her that I would write them up for her. She has continued to be my inspiration to create this book, this memorial to you, your friends and the unseen and unheard voices who found they had no choice in their fate.

The letters were tied with tartan ribbon, three bundles of them, written on whatever paper you could find, often written in pencil that has faded with time.

For some of the letters I needed to use a magnifying glass, but eventually I understood your writing, there were times when I would puzzle over a word only to have it mysteriously drop into my head. I feel we tackled this project together and now your voice is free for whoever wants to hear it. You also kept tiny little diaries that told another layer of your story; they told of your whereabouts, the action taken and always the weather, your letters were far gentler. Con jotted down the day your letters arrived, some got to her quickly and others dallied around. I think hers to you were equally erratic.

My hope is that between us we remind people of these words from George Santayana, a philosopher:

> *"Those who cannot remember the past are condemned to repeat their mistakes."*

With love
Sheila x

August 1916

Harold and teammate – date unknown

At its finest, rider and horse are joined not by tack, but by trust. Each is totally reliant upon the other. Each is the selfless guardian of the other's well being.

Author Unknown

5-8-16

1 August 1916

My own darling Con,

I got two of your dear letters last night and also the enclosed army form, which I shall probably fill up and enclose in this. Am very sorry so many of my letters have gone astray and do not know the reason why, unless the censors have torn some of them up, but do not think that I put anything in them for them to do so.

Dotu, thank you very much for sending that little snapshot of you two, I think that it is just ripping of you both and have got it safely in my photo purse. Do you want it returned, hope not, if you want another copy try and get it from Susan.

Pozieres* was a great take and one more slip on the long and slow road. They mention Delville Wood† a lot also, that is quite close to here and we gave a hand in the shelling of it and it did get a good doing.

Have just filled the form in and am enclosing it, so will you forward it to St John's Wood‡ to be filled in by C.V. *(compliance and verification)* and also send our marriage and Bindy's birth certificate. They should return it to you and then you will have to send it on to Blackheath. If there are any other questions let me know, sorry to trouble your dear old self so much.

The cake was very good, but too rich so when you send another will you send a lighter one. Also the butter arrived in excellent condition, but we can get plenty of it here, quite good stuff.

You are quite right about our signal and so it will have to slip. Sorry that Ethel is disappointed at you not being able to get down to Salcombe but she will understand, and if she does not, do not take any notice of her and it will soon pass over and be alright. It was very naughty of you giving that dress to Alice from me, it should have been from you or Bindy, and am sure that Alice would have much preferred it. Anyhow hope that she is pleased with it and it fits her.

I expect Bindy will soon be walking about and when I get home will be properly on her feet and a regular old chatterbox.

You need not put 30th Division on the address. Our work here on the whole is not very heavy, but at times we get long hours and usually turn in any time we see an hour or two in front of us.

---

*   Battle of Pozieres Ridges launched on 23rd July 1916.
†   Battle of Delville Wood July 15th – September 3rd 1916.
‡   Officer Cadet School.

Well dear one, hasta mañana and God bless you two dears.
Your loving
Harold

1 August –   *Incoming battery came to look at position. Quiet day, except for road being shelled.*
2 August –   *Came out of action to Bronfe farm (hurrah).*

8-8-16

3 August 1916

My own darling Con,

Yesterday I had only time to send a field postcard to you as we were very busy on the move, and now we have had a grand day of it on the banks of the river. I am having a real good slack, and am contemplating a dip in the river, which will be very agreeable as have not had a bath for over 3 weeks. It is really grand here and lovely trees all over the place, wish they would let us stay on here, but will be on the move in a couple of days. One cannot realise what peace is until one has come out of the fighting, and then wonders why one has never experienced such perfect peace before. Birds and cattle and everything in common around us, the horses all picketed close to one, it almost reminds me of the camp,* and now only wish you two had a wee tent and were here, as you would just love it, especially if you had old Rio Negro here and could have a good gallop in the valley, and there is lovely pasture land to get about on.

    I got two ripping letters from you last night, also a parcel which I have not opened yet, but will look at the contents before dinner and try them. I will finish this after dinner, so hasta luego.

    Just had my bathe, it was just fine and at last I feel clean, but must have another to get properly so. You will be pleased to hear that our battery has done very well, you have the battery number so just look out for it in the papers as I think there is sure to be something about it. All the officers have done very well and I can just tell you that I am proud of being with them, and that I was with them during the latter part of the time that they did so well. I will let you know all about it later on, anyway look out for the name of Captain Fraser-Tytler.

---

*   The camp referred to throughout the letters is Argentine countryside, in particular the land Harold both owned and rented for grazing his stock.

That is quite a good snapshot of you and Bindy, only the pity is that it is a bit blurred, you both look very cheery and ripping.

Am now in camita *(bed)* under rather a tiny tent, 3ft high and V shaped so you must excuse the writing, that is if you can read it. I do not expect that I shall get a letter from you for 5 or 6 days as they will be chasing us about.

If Eric goes home, tell him to keep his eyes open as we may be going somewhere up there and attached to the old division. Anyhow I will write to him once we are settled.

Well my own, night night to you two darlings, will write tomorrow.

      Your loving
      Harold

3 August –   Rested all day

      11-8-16

                5 August 1916

My own darling Con,

Am going to start this now but do not know when it will be finished as can only get little snacks here and there. I am right up north now and will probably pass through Calais and Boulogne, pity I cannot cut across for a couple of days, but it cannot be. Anyhow time will fly along and will get my leave as soon as possible. I did not know that Martin was at Albert,* anyhow we were a good way off him, and no chance of getting away.

We shall most likely be in it again by the 11th, but will let you know before. The Hows† get very little rest, in fact hardly any, the 18 pounders get much more, practically 1 week in every 12, but still I think that it is better working than having a fairly easy time, as time goes much quicker. Although I must say that I have thoroughly enjoyed these 2 days rest. Yesterday 3 of us went to Amiens and did some shopping and had a tip top lunch, we rode there, about 6 miles, and arrived back about 7.30. It was great getting back into civilisation again and having a look around the town.

I do not think it matters now saying a little about my work, as it is over and has all come out in the papers. We were in a position close to Trônes Wood and Guillemont

---

* Battle of Albert took place between July 1 -13 1916, the first two weeks of the Anglo-French offensive in the Somme.

† Howitzer heavy shell guns.

and during all that great struggle for Longueval and the two places mentioned. We were supporting the infantry by our fire, and one cannot realise what a struggle and amount of casualties there were before we took the places, but at last took them and going to stick to them. The Germans threw a lot of their poisoned gas shells over our positions, but did not do any damage, I got one little whiff which made me cough slightly but it had all gone in an hour. The helmets* we have are fine things and proof against anything. My work is entirely with the guns excepting when I have to go forward to observe, which is once or sometimes twice a week, in a way it is very interesting but then one has always the horrible feeling of killing. The country we have been in is all torn to pieces and the shell holes are tremendous, some 15 to 20ft. deep and 30 to 40 yards in circumference. Where the German first line was is now a mass of torn ground, ploughed up for about 8ft by shell, broken down barbed wire entanglement, machine gun platforms and dugouts.

The beggars have spoilt my slacks, they were hanging out to air and a bit of shrapnel went right through both legs, hope by now I have returned the compliment and torn theirs to pieces, the dirty dogs. We are working a lot of the prisoners now, chiefly along the roads, they are quite fine men and look very fit.

You must be wondering what is wrong with my writing but I am in a train and it is not very steady. I believe we are going up somewhere where Raymond is, so will try to keep on the lookout for his division. He did not get very long in the rear so expect they are doing some hard work but one never knows where one is here. You are told one thing, and half an hour after you are ordered to do exactly the opposite.

We are now passing through lovely country and exactly like parts of England, the crops are fine and turning a lovely golden colour, this mixed up with the green looks ripping. I have also seen several quite big alfalfa fields just coming into flower, they look fine but not nearly so well grown or luxurious as in the Argentine.

Before I forget, you asked if you could send potatoes, do not as we get any amount of them, they and bully beef are our most common food. The best thing to send is oatcakes, shortbread, biscuits, cakes, sausages, toffees, anything of that sort. The last parcel with oatcakes and tinned fruit arrived safely and we all enjoyed it very much. Up to now I have not had a letter from any one else except you, so am not going to write one line. I wrote Aunt Janie, a postcard. By the way did your receive my postcard written in Spanish, I want to know just to see if it passed the censors.

---

*   Hypo helmet or British Smoke Hood was an early gas mask. A khaki-coloured flannel bag soaked in glycerin and sodium thiosulphate to protect against chlorine gas. It has a rectangular mica or celluloid window for visibility. Harold may have been issued with a small box respirator, which replaced the helmet in July 1916, but were not fully issued until January 1917.

Well darling night night and hope this finds you precious ones in the pink, as it leaves me.

Your loving
Harold

5 August –   Rest at farm. Marched to Bois du Tay.
                      Fine.
6 August –   Marched to Douane.

11-8-16

7 August 1916

My darling Con,

Just a wee line to enclose with the recuerdo (*souvenir*), hope you will like it and there will be enough of it, let me know and I will get you more if necessary.

You will be surprised to hear that at the present moment I am with Eric, I found myself about 12 miles off so rode over, it was just ripping to see him and looking very fit. Our division is relieving his so you will know where I am, do not know where he is off to. I believe this is a much quieter part of the line, so expect to have an easier time.

The lace was got at "cannot tell you." There are two different kinds of lace, Bruxelles and Duchess, do not know which is who.

Have been with Eric since 10 a.m and now just off 5 p.m. Please excuse this short notita but must go.

Just heaps of love from us both.

Your loving
Harold

7 August –   Rest in Somme Valley.

12-8-16

8 August 1916

My own darling Con,

Yesterday I got a whole bunch of your letters, that is three, and today I got another, you are just a dotu in writing and it is just lovely to get them. Those photos of

Bindy are great, she looks a topper and very interested in life. Have had about 6 parcels from you, and you are great at sending what is best. The oatcakes were ripping and we all thoroughly enjoyed them. Sweetheart, there is just one thing wrong and that is very serious, you are sending too much. If you send 2 a month it will be quite enough, as Aunt Bella sends 2, and what with the other people sending we are overflowing. Two lovely cakes have just arrived from Ethel, I am at tea and giving them a trial.

In the country, where we were, we could not get anything as the country was desolate and no canteens anywhere near. But where we are now is a great agricultural country, practically right up to the guns, plenty of farms where we get fresh milk, butter, chicken etc., so expect to live life like fighting cocks.

I wrote you a short notita yesterday sending some lace, hope you got it. Wasn't it just ripping seeing Eric? It made me bound with joy and during the time that I was with him I clean forgot that there was any war on. We had a good old talk over the Argentine and things in general, hope to come across him again before he goes down to their new place, I think we have the better part of the the exchange.

It has been very hot here the last 3 weeks, today is oppressive and steamy and feels very much like rain. At present we are billeted in a fine old farm house and are very comfortable, and can get a bath whenever we like. There is a fine old apple and walnut orchard where we have some fine old slacks, and an occasional old cow comes to interview one and smell round. I had a great time the other day finding billets, I arrived at a station at 12 a.m., bicycled here at 3.30 a.m. and was 7 hours hunting around for billets for the brigade, and then was so dead that I turned in till 2.30 p.m. I got an awful shock when they told me off for the bicycle, and I think that I like it less than ever.

Wonder if you have any idea where we are? You will not be far wrong if you place me where Eric was or is, but of course in the front lines, I am not there yet. I do not remember whether I asked you to send me a small diary, such as yours, will you please do so as I want to keep up with the dates.

This evening we have church parade and as I am orderly officer am attending it and taking the men. This morning we were inspected by the General of the Division after which he made a short speech, which was really short but meant a great deal and was very complimentary and he seemed to be pleased with us.

I am enclosing a cheque on *Cox & Co.* for £50, cross it so that you can hand it into our bank and they will collect it. The boots from Taylors are alright, I made a mistake and found it was only a seam which had slightly opened. Remember when you pay my account to knock off 10%, that is what Tompson allows and think also Taylors, it is always something to get a little puchero *(pot)* with.

Parts of this country remind me very much of San Rafael, lots of the roads are lined with poplars and dykes on either side and they also water the roads in same way, that is with a bucket on the end of a pole. Every inch of the ground is cultivated and all the crops look A1, except that they want a bit of rain.

Well darling must close as have to get ready for church. So night night and just tons of love to you dears and God bless you.

Your loving
Harold

8 August –   Rest.
        Fine.

16-8-16

9 August 1916

My own darling Con,

Two of yours have just arrived and ripping chatty ones they are too. It is just great to hear of you both being so well and Bindy must be great company and getting more so every day, I just long to see you both. Your parcel also arrived with the cards etc., many thanks.

They seem to be pushing Donald about a good deal and not giving him much rest, hope he will have a good spell after Okehampton. Personally I think Okehampton a waste of time, and does not help one in the slightest, one learns in a week here more than 3 months work at home, but all the same the grounding you get at home is good for one. Practically all the formulas you learn are immediately forgotten, and one uses one's own common sense, the most important thing being map reading and telephone work, so tell Donald this.

You will be glad to hear that unless anything unforeseen turns up we will not be going into action for 3 or 4 weeks, which is great.

During this weather it must be grand on the river, hope you are getting quite a lot of it, canoes are ripping things; we must have a go sometime together on them. Last night we had an open air concert given by one of the batteries, all who performed were Tommies, except for an officer who sang well, it was quite a success but not enough good songs with a good chorus to them, anyhow it was a change and the R.S.C. (*Regional Support Command*) provided a good band. Two of the maids of the village played, but it was a dull strum and no mistake.

By the way do not worry any more about the watch glass as I got it repaired in Amiens, now that I am more up the line it must easier to get things done. Please thank your Dad for the book which am sure will be very interesting, and tell him I will write as soon as I can, but as we are on the move tomorrow it will not be for 2-3 days.

There still seems to be quite a craze on going to San Rafael, and will soon have the whole place loaded up with English people, anyhow they are lucky beggars to be out there, and we must soon join them, that is at *Lucero*.

Am glad to hear that Peter is doing so well and he will soon have caught up with Bindy at the pace he is going. I will keep all the snap shots, but remember I want some of you as well. Just fancy Bindy being nearly 1 year old, how the time flies. Yes, it is a very good idea of yours giving her that corral and do so by all means, and hope it will be enough to keep her safely in. I should get a fairly high one and a nice nursery carpet for it.

About the nurse you are talking about, you know a lot more about it than I do, so if you think it as well to arrange it now do so by all means, but I should think you could easily wait for another month or so, but do not leave it too long. When getting a nurse get one you really like, also the very best of them. Also another thing is to know where you would prefer to have it, that is whether in a home or at your Dad's, but this you can arrange with him later on, that is in 4 months or so and the doctor must be thought of etc. Anyhow the first thing to arrange is the nurse, so do this whenever you like. Also I know Susan would be a first class person to confide in and will help you a lot, and I should think that in some round-about-way you could get hold of Eileen's nurse, say that you know someone who may require one.

About the munitions works, am afraid that you will find this very heavy work and now you are expecting you must be very careful and not overdo it, and keep very fit and well, as you will have a lot to go through dear one. So think well before you do anything.

Well must close up, just heaps of love and hope that this finds both of you in the pink and that you are having real good weather in Blighty.* Love to all and great big hug to you and Bindy.

Your loving
Harold

---

* The name often used by soldiers for Great Britain.

9 August –   *Rest.*
10 August – *Went to Croix Marcheux and Haverskerque billeting.*
               Fine.
11 August – *Battery arrived.*
               Fine.

16-8-16

12 August 1916

My own darling Con,
Sorry that I could not get a letter off yesterday, but we were on the move, and as I was also orderly officer had no time for anything else. We had about a 4 hour journey, and then when we arrived we had to get all the men billeted off, cleaned up, new horse lines etc. This part of the life I like very much, as am always with the horses and among my own men. In my section there are about 60 horses and somewhere about 50 men. At present it is very hard to get the run of them all and all their different ways, but hope to get into it before long. Our work chiefly consists of stable feeds, exercise, harness cleaning and also cleaning of guns and wagons. Next week we start dismounted drill, gun laying and marching, also lectures which the Captain informed me I have to give once a week to the men, but am going to do my best to get out of this.

You would be very amused, at the hours when we feed the horses, they know as well as any of us, and when the Sergeant Major or one of us shouts this out they begin to neigh and prance about like 2 year olds.

Coming along the road yesterday with our column we met Eric's on the move, so we had a short chat with him, our horse lines are only about 1000 yards off where his were, is a pity that he could not have stayed on and so been near one another. I believe he goes to somewhere where we came from.

Up here we nearly always get the papers of the day before, which is a great change as in our other position we got them 4 to 8 days later. *The Times* arrived about a week ago, since then no other has come to hand, I think that you said that you had ordered it to come regularly, so please let me know.

I am enclosing a programme of the concert we had the other night, I have scratched the ones out that did not come off and marked the good ones. The active service one was quite good, it was a skit on what one may expect.

I see by the past papers that Italy has got a move on and inflicted a severe blow on Austria. Austria must be very fed up with it, I only wish that she would chuck it up, as it would mean the greatest blow of all to Germany.

About asking Miss Young to go and see the gardens of *Lucero*, I do not think that it is worthwhile at present, as they are in the middle of winter and there would be nothing to see, so it would be as well to wait for the spring and then see how things are going. I will write to Johnnie and see what he says.

Also I must write to *L. & Co.** and get them to send some £.s.d.† as we shall require it for when your time comes, and only hope that I shall be in England for it. Will have a very good try for it.

How's wee Bindy? I hope that this hot weather is not too much for you, and you are not overdoing it. Goodbye best of all, and heaps of love to you dears.

Your loving
Harold

12 August – Rest.
Fine.

☆☆☆☆☆☆☆☆☆☆☆☆☆☆☆

18-8-16

13 August 1916
Sunday

My own darling Con,
Just a wee line to say that I got 2 parcels from Harrods, were these from you, as no note came with them, if so darling thanks very much and such ripping things in them. Well dear heart, wonder how this finds you, hope in the pink as it leaves me, excepting for one of my crowns that came off yesterday, it is sickening as there is nowhere where I can get them renewed.

The Captain has got his leave today and goes to Blighty for 10 days, and he well deserves it. He also said that if possible he would run down and see you, that is if he can get, or otherwise has time, so hope he does and you will be able to get all the news from him. I am very bucked at him getting his leave now and hope the rest of the officers do so soon, as that will mean there being less delay in my leave.

I am enclosing a letter I wrote to Susan, will you please send it on as I do not know her address.

---

*   I imagine this was Harold's agent in Argentina, but can find no clear reference.
†   British pound, shilling and pence symbols.

We had a great morning of it drilling the men, they have got very much out of it during the time we were in action, and now we have to get them up to the mark again. It has been scorching here the last few days, and are longing for a drop of rain.

We are just going to have dinner, a cold one too which reminds one very much of Sunday suppers at home, I expect you are having the same at 8 p.m., and hearing Bindy in the distance, probably pulling Alice's leg. Am afraid this is a very short notita but have no news at all.

So goodnight my own, and just heaps to you two dears.

Your loving
Harold

13 August –   Rest. Haverskerque.
Fine.

19-8-16

14 August 1916

My own darling Con,

Another day gone, had a big day drilling my men, and found that I have as much to learn as most of them, but there are one or two brainless chaps among them and wonder if I shall ever be able to knock anything into them.

We had a fine shower at midday, but it still feels as if more is coming, hope so, but do not want too much as this is a very muddy spot and in winter one has to wear thigh boots. They are now hard at work getting the crops in and it is very nice to hear the old harvesters cutting away. The crops appear to be quite good and very well kept.

No post has come for the last 2 days, at present they are very erratic and get mislaid, think a great deal must get lost. Our Captain will now have arrived in old England, and hope he will have time to go and look you up, but hardly think so as he will be in Scotland most of the time, and having a pot at wee birdies.

There is a fine town near here, which we occasionally go to, I expect you will know which it is, one can get almost anything there, but they do stick on about 4 times their value. That little bit of lace I sent you was bought at this place. I think Eric sent Susan some hankies from there, I would have got you some but they had none.

Afraid these are very uninteresting notitas, but really nothing to talk about, as at present it is a very quiet existence and nothing to liven one up.

Well my own, night night and hope this finds you just A1 and that you are not feeling any bad effects as you did last time, wish I was there to look after you. Heaps of love to you two dears.

Your loving
Harold

14 August –   Went to see Eric at Choques.
Fine.

22-8-16

15 August 1916

My own darling Con,

Three of your dear letters arrived today, also a parcel and some illustrated papers, it was just ripping to get them as we have received no post for 3 days. I cannot understand why my letters do not get to you, and also why they should be so late, I do not think I have missed more than 2 days writing since I have been out here, and do not think that the censor would stop them as I have said next to nothing in them. Also all the letters I have written were dated correctly, and the one I wrote before the one from the river should have arrived much sooner.

Anyhow, the indi was bad for a couple of days, and then I got rid of it and have been very fit since, but I will always let you know when there is anything wrong, but think that I have got over all that sort of thing now.

The gumboots arrived fine and many thanks, I mentioned this in a letter about 10 days ago, but it must have gone astray. Do not trouble about sending my photos for me to see, they will only get lost, I thought probably the proofs would be useless and so could see them.

I got Johnnie's letter and the news seems quite good, but they seem to be having another very hard winter, hope it will not do too much damage to the monte *(woodland)* but am afraid that a lot of the paraíso trees* will go, and probably a few of the more delicate plants, especially as the soil is very dry. By what Johnnie says I think that the cattle will pull through, but am sorry that he did not sell more, even at a low price, as there must be a big lot of calves, and they till a great deal at this time of year. It does make me ache to get back.

---

*   A popular tree in Buenos Aires as it provides shade,
    the berries loved by birds but toxic to humans.

The capataz *(foreman)* has also got married, hope she is a decent woman, she should be as she comes from a good crowd. Poor old George, he has got bad luck, but hope that the fall will not do him damage, they seem to be playing polo, wonder who they get, but totalling them up there must be quite a crowd of them, Emerson, Bill, Hoan, Anderson, Ackerblood, Bridges, Tyson, Lindell, Wood, Lacey and probably one or two others I have forgotten about. It makes me think of our dear ponies and expect they are as fat as pigs and careering about the paddock for exercise.

What is the depot you are working at, is it bandages, munitions or what? I cannot make it out and hope you are not overdoing it, and that the heat is not upsetting you, do take great care of yourself. You ask if I take much care of myself, you may bet that I take all the precautions I can and if I hear of anything unpleasant near I drop into a shell hole at the double, then we get up and laugh, or if very near, a dull smile. Where I am now there is nothing of this sort.

Well darling will answer the rest of you questions tomorrow, so with heaps of love to you dear.

Your loving
Harold

15 August –   Rest. Haverskerque.
                Fine.

22-8-16

16 August 1916

My own dear Con,

Am afraid that this will be a very short notita as there is absolutely no news, and so far no excitement. We have had quite a nice little rain at last, which has cleared the air and freshened things up a bit.

I do not think that you could have got my letter describing our battery mascot as you have never made comment on it, but will not describe it here, as you may have done so, so let me know. All our guns are named, my two are called Mary and Sybil and are behaving very well and doing good work, that is when we are at it.

We get plenty of baths here as we are alongside a canal, but no hot ones as there is not very much firewood knocking round. The old canvas bath comes in well and is really a great substitute for a bath.

Expect that Donald will be back by now and waiting for his commision, hope they will give him a good holiday as he well deserves it. It is curious that he should meet Mr Greenslade, I should like to come across him again. Did Donald shoot with 50 pounders at Oakey? There were none of these during my time, only 18 pounders.

Well darling, will close as there is no news or else my old brain will not work. Night night and will try and think that I have you in my arms, a huge hug for you and Bindy.

Your loving
Harold

16 August –   Rest. Haverskerque.
              Fine.

☆☆☆☆☆☆☆☆☆☆☆☆☆☆

22-8-16

17 August 1916
No 1*

My own darling,
Yours of the 13th and 14th have just arrived and just ripping to read. Am afraid you will think that I am very bad in writing, but something must be very wrong as I write regularly every day, bar two which I missed. I am now going to number my letters, so let me know the ones you do not receive. Also the two photos of yours truly came. In one I look as if my left eye had gone groggy, otherwise they are fairly alright. Am returning them tomorrow, if you want to send one to Mrs Emerson I should send the full faced one. But do just as you like about it.

So Donald has arrived back and likes Oakey, I got very fed up with it and expect in a couple of weeks he will be a full blown 2nd lieutenant. What about Raymond? I have not heard of him for a long time, let me know where he is, he must be a good deal further north than this.

I have had no letter from Flurry, but hope that it will turn up soon and hear what he is doing. He will be very bucked to get a hamper, he has had a rotten

---

*   Harold started to number his letters, but was not consistent as he did not remember to number them all. Some are written on consecutive days with no number – others are probably missing.

time from his point of view. Yes, I heard of his accident through Eric, it appears a barn exploded and a splinter went into his eyeball and he was afraid of losing his sight, but luckily it did not turn out so, but expect it will cause him some pain for sometime.

They seem to be going strong with polo and tournaments and glad to hear that Miss Young is moving about, and her brother ought to jolly well take her too, afraid that he is a slacker in that way as in others. Pity he will not buck up, as it would make such a difference to the place and much more pleasant.

Am now writing in my room, the window looks right out onto the horse lines, they have just had their feed and look peaceful, but just before their feed they neigh and prance and kick like 2 year olds, which decidedly they are not and never will be again. With this rest they are beginning to pick up and take more interest in life, as they have been rather overworked before. Really, looking at them and the country one would never know that there was a war on, excepting that one knows what they are there for.

Well night night my own, just heaps of love to my own two dears.

Your loving
Harold

17 August –   Marched to Essars – 5 hours.
                     Essars.
                     Fine.

23-8-16

18 August 1916

My own darling Con,

Another day gone, and a most peaceful one too, only heard 2 or 3 guns go off, and those a long way off too. It has been a dull day with one or two showers and very moist, and one has that clammy feeling. No post again for two days, there must be something wrong somewhere, probably it is on account of our move, but should have settled down by now.

I had a ripping ride before breakfast, took the horses out exercising and then had a good trot home, gave me a thundering appetite, and since then I have had an easy day of it. I now have one quite nice horse, a tostada *(tan)* and got a good trot. The other one is no good, so am having a good look round for one to replace it. I have a young lad as a groom, he knows nothing about horses but is keen and keeps my harness in great order, might be turned out for Hyde Park. He is a good man with cars, also repairing them so will keep my eye on him for after the war, whenever that may be.

Sweetheart you must not expect me to get leave at 3 months from the day I left England, it starts from the day I joined the battery, 16th July. Do not be disappointed if I do not get it then, I will do my very best to get off, but it all depends on what movement there is. I want to get off as soon as possible, so that my next leave will be just about the time you are expecting.

How well the Russians are doing, fancy 350,000 prisoners from 5th June till 10th August, it is very fine and hope they will soon get another haul.

Lucy wrote me a short notita, all he said that he was moving to Epsom, he might as well have written nothing at all, I will get on his track about it. Glad to hear that Beatie is so fit, the work must be doing her good, and if Helen goes in there it will be very nice for them both. They seem to be very hard-pressed for nurses now, but hope that it will soon lighten off.

Well this is full of nothing but cannot think of any decent news or subject to write about, so hasta mañana *(until tomorrow,)* and with just oceans of love to you two dears.

Your loving
Harold

18 August –   Orderly Officer, exercised horses etc.
      Essars.
      Showers.

24-8-16

19 August 1916
No 3

My own darling Con,

Only a very short notita tonight as the room is very full, it is almost dinner time and we play cards after, it fills up our time for the evening. We either play poker, snap or patience, and I am becoming quite a nut at the game. It has been a very rainy day, mud up to our ankles and looks like going on, although it is fine at present.

This afternoon's mail brought 2 of your letters, and the closed postcard you wrote in London. Glad to hear that you liked the lace, but hope it is good as I know nothing about it. I can hardly realise that it will be Bindy's birthday on the 6th September, I must try and get her a wee recuerdo, veremos *(a present, we will see)*. Many thanks for the diary and dictionary, which are just the things, afraid my French is going, as we do not get any practice here. Your letter with the diary came open, so do not know if there was anything else in it.

I wore the boots from Manfields today, afraid they are very big, but will do fine for winter, and will start to break them in, have put the 2 pairs of socks in them, but still there is room for more.

That is very quick for men to get commissions, but just shows how much they require them, there is a tremendous lot of artillery all over the country, and that is the reason. You say that you think Raymond may be in the 9th or 30th, if he is in the latter it is our lot, so he must be somewhere near here. I think that you must be mistaken, but hope not, as it will mean my seeing him. I do not know where Eric has gone, but think somewhere south.

Am so glad Mrs Watts went over and was so nice, and I must meet her when I get home, the Captain said she was a good sort and believe that she has a very nice place. It was very sad about Peter Fraser-Tytler's death, he was only lunching with us 2 days before and very cheery about everything, his battery was only about a mile away.

I do not know why they say that the Somme is so unhealthy, it is swampy by the river, but there was no sickness when we were there, anyhow the battles of the Somme cover a big area, and we were most of our time on high ground, and well away from the river. It is much steamier here, and I should think not quite so healthy, but so far have heard of no fever or diseases, so you can set your dear old mind quite at rest about that.

Am very glad to hear that you are fitter than last time, but dearie do take it easy on your off days. I expect you think that I am very fussy about it, but one never knows what it might lead to if you do not take precautions, so sweetheart do be careful for all our sakes and make him behave himself.

We never went anywhere near Boulogne, but if I do will look up Kathleen, perhaps when on leave.

Glad that boiled water and brown sugar is so good for Bindy and it will be just great if you can get her alright. Well dear one, night night and just heaps of love to my own two dears.

Your loving
Harold

19 August –	Men inoculated.*
	Essars.
	Rained morning, fine evening.
20 August –	Orderly officer, general routine.
	Showers.

☆☆☆☆☆☆☆☆☆☆☆☆☆☆

---

* The men were inoculated against Typhoid Fever

Nelson
New Zealand
2017

Dear Harold,

In amongst your letters was this delightful letter Con received from a Mrs. Watts, inviting herself over for a visit, which appears to have been successful. She was aunt to your Captain, Neil Fraser-Tytler, who made the connection that the ladies were near neighbours. He described her a good sort with a very nice place. I wonder if you ever saw the letter, or if you also met her, as you hoped to.

Thursday Aug. 10. 1916
LIMNERSLEASE
GUILDFORD
(3 miles)

Dear Mrs. Musson

Several times in letters of recent date, my nephew Neil Fraser-Tytler has spoken warmly of the help your husband has given him. Today I have a line telling me you are a neighbor of mine. May I come to see you tomorrow rather early after luncheon, about three? I should much like to find you at home – I will come on the <u>chance</u>, but must mention it.

I can indeed feel for your anxiety, and I know Lieut. Musson is one who has travelled far, that he may give his helping hand in this terrible crisis.

My dear and only nephew evidently finds comfort in holding that hand.

Yours truly,
M.S. Watts

(Mr. G.F Watts)*

P.S. You may have seen my old name (and your husband's captain's) in The Times *today – Peter Fraser-Tytler was both a cousin, and yes my brother's stepson. I think you might fear it your husband's brother officer if he has mentioned Neil to you.*

My investigative whim came to the fore; I searched for Limnerslease and was surprised by my find. Neil's Aunt Mary, known to the family as Molly, had married an acclaimed artist, George Frederic Watts. He was thirty years her senior, Molly was his second wife, and she cared for him through his ailing health. He died in 1904 and was referred to as 'England's Michelangelo'. Both George and Mary, who was also an artist, held the view that art was for all,

---

*   A referral by Molly to her husband, George Frederic Watts.

Mary sharing her pottery skills with all who were interested. That 'very nice place' that you mentioned in your letters is now open to the public to explore and view the work of George and Mary.

George and Mary also designed and built the Watts Cemetery Chapel, in the village of Compton, completing it in 1904, just in time for George's memorial to be held there. It holds Celtic art, angels galore, and the villagers, including local school children, contributed to its wonders. One description gives it high praise: -

> 'It is no exaggeration to say the Watts Cemetery Chapel is one of the most beautiful, extraordinary, original, marvellous and magical buildings in the whole of the British Isles!'
>
> Lucinda Lambton

Mary dedicated the chapel to: -

> "The loving memory of all who find rest near its walls, and for the comfort and help of those to whom the sorrow of separation remains."

Perhaps Con too found some comfort and consolation there when she needed it. It certainly sounds like a place I would like to visit one day. You both certainly met some interesting people and I am so glad I have been able to find them for you.
With love
Sheila x

26-8-16

21 August 1916
No 4

My own darling Con,

Just a wee palabra (*word*) to wish you how do, and thank you very much for the parcel from Stewarts, quite reminds one of bonnie Scotland, and will tuck into them tomorrow. No cartita (*letter*) from you but expect 2 will arrive tomorrow, you are just a darling at writing, but do not write every day if it will ease you off a bit, but I just love getting them.

I had a ripping ride this morning all on my own, about 2 hours of it, and just a perfect day, I wish you would have been there to have enjoyed it with me. As we are at rest I get a lot of time to myself, and so fill it up by going for walks and rides.

Yesterday I got a ripping letter from Aunt Janie, she seems to be much better and expect Scotland will do wonders for her. If possible I am going into town tomorrow to do some shopping and will try to get something for Bindy, but do not expect that there is much of an assortment although there are some quite good shops and a very first-class tea house.

Well dear, will close as there is no news at all. This takes all my love to you two dears and hope it finds you very fit and Roderick has not too much to say for himself.

Your loving
Harold

21 August – General routine.
           Fine.

25-8-16

21 August 1916
No 5

My own darling,

Your dear notita just arrived and also one from Aunt Janie. Oh, I was so sorry to hear that Martyn had been killed, it is just rotten luck, and so many fine men here gone the same way. I will write to Mrs Williams as soon as I can. He must have been somewhere on the push, there have been a lot killed in that region. Am very glad we are out of it, as it was getting worse every day. Where we are now is quiet, sorry I cannot tell where we are, but they are very strict and quite right too. Do they open many of my letters?

About *The Times*, it has only arrived once so I think that it will be as well to stop it as we get papers here only one day late, and it will also save a little £.s.d. I was very glad to get Patsy's letter, he seems pretty fed up with his lot, but lucky he has a decent C.O. *(commanding officer,)* he must be somewhere round here and will try and find him out.

Yes, as you say we hump our guns about and nurse them well, and now getting them overhauled one by one as they have a great deal of work to do. John Campbell has got into one of the hottest parts of the trenches, about the same as we were, and can promise you that it is warm. The French, who were up alongside us, had been at Verdun and they say that where we were was far worse that anything they had seen. Am very fit and eating too much, we get very well done here.

Will write you a longer one tomorrow, so night night.

Your loving
Harold

27-8-16

22 August 1916
No 7

My own darling Con,
Just a very hurried notita as we have just got back from town, and dinner is just coming in. I could not find a single thing for Bindy, hunted high and low, so the wee one might well have to wait and I will try and get something as soon as possible.

Have just got your letter of 17th, am afraid Bindy is a terrible flirt, but do not know why you think that she takes after me, but really expect she is like most girls and loves the men, what say you?

Wonder if you met the Captain, but I do not think that he would have got down from Scotland by then, as am sure he will put all the time he can in Scotland.

Am very glad to hear that Gordon is so much better and able to get away from hospital soon, great idea getting a farm, and a fine life too.

Up to now have not had to give any lectures and do not expect to have to do so now as we shall probably be up in the lines again by the end of the month, but one never knows until one is there.

Just heaps and heaps of love to you both.

Your loving
Harold

22 August –   MacClean and self to Bethune. Mac and self to Beuvry.

☆☆☆☆☆☆☆☆☆☆☆☆☆☆☆☆

27-8-16

23 August 1916
No 8

My own darling Con,
Am glad to say that your letters are coming very regularly now, and it is just ripping getting them.

You ask what I am in charge of. It is a section that I am in charge of; that is 2 guns complete, but of course the Captain and 1st lieutenant are over me and see that my work is up to date, and also give me all my orders. It is interesting work and a certain amount of competition between the the 2 sections.

I see by yesterday's paper that Robin Le Begg has been wounded, hope that it is not serious and he will soon be fit again.

It has been a lovely day and had very little to do, finished it off with a fine hot shower, the first I have had since I was at Rouen. I must say I did enjoy it and felt just like getting into a train and paying you a visit.

Glad to hear that Bindy is such a good visitor and entertainer, she seems to enjoy herself alright and seems to get more cheery every day by all accounts.

I got the ruler alright and many thanks. Well sweetheart, night night and a great big hug to you both.

Your loving
Harold

23 August –   Stables etc.
            Essars.
            Fine.

29-8-16

24 August 1916
No 9

My own darling Con,
The Captain has arrived back and seems to have enjoyed his paseo *(trip)* very much, but had the misfortune to strike bad weather in Scotland where he had only 3 days

of it, but on the whole had quite good sport. Seems quite cheery at getting back, he is a great person for putting go into things.

The day before yesterday I was in town and ran across Arthur Le Rossignol, it is very curious as when I was in Rouen I met him and now for the second time here. I should like to tell you the name of place, but cannot, I am going to have lunch with him tomorrow. I believe his sister is nursing in a hospital at Dieppe.

What a funny dream of yours about Bindy talking, expect she will soon be able to, and then you will have a time of it. Glad to hear that they all enjoyed themselves at the theatre and that it was such a good piece.

Looks as if Donald is going to get quite a good holiday, is he keen on coming out? I should not be although I must say that it is very interesting.

When we were in our old position I was sent out one morning to observe from the front line trenches, was going to be a special day and a big advance. I got up there about 4 a.m. and the advance took place, but unfortunately there was a thick mist and could not see a thing of them after they left the trenches. The mist lifted about 3 hours after and then I could see our lot had done fairly well and were some way ahead. Cannot give you any detail but after the war will let you know about it.

Am afraid that we can never get leave as John did, it is only cavalry men that can do this as they have not much to do at present. It is a few of the luxuries of war, and do not think it will come to anybody except their lot, or anyone who is very lucky and knows how to work it.

Well dearie, night night, and a huge hug to you and Bindy.
                                          Your loving
                                          Harold

24 August –   Orderly officer, general routine.
                Essars.
                Fine.

25 August 1916
No 10

My own darling Con,

Just a very quick scribble as the post is just off, and had not time to write, these are very fashionable postcards round here. Do you like them? I went and lunched with Arthur Le Rossignol yesterday and had a good chat with him. Had quite an exciting lunch as a Hun aeroplane was over and empty shells from our Archies *(anti-aircraft gunnery)* were falling all round. Well best of ale, must close, with shoals of love.

Your loving
Harold

25 August –   Orderly Officer, nothing doing.

☆☆☆☆☆☆☆☆☆☆☆☆☆☆

30-8-16

26 August 1916
No 11

My own darling Con,

A clearing wind today and hope that it means a clearing up of the weather, as we have had quite enough rain for the present and can do with some more fine weather. Glad to hear that you all had such a nice day at Hindhead, it must be just grand up there and can imagine you all thoroughly enjoying it, but you must just forget all about our time up there as it is now all done with, so not worth thinking about.

I am now living in a tent, as am fed up with the room I had, it was small and stuffy and occasionally a bit smelly, so all today have been fixing the tent and now going to get a bed made and rigged up, and get into it as soon as possible. MacLean is sharing it with me.

Pity about Donald not being able to get over to Ireland, if I had been him I should have gone, as it makes no difference when you are called up, that is they must give you time to come from wherever you are without worrying one.

Hope Bindy has got over her fright, poor G must have been in a great state and it will teach him to be more careful. Then he did not go out after all to Buenos Aires? I thought that they had arranged for him to go.

You still seem to think that I am in the 9th Division, why I do not know as have never been anywhere near it, ours is the 30th.

Raymond must be much further north. Glad to hear that Hugh is fit and will be very bucked at getting down to Salcombe, you did quite right in not going dearie, as am certain it is your duty to stop and look after your Dad.

Today I am all alone here as it is a ½ day holiday, and all the others have gone out visiting a paseando (*parade*). Fancy M. Begg and Gould getting the M.C., as you say the Argentinos are doing well and will get a fine old name for themselves.

No news, so night night and heaps of love to you two dears and remember me to all.

Your loving
Harold

26 August – Nothing doing.

2-9-16

27 August 1916
No 12

My own darling Con,

Sunday nearly gone and have had a quiet day of it. This afternoon we have been around looking for furniture for our new billet, but no luck. So will you wrap that chair up that Ethel gave me and send it along, that is if the post will take it, if not do not worry as it takes such a long time, and we may be anywhere by then. Also get me 20 packets of Reine Victoria,* as I am nearly out of them, but do not worry about going to town for them, if you write and enclose a cheque it will be quite alright.

Glad to hear that Monty had an easy time in the trenches, but must have been in a quiet spot, or else nothing doing, as where we were they would not have got off so easily. Just fancy Mabel getting up to the front line, she was very lucky and must be a good pal of the General, although I think the General an old fool for taking them, as it is no place for them. I do not think that it could possibly be done in our trenches, and if it was done, there would be the very devil to play if found out.

My batman does not act as my groom. I have also a groom, one gets well looked after and as they have plenty of time, if you find that they are slacking you give them what for, but they look after one well as it is an easier job and they get a little extra and more food.

I think the account for Negretti and Zambra† was £1, and they must have added 10 shillings on for the extra cleaning they gave them afterwards, if this is so do not pay it, as it was badly done at first, so get them to send a detailed account and wipe it out. Also re Thompson that £2.10 I do not understand, so please tell them to send a detailed account and then we can see. Sorry to trouble you dear about these trivial things, but you can easily leave them until my return.

We have just finished a great game of cards and very late. So night night my own and a great hug to you and Bindy.

Your loving
Harold

27 August – *Nothing doing.*

---

*   Harold's preferred brand of cigarettes.
†   A company that specialised in the production of scientific and optical instruments. It was also a photographic studio in London.

☆☆☆☆☆☆☆☆☆☆☆☆☆☆☆☆

2-9-16

29 August 1916
No 13

My own darling Con,

Your letters are coming regularly now, it is ripping to be getting them and hearing all your news. Am afraid that you are not feeling very fit and having rather a rotten time of it, although you do not say much about it dear one, I hope it is not too bad, and that it is not weakening you, and it will soon be over. It is rotten luck and I was in hope that it would not have much effect on you this time, anyhow hope that you will be thoroughly repaid for it, and what a time we will have with them. When we get back to the camp Bindy will be ready for her pony. By the way when you write to Winnie remind her about the pony and tell Bill to get it broken in by someone, as we must not loose the opportunity of getting him, as good ponies are very hard to pick up.

Have not had a line from Eric since he left, but expect that he has been very busy getting into his new position and organising. It is a wretched day and raining steadily, hope the weather is not going to break up on us yet as it is still very early and would probably mean a long winter.

I hear that we have got very comfortable billets in our new gun position, a good house, so if we remain there it should be very comfortable. We are having it well cleaned and whitewashed, and then with a little furniture it should be A1. It has also got a good stove in it.

What a dirty bit of paper this is,* must apologise for it, but as am in a hurry had to pick up the first piece that came along so como las gente dicer disculpe me (*pardon me*).

They should be soon over the winter in the camp and by now may have got some early rains, just fancy seeing everything coming into bud and that ash tree of ours, wonder how it is looking. If they have a good year we will hardly know the place when we get back, especially if the new willows they are putting in come away well. Am not going to say another word about it as it is no good.

Well darling must close with heaps of love to you two dears and God bless you.
Your loving
Harold

---

* The paper was a torn in half sheet with a list of battery staff written on it.

28 August –   Orderly Officer, nothing doing.

3-9-16

29 August 1916
No 14

My darling Con,

It is just pouring, like a very heavy storm in the Argentine, has been doing so for ¾ of an hour, and still hard at it. I do not know what the mud will be like, but shall not be able to leave the roads for sometime.

I do not know in the least when we will be going into action, there are all sorts of rumours flying around, we may remain out for a long time, yet another is that we go to another part of the line, another we may go to Egypt or India, none of which I believe. All these rumours come from nowhere, they are worse than living on board a ship.

Well Romania* has at last come in, wonder if that will help to shorten the war, anyway if their army is well equipped it should be able to do some good work in the Balkans, or assist the Russians against the Austrians. Anyway it is another knock for the Germans, although I am sure that they have known it would be so for a long time back.

I went for a short ride this morning, but not a very interesting one, as it was mostly through the suburbs and to an old coal pit about 4 miles off.

You ask when you can send more parcels, we are done so well here that really we do not want much, just some little odds and ends occasionally. What I would just as soon have are some toffees or hard sweets, they are appreciated as much as anything, and are great things to have at odd moments, but if possible do not get anything with acid in, what would be nice are some peppermint creams, or those green things, anything like that.

Must go now and give a look round and see how the horses are, they will most likely be like drowned rats.

Goodnight my own and heaps of love to you both.
Your loving
Harold

---

*   Romania was initially on the side of the Central powers, but changed sides in 1916 to fight with the Allies.

29 August – Played cards all day.
　　　　　　Rained all day.
30 August – Nothing doing. Bath.
　　　　　　Rained all day.

31 August 1916

Darling Con,
Just a hurried notita before I go out. Am off to our new position but do not expect to be in action for sometime. It is just a glorious day, fresh and nice after the rain, except for the mud, which is very bad. That is very nice for Vi being so near you

all and glad to hear that she is so much better and able to start work again, expect she will very much prefer being in a hospital. Well dear must slip off as the Captain is waiting for me, so haste hugs and best of love to you both.

Your loving
Harold

31 August – Captain & self went to new gun position and to Observation Post at machine gun house Festubert. Mac D left for Blighty. Fine.

☆☆☆☆☆☆☆☆☆☆☆☆☆☆

Nelson
New Zealand
2017

Dear Harold,

It seemed quite wonderful that you could be in the theatre of war and come across friends and acquaintances. I have found some of them and others have proved a mystery to me. They will pop up through my letters, as I am able to fill in some gaps for you. I loved how you kept in close touch with your brother Eric, and you were so fortunate to see him from time to time.

Before you had got to France I had lost a great uncle, Wilfred Cantral – I only met him because of your letters, so thank you for inadvertently introducing me to him. His mother, my great grandmother Sarah seemed to be quite a woman, she and her husband John were dedicated to the Salvation Army, working with the founder William Booth. Sarah became a widow in 1898 with John's premature "promotion to Glory" as "he passed over the River at ten o'clock on Thursday morning" – I have taken these wonderful words from their obituaries. I think my grandmother was born after John died and Wilfred would have been two. Sarah spent the entire war in France; I imagine as a nurse, your paths may even have crossed. Wilfred died in the Battle of the Somme on 1st July and is remembered by his regiment.

The Fallen of the 1/5th London Regt. (London Rifle Brigade)
1st July 1916
"We will remember them"

2907 Rfn. Wilfred Herbert Cantral
Aged 21 Son of Mrs S Cantral of 22, Pembury Rd., Clapton, London, previously of 85, Downs Road, Clapton
Thiepval Memorial

Died 1st July 1916

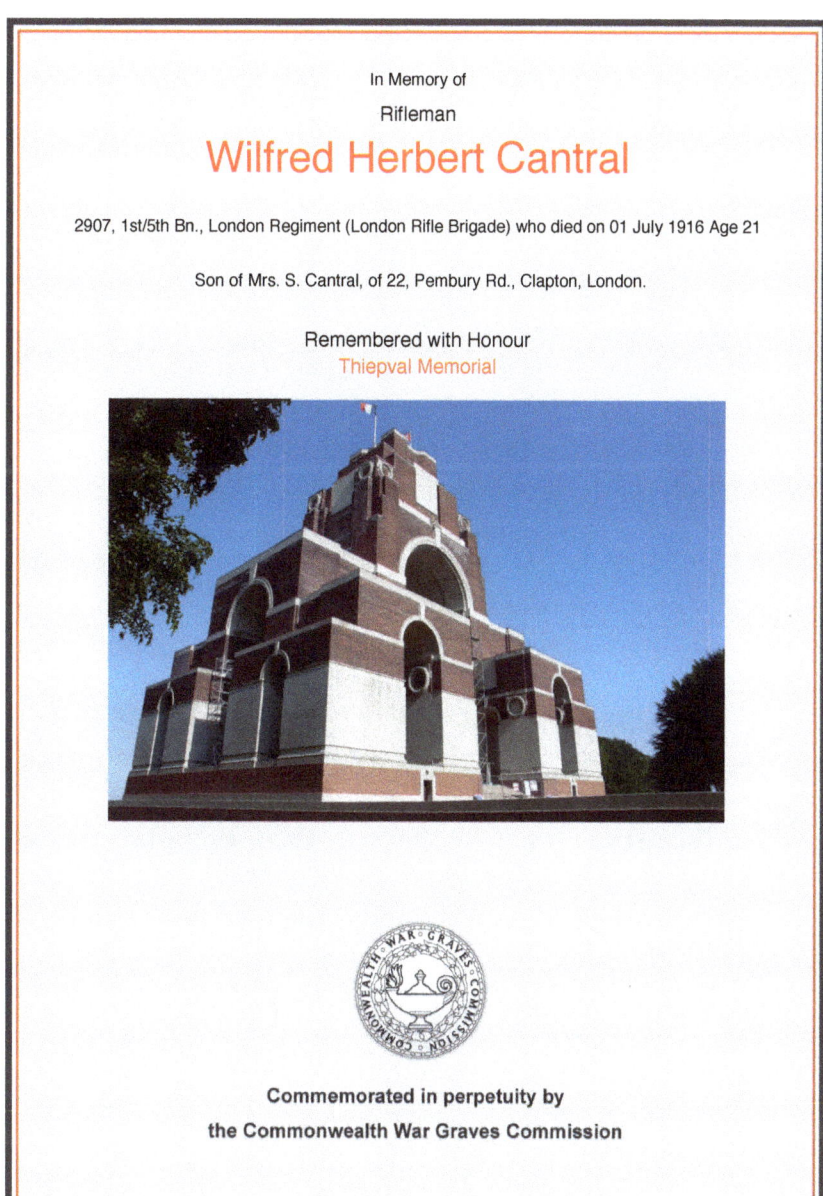

Wilfred would have died on the first day of the Battle of the Somme; he was one of 19,240 men who died on that day alone. Another 57,470 men were injured. It was the worst day in history for loss of life and injury; it does not bear thinking about, all they gained was three square miles of land. I imagine that so many of these men knew that their end was inevitable, as they watched their comrades' fall before them.

The War Graves Commission created certificates for all of you who died; I think they are a great memento for you all. Many of you expected adventure and daring-do, and instead you got nothing but horror, often too great to remember for those who survived. So many never told their story, as you never really did, your letters to Con were gentle with little detail, but your diaries told a little more.

I was so pleased to find Wilfred remembered and I am sure his mother gave extra love and care to all those in her care as she nursed them, and helped them heal from injuries and disease. Wilfred is remembered at the Thiepvil Memorial in Northern France, which is dedicated to all those who lost their lives in the Battles of the Somme, it would have been impossible to bury all those who died. Many of them would not have complete bodies to lie in a grave. The words engraved onto the memorial say:

> Here are recorded names of officers and men of the British Armies who fell on the Somme battlefields July 1915 February 1918 but to whom the fortune of war denied the known and honoured burial given to their comrades in death.

As we are now 100 years on from all the horror of the Great War there is an increased awareness of the importance of remembering and honouring all of you, some of us stumble into it, as I did, and others have made a conscious decision to do so. One such person is Rob Heard, who has committed to making a shroud for each of the men lost in the Somme who have no grave. Rob is tenderly wrapping every man whose name is carved on the Thiepvil Memorial in a hand-sewn shroud. The twelve-inch figures lie in different shapes, and each man is remembered as his metaphorical body is gathered together once again. Rob intends to create a display of the shrouds on Armistice Day, 11th November 1918, as a stark reminder of the ultimate sacrifice made, but not necessarily chosen. Wilfred has already been gathered into a shroud, as those who died on the first day of the Somme have already been laid out for others to view. As I discovered this project I sat with only tears for company, and I am proud to say that I have will eventually get Wilfred's shroud.

Photo thanks to Shrouds of the Somme

I can also tell you a little of your friend Arthur de Rossignol, who you bumped into a couple of times. He survived the war; his correspondence with his sister Ethel is stored in the American University of Notre Dame as part of their collection. Ethel turned to spiritualism after the war and produced some amazing paintings that are still exhibited; they are kept in the College of Psychic Studies in London. Her inspiration was a spirit guide she called J.P.H. and her intention was to demonstrate life after death – you would know if there is, I hope so.

Other friends and family will have their own letters with the stories they revealed to me; I have really enjoyed my detective work.

With love

Sheila x

September 1916

Bindy - 1917

Those building blocks on your life journey
can either be roadblocks or building blocks.
It is up to you to choose.

Author Unknown

8-9-16

1 September 1916

My own darling Con,

Am not quite sure whether I mentioned in my letters that I received the ruler alright, and it is A1.

Well yesterday I went up to see the new billets, they are going to be very comfortable. It is a small farmhouse that the inhabitants have cleared out of, well built, a stove in it and consists of a good mess room, 3 bedrooms, kitchen, servants room and store room, a big loft and a fine barn for the men, so if they leave us here for the winter we shall be well off.

It is 5.30 p.m. and at 6 p.m. there is a football match on between our battery and one adjoining this, the men are as keen as mustard and I think that it will be a good game, will let you know the results either by this or by tomorrow's letter.

Your photo came and very many thanks for it, it is just ripping and am going to get a small frame for it, as they get rather dirty in the pocket case, the celluloid gets rather scratched so will keep it for my best, and in my room. I have all of Bindy's pinned up, and they look fine, and the more I look at them the more cheery she seems to be.

I see by yesterday's *Times* that Donald has got his commission and wonder when he will come out, hope he comes to this region, although I expect he will want to get a more lively place. You are quite right in your first guess about where I am, I see by the papers that it has been shelled. Another of the officers has gone on leave, so the sooner the others go the better, and the sooner mine will come round.

Send me Kathleen's address as I have lost the last one and have now started an address book. Raymond must have been very bucked at getting to see her and expect they had a real good time of it. It would take me from 2-3 hours to get to Boulogne on a motorbike, but I am not going to try it as it might effect the leave. I have not been to the club yet, as have not had time, but will do so when I am next in town.

Will you please get some of my remedio made up and send it out, as I am nearly at an end of the stuff I have got. I do not think that I shall require any warmer clothes before end of November as I have got that thick sweater and muffler, if I require anything I will bring them out on my return from leave.

Yes, it is great the Romanians coming in, but I doubt very much if the war will terminate sooner, hope so but expect the Germans will still have a lot of fight in them, it all depends on how long the Austrians hold out and think that they have got their tummies full.

I have written wee Bindy a long letter and enclose it in this, could not help writing for her first birthday and hope it will arrive on the day. You must write and tell me all about it and how she likes her corral, and hope she does not feel too infra dig being penned in.

The football match has just ended and we were beaten by 3 goals, half the ground was dry and the rest partly lake and mudhole, but must say that the better side won.

About *The Times*, will you please stop it as the mess now gets it, and send me turn abouts - that is one week *The Field* and one week *Land and Water*.

Well my own, must close, with just heaps of love to you and a great big hug.

Your loving
Harold

1 September – Orderly Officer, nothing doing. Football match at D149 Essars. Fine day.

2 September – Captain W and self to Bethune afternoon. Football match against Manchesters, lost 2 goals, good match. Essars. Fine.

7-9-16

3 September 1916
No 16

My own darling Con,

I quite missed writing yesterday evening, but as the post is just off, will scribble this notita and will try and write a longer one this evening. Yesterday we went into ~~Bethune~~ and had a ½ day shopping and walk about. I got a frame for your photo, which does, but cannot say anything more for it. I joined the club and spent a couple of hours there, but saw nobody I knew, still it is quite a nice place, and plenty of deck chairs about which one can roll into and have a read.

Yesterday we had a football match against the Manchesters and were beaten by 2 goals, but it was a very good game and they had a hard tussle for it. Well no more for the present but hasta luego, and just heaps of love.

Your loving
Harold

8-9-16

3 September 1916
No 17

My own darling Con,

It is good news to hear that Jack Williams has arrived back and hope that the experience has done him no harm. The trouble is that he is so young that it might have been too much for him, but expect that a good rest in Ireland will do him a lot of good, and will be quite his old self before long and none the worse for his outing.

I have not heard of anyone here using body shields and do not think I shall worry about them as they must be rather heavy, and trudging around in the mud one wants to be as light as possible. Yes, whenever we are near the firing or under fire we always have the steel hats on, they are a great saving to life and head wounds. We are not in action yet and do not expect to be for sometime, but one never knows, will put it on when I am.

John Campbell is a lucky man to get away and then have leave on top of it, expect that they had a great time of it, and now they look forward to another 10 days of it. Our men only get 8 days, but hope that will be extended by the time that I get my leave.

Expect that Donald will be in his uniform by now and wonder if he will go to Winchester for another course, he may be rather sick of it, but if I were him I should not worry, as he will see plenty of fighting before the war is over.

Surprised to hear that it is so cold over there, here it is quite warm and at nights only have a thin blanket over me, it is still very heavy here and expect to get more rain before it clears up.

What say you, I bought a pipe and baccy yesterday to see if I can used to it, but think I will have a job as had a go this morning, but must say that a cigarette knocks spots out of it.

The Captain brought a typewriter out with him and he is at it all day, just like a kiddie with a new toy, am very fed up with it, as he works in the mess so there is a continual click clack. I will have to get at it on a quiet moment and put it out of gear. He also brought out a fly killer, the same as we had out there, you will remember it, and when he is not with the typewriter, he is falling over everything trying to kill flies. He is a clumsy beggar about the feet and flounders about, decidedly worse than Helen.

Our motto on our Badge is "Ubique Quo Fas Et Gloria Ducunt"* which means

---

*   In Latin Fas implies sacred duty.

"Everywhere That Right and Glory Lead." I always meant to let you know this, but clean forgot.

Have just got up from siesta and read of *The Times*. Russia seem to be pushing ahead and there seems to be a general move for the better, and if Greece comes in, and have a well equipped army Bulgaria's number should be up, and that would finish Turkey up. It will be interesting to see what the next 2 months bring forward, now that Hindenburg* has been made German Chief of General Staff. I do not think that he is, by any means, such a fine man as the man he relieved, can't spell it, but beginning with a F – Falkenhayn,† and I think this is the general idea.

We have another football match on at 6 p.m., right section against the left, there is a lot of excitement about it and they are all as keen as mustard, will be a good game but not up to a very high standard.

Well dearest must close now, with heaps of love to you two dears, and darling your photo in my room is just grand and made a heap of difference.

Your loving
Harold

3 September – Football match R vs. L section.
                     Dull and heavy.
4 September – Nothing doing.

---

*   Paul Von Hindenburg – German Chief of General Staff August 1916 – July 1919.
†   Erich Georg Anton von Falkenhayn - German Chief of General Staff September 1916 – August 1919.

9-9-16

5 September 1916
No 18

My own darling Con,
Here we are having lots more rain and still looking very bad, hope to goodness it will clear up soon. No notita for 2 days, but everything in that line has been going wrong lately, such as papers etc.

This month is gradually creeping along and there is a rumour that leave is going to open shortly, but one never knows. Wonder if Eric has been able to get away yet.

Went for a 7 mile ride yesterday before breakfast, which did me a lot of good, I go out for these every 3rd morning, that is when I am orderly officer.

Here we are all very keen to see what Hindenburg is going to do and if he will make any of his hammer strokes on any of the fronts, or whether he will shorten them, he has got a very big problem before him, and a difficult position to keep up.

Well dear must close as it is just on time for drilling, so hasta luego and heaps of love to you two dears.

Your loving
Harold

10-9-16

6 September 1916
No 19
Bindy's first birthday

My darling Con,
I got a ripper from you yesterday. Yes I am afraid that Mr and Mrs Glynne will feel it very much and am sure they are a very plucky couple, it is hard luck losing their eldest son, but considering so many have gone, I consider the family very lucky who have not been effected by some loss or other. Anyhow we hope there will not be another year like this, of such terrible losses. The longer one is out here the more one sees the reason why there should be such a great quantity of artillery, the more we have the less loss there will be, and every man that is taken into the R.A.O.T.C. (*Royal Artillery Officer Training Core*) should do his utmost. When one is at the R.A.O.T.C. one hardly realises what is before one, in fact it would be a clever man who could thoroughly picture it.

Glad to hear that you got a nice corral* for Bindy. Just fancy it is her birthday today, bless her. One can hardly realise that she is one year old. I expect she can almost walk about and will have a lot to say for herself. I wonder what you are all doing, expect giving the day for her, and having a great time of it. Hope it is fine and you will be able to go out. Here it is a misty damp morning, everything is wet and sloppy. I am having a day of drilling the men at the guns for this competition that is coming off on Friday.

Your Dad is far too good to Bindy, but it is just ripping of him to give her such a present, and expect there will be no holding her in for her uppishness, with all the swagger things for her own wee self.

We had to clear out of our tent as the weather got so bad and went back to our old room, which is not as bad now as the weather has got cooler. Mr. MacLean is one of the junior subs, one above me, an Irish man and a fine fellow.

Well bye bye, whistle just gone. Heaps of love to you both.

     Your loving
     Harold

☆☆☆☆☆☆☆☆☆☆☆☆☆☆☆☆

10-9-16

September 1916
No 20

My own darling Con,

Here we are, 7 a.m. and a gorgeous morning, a grand sun and heavy dew, just like a spring morning in the camp, and only just have to think of having a gallop over it.

Well Bindy is over a year old now, really I can hardly believe it, am certain she will be on her feet by the time I get back. All leave is stopped again, at least that is the rumour.

We seem to have done some good in the Somme again and with the French have taken 10,000 prisoners, it is good and hope will lead to better results.

I had a long letter from Eric, nothing much in it, except that they have had bad weather and one storm washed most of their tents and bivouacs away, and the remaining ones got well swamped, the rain must have been excessive. I do not know where he is, but anyway not where I was, but should say about ¾ of the way down from here. I will enclose his letter, he seems to have good news of Susan, and Peter must be getting a fine boy and will an armful by the time Eric gets back.

---

* A playpen.

I have not heard a word from Lucy or Flurry for a long time, wonder if either of them are out here and whereabouts, wish I could see them and that if they come here they were put into this division, but that is too much to expect.

Well sweetheart the best of good luck to you both and keep very fit. Love to all and must try to write to your Dad today or tomorrow, but it will be a very poor letter as there is no news at all, but may be some shortly.

Your loving
Harold

7 September – Nothing doing.

13-9-16

8 September 1916
No 21

My own darling Con,

Another day gone and a fine one too. We have had an interesting day of it, first of all we had a competition between the 4 sub-sections, for who turned out the quickest to action and with least mistakes, it included best groomed horses, best kept harness, correctness in saddling up, smartness in all the movements and laying. The whole thing went off well, but up to the present do not know the results. I am in hopes that one of my sub-sections get it, they all worked very hard and the turnout would be a credit to any battery considering the very few conveniences we have for our general work. The prizes each sectional commander gives himself, so this month we will not be drawing much pay.

I had a long letter from Aunt Janie, they seem to be having a grand time of it, the moors must be just perfect now, but there do not seem to be a great quantity of birds.

You need not worry about us going abroad, it is about 1,000 to 1 against it. We will be going into action in about 3-4 days time.

Bindy must be a great nut in those bombachos (*baggy knickerbockers*) and expect she is hugely delightful with them, and must have been very fed up with her skirts, I expect she will be a powerful lassie, and later on keep us in order.

I would not trouble to write to Winnie, especially as she has not answered any of yours, she is a funny girl and really not worth troubling about.

There are lots of guffaws from the guns tonight, in fact from the noise they seem to be going it some. We play bridge every night now which passes the time away and are all getting very keen on it. By the way if you hear of anybody wishing to send out games for the men tell them to send some out to me as we want a few for the winter, games such as throwing the dart, rings to throw on hooks or anything they think might amuse them. Am going to write to Uncle Fred, expect he will send some of the old ones which are accumulating at Milfords. About the chair do not trouble at present, will let you know the reason at some future date.

Well my own, must close up as it is very late and must get to bed as am off early into town. The Captain has a new stunt on and is making me open an almacén (*canteen*) which I have got to run, cheer ho, what a muddle there will be. I sell tinned fruit, boot polish, buttons, cigarettes, matches, soap, bread, writing paper, beer, cake, pencils, tinned fish and about 20 other odds and ends, so you can imagine me with a white apron on and hacking away at a lump of cheese.

Well night night my own two pets and heaps of love to you both.

Your loving
Harold

13-9-16

9 September 1916

My own darling Con,

I got yours about Bindy's presents, she is a lucky girl, and you must not spoil her, or else we will require a couple of boats to take her with all her baggage out. It was great having a fine day for it, and expect she will be in great form. Glad to hear that you and your Dad were going down to Folkestone, it will do you good and you will both enjoy it. Wish you could popple over here for a day or two, as we could have quite a good time of it.

The packet with pyjamas and also the cigarettes arrived safely and many thanks, I thought that I had answered about the former. Clothes get lost very easily here, and am short of quite a lot of things, but this does not matter, as I had too many, and also whenever I require anything I can get them out of stores.

Tell Donald to bring as little as possible, 3 shirts is ample and 4 pairs of socks, so the rest in proportion, if he finds himself short, he can get them out here. Donald need not get uneasy about not coming out at present, as there is no doubt he will come, and have quite enough of it by the end of the war.

I am quite close to where Eric was billeted, about 10 minutes ride. We have church parade in a quarter of an hour, about 40 of us going, it takes about an hour to get there and back, that includes church.

Well dear, hasta luego, y con mucho suerte y cariños (*so long, and much luck and love*) to you both.

Your loving
Harold

9 September – So very good footer match, Bedford vs. 149 Brigade.
　　　　　　　Fine.
10 September – Church.
　　　　　　　Fine.

☆☆☆☆☆☆☆☆☆☆☆☆☆☆

16-9-16

11 September 1916

My own darling Con,

Hope that you had a good time of it at Folkestone, it must be quite nice there, but you got among a very energetic family, and hope they did not run you off your legs. How does the G.W.K. run now, have you to push her uphill or down.

　I wish we had a little runabout for you, it would be great. Pity you could not stop there longer as your Dad must have enjoyed a good chat with Mr. B.

Photo thanks *to Grace's Guide to British Industrial History*.

Where did A get wounded? I hope it is not serious and that he will get quite over it.

I am off up to the front lines today to have a good look round, and see what the country is like, have hardly heard a shot since early this morning. By the papers the French seem to have done well down South, and we also, hope that they keep it up and get a big move on.

8 p.m. and just come back from forward, had a very easy time of it, can hardly call it war, compared to the other place. Sorry I cannot tell you anything about it, but at the end of the war it will do.

It was just ripping getting your letter with Johnnie's enclosed. Hope the journey did not tire you out too much and expect that Bindy will be in great form when she wakes up and sees you.

The grouse Aunt Janie sent have just arrived and in fine condition, we are going to enjoy them tomorrow. Round our new position there is a fine apple orchard, just full of them, in fact some of the trees are too crowded, some of them are just ripe and very good too, so we will have them all sorts of ways, we have quite a good cook who does us very well.

We are going to have a battery photo taken, so if they turn out any good I will send you one, it will be of the whole battery and so will be quite an interesting recuerdo *(souvenir)*.

Well it was very nice to get a cheery letter from Johnnie about the camp and hear that at last all was well. The price for the cows seems quite good, and if he is able to sell the remainder at that price, should do very well. That big rain we had in April and May seems to have pulled us through the winter, and with all that good hay we cut just before leaving should keep them in good condition. The monte *(woodland)* cannot have suffered much through the locust and drought, and by the time we get back it should be quite a fine place. What luck that the capataz *(foreman)* has turned out such a good man. His wife will probably be very useful as a washerwoman for us, but there will be a crowd on the place what with the capataz and family and Jose's family, we will be swarmed out. Something will have to be done to thin them out, or turn some of the kids into servants, and make Pedrito our buttons or butler, or maybe chauffeur. Johnnie has not said much about your mares, but expect that in his next he will let us know all about them.

Poor old George seems to have had a bad time of it, and should he much more careful, as am afraid that these falls must upset him a lot, also Mrs Emmerson will be very worried, and now with Tiny getting his arm bust, the little devil, expect he was up to some mad trick.

The Halsey polo tournament am afraid will not be very great, as all the old crowd are away, but expect that they will struggle along somehow. When we get back there will be a great bust up. But think it will be hard to get us to move from *Lucero*, especially with the huge family.

Well darling night night and just heaps of love to you and Bindy and sleep well.

Your loving
Harold

17-9-16

12 September 1916

My own darling Con,

Well dearest I never told you how the competition finished off, am glad to say that one of my subsections won, C & D are mine, and it ended up C-382, A-379, D-376, B-372 so that there was very little in it, anyhow the sergeant of C sub got the fifty francs. The show was very good, now I come to think of it I have told you all about it in a letter some days ago, so no more.

They make all sorts of uses of one here. Today they made me attend a court of inquiry and had to pass my judgement on a case of the disappearance of a bicycle.

The canteen is going strong, and doing quite a brisk trade, we have started selling beer, on which there is a great run, in fact there is quite a big block in the door way. It is quite a job keeping up accounts, and expect that there will be a dickens of a muddle by the end.

We had another great football match today, our battery against the mighty grout of the Bedfords, a most exciting game and very even. We won by 1 goal amidst great cheers, quite a crowd of spectators. We supplied our men with white knickers, and light and dark blue jerseys, in fact they look quite a fine lot and are very fit. Luckily the rain kept off but has been coming down hard the whole time since.

Poor wee Bindy, I wonder what she has done to her wee self, I do not expect it is much but hope that she has got nobly into it. It is hard luck at that age, especially as she cannot express herself.

That will be great Ethel and family coming to Eastbourne for the winter, and it is very sensible as it must be very brisk down there. By all accounts Uncle Bof seems much better, can even have a game of golf.

I am becoming quite a cyclist again and go out nearly every day for some little run or other.

Must close now, so night night and just heaps of love to you two dears and God bless you always.

Your loving
Harold

12 September – Went to frontline, very quiet. Wrote Johnnie.

☆☆☆☆☆☆☆☆☆☆☆☆☆☆☆

17-9-16

13 September 1916

My own darling Con,

Just a tiny notita as am very sleepy and just off to bed, and tomorrow will have no time before the post goes. As you say, days and months are gradually going, which means always a little nearer to you, I know we both long for that day, and when it comes we will very soon forget about all this time, and if we don't, we can look back to it with square shoulders, so do not worry and it will soon be gone.

Well the Captain has got the D.S.O. and MacLean the M.C. so this battery has done well for itself, and there are 2 more men in it that should have the M.C., but the Captain, he does deserve it, no mistake. We are all very bucked about it.

Glad to hear that Beatie is so fit and got 4 days off, she will enjoy it, and be ripping for you two being both together.

Bindy must look fine in her pen, and I can quite imagine her poking around for an opening and then consoling herself with the marbles, and then get on her high chair and inspect you all at your meals, with some of her gurgles to cheer you on, and expect wanting to have a lick of lobster, or some such high coloured thing. Wonder if she will know me when I come back, she is too young to remember.

We had a fine hot shower bath this evening, so feeling very clean and comfortable.

So Donald has been posted to a battery in England, wonder where it is near and if, with any luck, near you.

I do not think that I mentioned that last Sunday I went to church with my men and heard one of the best sermons I have ever heard, it was on perseverance and putting one's might and main on trying to do a thing, and doing it well. He had everybodies mind fixed on him, and one could not help listening to him, in fact I would go a long way to hear him again.

Well darling, night night and just loads of love to you and Bindy.
Your loving
Harold

13 September – Orderly Officer. At gun position all day. Went to court of inquiry. Fine.

19-9-16

14 September 1916

My own darling Con,
2 of yours arrived this evening, with Johnnie's second letter, he will be overdoing it if he is not careful and get a stiff forefinger.

So sorry to hear about wee Bindy, but glad that it did not last long, and expect she is quite her wee self by now, wonder if it is teeth or the hot weather, hope it is not the latter.

What a popular place San Rapheal is getting, the Lindselles going up for the summer, it will become quite a summer resort, and we will be able to let our house for untold rents. It is good news that Johnnie sends about the camp, and I think that the capataz knows something about his work, am very bucked about it, and will be a fine thing for us if he turns out to be a thoroughly reliable man. What a time we will have next year.

A new charger has just arrived for me, fairly good looking beast and hope he turns out decent. I think that he must have had a good rest as he has a bit of a tummy on him, but will soon get that down, and hope to get him in good condition by the end of the month.

Has Donald been posted to a regular battery or what, and are they 60 pounders? Winchester is not very far off you, so you may see quite a lot of him.

When I write to Johnnie I will ask for the fox skins, am sure he will have any amount of them and so he will fish out some of the best, but do not know how he will be able to send them home, unless by luck anybody is coming.

Thanks very much for your little bit of French, I can get through it alright, but am afraid it is not getting on at all well as I never get a chance to speak it.
Well dear, night night and just heaps of love to you and Bindy.
Your Loving
Harold

14 September – At gun position, fix up pits etc.
  Very cold.

19-9-16

15 September 1916

My own darling Con,
Just a little notita, as I have at last just written to your Dad. I ought to have done it long ago, but somehow time seems to have slipped along. You need not worry about me going into action yet awhile, as I do not believe it will be for at least 3 weeks, and then probably somewhere far away from here, but do not know in the slightest where it will be.

We had quite a party here to dinner, 9 of us and had grouse for dinner, some of which we sent to the Captain. We have also borrowed a gramophone and have had it going all evening, and have all enjoyed it very much. It is a very craggy old thing, but just makes a noise.

Tomorrow the General is coming around to inspect our horses, so will have a busy morning getting all ready, and try to put up a decent show. We are on the move again in two or three days time, where I do not know.

What good news in the papers yesterday about the French advance, they have done well, and deserve a lot of credit for it. We are very keen on getting the papers this morning to see what is doing.

Last night we had a little rain and of course the only leakage in the tent was right above me and got me on the head, so had a hasty retreat to the other side of tent, where I was left in peace. Luckily it did not rain much, but now looks very like it.

Wonder how wee Bindy is, hope quite alright by now. Must close, with just heaps of love to you both. God bless you.
      Your loving
      Harold

15 September – At Festubert, gun position, firing up gun and ammunition.
  Not too cold.

21-9-16

16 September 1916

My own darling Con,

Two days gone and no cartita, so expect the post has gone to glory again. This morning we went and had our photos taken, a group of 5, so as soon as they come I will send it along. It is of the 5 officers, hope that it turns out well. There are just two of us here this evening, as the Captain and MacLean went to have their medals presented to them, and are having a dinner in town after, so quién sabe (*who knows*) when they will be back.

Tomorrow we will be very busy getting everything packed up, and then on the move, so expect that the post will be very erractic for sometime, probably you will get my letters fairly regularly but yours will be very spasmodic. In a way I am glad to get a shift on, as we are tired of rest, and time passes much quicker when we are trying to biff the Bosch.

This evening we have the gramaphone on and playing The Girl in the Taxi.* It did take one back to old times, especially that time we had that glorious Boston at the Savoy, it just made me long to have another whirl with you, dotu we must have another soon, and we will have one, and hope many more.

I had a ride on my new charger this morning, he is quite nice, but is very nervous of motors and flies clean off the road, but hope to get him out of this, he stands about 16.1 hands, so is quite a good climb to get on his back.

The oatcakes, toffee and peppermint lumps came and many thanks for them sweetheart, they are just lovely, also the caramels, the latter the Captain is very fond of and puts them down well. He is very keen on a trip out to the Argentine, and so one of these days we may see him out there, I have been telling him of the trips etc., and he now wants to make one outing of it, from Tucuman right down to Nahuapi in the south, that is SW of Neuquen. He is a most energetic fellow and cannot keep still for a minute.

Well my own, must now close with just heaps of love to you and wee Bindy, sleep well and bless you.

Your Loving
Harold

16 September – Orderly Officer. Photo taken. Orders for marching.

---

* A musical performed at the Lyric Theatre in London from 1912 – the magazine *The Play Pictorial* called it the "the merriest of musical farces".

☆☆☆☆☆☆☆☆☆☆☆☆☆☆☆☆

28-9-16

18 September 1916

My own darling Con,
Another pouring day and no sign of clearing up, it rained practically the whole night, and there is a grand old slush this morning.

Wee Bindy must be having a rotten time with her teeth, hope they will soon come through and she will have no more worry, it is hard luck. I have again lost one of my front teeth, so will have to have a real good go whenever my leave comes, it is the hard biscuits I eat, but as I much prefer them to bread and are better for me, it is worth giving up a false tooth or two.

Afraid you had awful trouble finding that wretched chair and sorry I gave you so much trouble in finding it, and am now afraid that it will not be of much use to us as we shall be very unsettled for sometime to come, and there is no room on the wagon to take things about on, so will probably have to leave it behind.

It must have been rotten in the empty flat, I thought that Mrs Ennor was going to rent it out for a few months.

You must try and go to see the Somme films, they all say that they are very good, but of course there are lots of other sights you will never see. I only wish I could go with you and point out the different things. I believe they were taken just a little further north of where we were.

In one of my last I wrote and told you that I had written to *L. & Co.* to send £150 to you so that you will be able to plug along alright. Am very glad you got your musk coat fixed up, of course it was well worth it and you must get yourself well fixed up before the winter comes on. If Donald comes over this winter tell him to bring a British warm *(greatcoat)*, as he will require it as much as anything. I will get one when on leave.

Must close am just off to parade. Well darling hasta luego and best of love to you and Bindy.

Your loving
Harold

18 September – Went to theatre Bethune, The Pedlars, good. Rained.
19 September – Marched from Essars to Marles-les-Mines, Auchel, Pernes, and Sangray. Heavy showers.

28-9-16

20 September 1916

My own darling Con,

2 mails have gone and I have not written, am so sorry, but we have been on the move and had no time to oneself, and looks like getting a very little for some days to come. We marched about 24 miles yesterday, and had heavy showers the whole way but arrived quite dry. It has rained ever since, and the whole place is covered with inches of mud, and everything is in a frightful state. Expect we shall be on the go for 3 or 4 days and then have a few days rest. The marching I quite like and we pass through some very fine country, and are now out of all the low country.

This battery is doing very well in the line of medals, 2 more men have just been awarded the Military Service Medal and both of them are in my section, they gained these before I joined the battery, in assisting to save one of the guns (May) when the pit was set on fire, that was a month or so before the big advance set in. The Captain is very bucked about it, well he should be proud of these men as they are a fine lot and there is nothing that they would not go through, expect they will have to do this before very long.

Yes I can imagine Mr Kennard's son not liking it very much and the animals going for him. One has to be very careful, and take care where one goes, as once you get them, they are very hard to get rid of, the only way is to chuck all your kit away or get it boiled and have a real hot disinfectant bath oneself. I expect he is a gunner and will have a fairly heavy time of it.

I wonder how you two dears are, am longing to hear, but do not expect a letter for at least 4 days, but may have a bit of luck and get one before that, veremos *(we will see)*.

I got yours with Lucy's enclosed, so he is out here at last. He went to the same place at Le Havre as I did, I may meet him as am on my way south again. Will finish this later, as stables is on.

Two of your dear letters have just arrived and it was just ripping to get them. Am sorry to hear that Bindy has taken too much to Alice, but expect that she will soon change when she gets a little older. I think that most of them are taken that way if they have a good nurse, and very naturally too, as they are continually with them, and do most things for them. Wonder how she will like the birthday party, expect she will thoroughly enjoy it, and be a great nut.

I got the medicine alright, and in one of my former I told you that the cigarettes had come. Will you send another lot, afraid am smoking a good deal, but the pipe has not come into work much, and do not think it will for sometime to come, as I do not appreciate it.

The photo I had taken was so bad that I did not get any so will have another try when I get to any town.

Yes, the Somme battle goes along well and hope that they will get well through, but it is a very fierce fight and a good many fine men have gone west.

Aunt Bella has just sent two squares of honey, it looks grand. She is a dear kind old thing.

Well darling, will close, just heaps of love to you both and God bless you.

Your loving
Harold

20 September – Rained.
21 September – Marched through Hernicourt, Croix-en-Ternois, Siracourt, and Croisette.
22 September – Marched through Vacquerie-le-Bouck, Bonnieres, Barly, Occoches, Mont Plaisir (now Rue de Mont Plaisirt, Longuevillette.) Arrived 1 p.m., good billets. Fine.

28-9-16

23 September 1916

My own darling Con,

We have been marching the last 4 days and have had very little time to oneself. Luckily the last two days have been lovely, and I like that sort of weather, the marching is quite nice, I do not know in the slightest where we are going to, or when we are going to get there.

The chair arrived today and many thanks.

Had a march of about 14 miles and the country we have gone through is very fine, but gets more open as we get along and less populated. The last two nights we had very comfortable billets – but tonight everything is full up, and so are going to sleep in the open, hope they do not keep us here long. I must have passed somewhere close to the division Eric is in, but had not time to look for him, and from now on will be gradually moving away from him.

That boy I had as a batman turned out an awful little ass and conceited pup, so have kicked him out, and now he does odd jobs with the horse lines. They are fools, as a batman they get very little work and all their food is much better and on top of all this they get lazier and slacker until at last you have to kick them out, they are much worse than the servants one gets out in B.A. Have now got an older man, and hope he will have a little more sense, I think he will. He is a peculiar chap and in his spare time writes short yarns and sends them to some lady friend at home. They are not very good, but should think with a little training he would improve.

I expect that Lucy has by now joined his unit, but do not think that he could have gone through that big doing they have had, probably he joined after it.

Am afraid this is a very poor notita, but do not seem to be able to think of anything today, so will close. Just heaps of love to you and Bindy and bless you both.

                Your loving
                Harold

23 September –   *Marched through Doullines, Beauval, Rubempre, and Pierregot. Bad billets, stopped three nights. Tested sights etc. Fine.*

4-10-16

24 September 1916

My own darling Con,

Such a grand post today, 3 from you, one from Susan, also one from Eric and *L. & Co.*, so have had a rare old afternoon of it, and thoroughly enjoyed it. Those snaps of Bindy are very nice, but I think that the best of the lot are the ones you sent before, of her in the pram, and on the rug crawling along. I had them all pinned up in my room, but as we had to move I took them down and packed them away. She is getting a regular old mop of hair, hope she is not going to take after me, if so she will have some trouble with it. She seems to be great on her feet, and the cheer of her walking about and taking the corral where she likes is about the limit, suppose she will soon be rolling it over, you will have to anchor it down and then there will be a tussle. Yes, I am longing to see you both, and wonder when that will be.

Glad to hear that Hugh is so well, and will feel very bucked at having Ethel and children at Eastbourne. Salcombe was so far away and such a place to get at.

I would most certainly have a good photo taken of Bindy now, and then we can have it taken at the end of each year, get it done by some good childrens photographer. Is Lina Connell any good at that sort of thing?

I do not think there is any difference between English time and this, if so it is only a few minutes.

Yes dear, please send my fur lined gloves, during the early mornings they will come in very well. Also send a bottle of Syrup of Figs.

About the canteen, I raise the few francs from whoever will lend them, about 300 francs, and all the profits go to the benefit of the battery. In the first 8 days we made 100 francs, not so dusty. It is an easy job, a very few accounts to keep, the benefits are to supply them with footballs, boots and short pants, and anything they would like, and probably at Xmas give them a good dinner.

Glad Bindy enjoyed the party and expect she was in great form. The grouse Aunt Janie sent me arrived in fine condition and were very much enjoyed.

My last batman's father has sent me out 4 little paintings which I think are very nice and well worth framing, so am going to send them on to you. The boy says his father has some paintings in the Academy, his name is Palmer. I feel rather a beast at turning the boy out, and think that the old man must have sent them to me on account of me taking the boy and looking after him, but now have turned him out on account of being so slack. But anyhow am trying to get him home on account of him suffering from rheumatism.

Well dotu, will now close, just heaps of love to you both, God bless you.
Your loving
Harold

30-9-16

25 September 1916

My own darling Con,
We are still having grand weather, and only hope that it will keep up for a month or so, when it is like this it is glorious.

We are on the move again tomorrow and will not be sorry to leave here, as it is a very poor place, and billets are not good, but the great thing is that we have a good roof over our heads. The last 2 nights we have been sleeping on the floor, but nowadays it makes no difference and my hips do not ache any more, one gets used to these things very quickly. This morning we were out in the fields, practising with the director, it is extraordinary how quickly one gets out of it.

Yours of the 20th has just arrived. Bindy must be a handful, and make no mistake, it makes me long to see her, but much more you. I do not expect you will get many letters from me for a few days as we are going to be very busy getting all ready.

No, the guns are not 60 pounders, they are 4.5, about 35 pounds.

There is a great scrummary outside the window, as all the men are being paid, and are very bucked about it.

I still have my sweater and all my warm clothes, so will be alright for sometime to come.

How did the picnic go off? I expect your Dad enjoyed it, and will have done him a lot of good.

I met one of the boys who was with me at St. John's Wood, and he says that I am getting much fatter, I shall have to diet myself, or else you will hardly know me, I am sure I am as have to let my belt out, especially after meals, so you can guess what an appetite I have.

We heard this evening that 2 zeppelins* had been brought down in England, that is great news, and hope next time that it will be three or more. The Huns are getting nasty knocks on all sides, wouldn't it be grand to see them crumpled up.

---

* A rigid airship invented by Count Ferdinand von Zeppelin. Germany used them as scouts and bombers, killing over 500 people over the course of the war.

I sent you those small paintings and hope you will get them safely and like them. I really think they are quite good.

Well sweetheart must close now, just heaps of love to you and bless you both, and keep well.

Your loving
Harold

25 September – Practiced with director.*
    Pierregot.
    Fine.

☆☆☆☆☆☆☆☆☆☆☆☆☆☆☆

4-10-16

26 September 1916

My own darling Con,

Here we are again, very near where we were before. Dotu I am glad, the news that is in today is the best we have ever had, and darling I think that it is better than we could have hoped for, and the Bosch is down down down. There is a different atmosphere in the air, and all the troops are cheery and right on top, and dotu we will be in action tomorrow, and are longing to be, and dotu it will be much better than last time, I must not say anymore as I will say too much.

We have had a long march today, but nobody can be tired on account of what our troops have done, good luck is with them as they deserve it more than anybody in the world. The only thing we want to help us now is the weather, and may it keep fine.

This spot we are in now is really a wonderful place, where it used to be peaceful farm land is now a mass of roads, horse lines and swarmed with troops, it is a sight one could hardly believe, it is a sight I would not miss for anything.

Well dearest, am off to bed, God bless you both and will write as soon as I can, but quien sabe (*who knows*) when it will be.

Your loving
Harold

---

*   Directors were used to orient the guns of an artillery battery on their zero line. In The Great War most directors were optical instruments.

26 September – Marched through Molliens-au-Bois, Saint Gratien, Querrieu, and Dernancourt. Slept out the night.

27 September – Marched to new position at Longeuval. Quiet. Fine.

☆☆☆☆☆☆☆☆☆☆☆☆☆☆☆☆

Summer / Autumn / Winter 1916

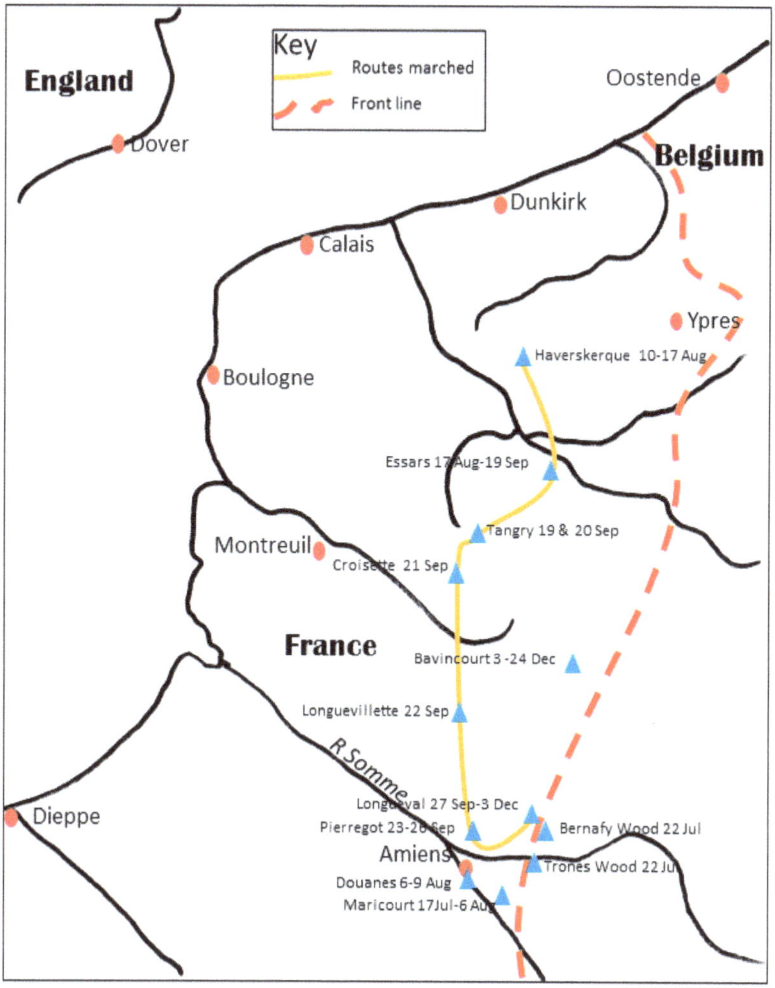

© Sheila Kennard 2016

Places and dates mentioned in Harold's diary of 1916 – including the route marches.

4-10-16

28 September 1916

My own darling Con,

Here we are in our new postion, which is very much the same as the first one I went to when I joined the battery. The whole place is an extraordinary sight, and only wish I could describe it to you.

I had the luck to come across one of the "Tanks" yesterday, and was shown all over it. They are wonderful and look like a block of iron moving about, and are of this shape:

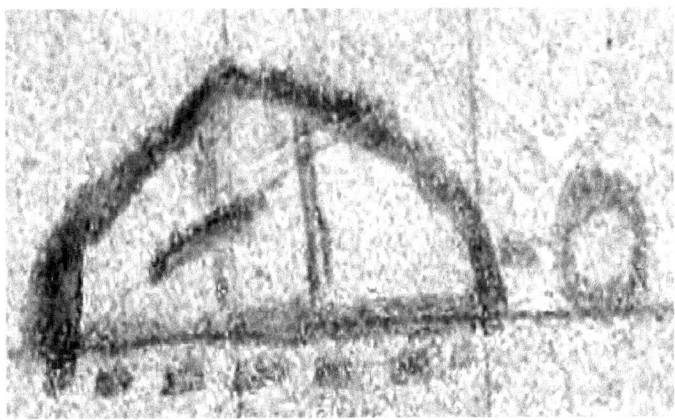

The little circle is the steering wheel and it runs on caterpillars, the one I saw had two 6 pounder quick firing guns, and then several little slots where they can put a machine gun in and blast away. They have a periscope and are chock full of ammunition. They are driven by a high power motor engine. On each side there is a turret, and a quick firing gun. The quick firing gun is the little mark I have made on the slant. I have not seen one go into action yet, but hope to do so soon, they must be a funny sight, and must have been a great shock to the Bosch when they first came on the scene, and hope that they will cause them a good deal of trouble.

Do you remember Gorton who died at San Rafael? Curiously enough, I was standing on the road by our guns and who should come up but his brother, he is a lance corporal in the New Zealand engineers, and I think that this war must have done him a lot of good, he looks very much better for it. He used to drink a great deal before, but now does not get much chance of that, and is quite a good hand with a pick or shovel.

When I wrote you my last letter we were all very much elated at the success our troops had achieved and probably I was too glowing, anyhow they did very well and the Bosch had a very rotten time of it. But you must not think it will shorten the war unless we get a very big move on from now.

We had a little rain last night but luckily not very much, hope to goodness it keeps off.

Must close now as am going to have a look around, so hasta luego and very best of luck and heaps of love.

                          Your loving
                          Harold

28 September – Quiet.
           Fine.

                     5-10-16

                                                      29 September 1916

My own darling Con,

I had a ripping 3 letters from you, and one from your Dad, dated 23rd. But darling, I picked up *The Times* of the 28th, and can it be true? I saw that your dear brother Raymond had died for his country on the 18th. I cannot put words how I feel about it, and has given me a great shock, it is just a wicked war. I will not write to your father until I hear from you, I hope it is one huge mistake, and that I may get a letter from you very soon saying that all is well. If it is true, you will all know that he died with his face to the enemy, oh it is so hard to think that he has gone.

Here the country is in an awful state, and hardly an inch which has escaped our shell fire. The work that is going on is tremendous, and is one big strife and struggle, and the one point is to kill the Hun, how I wish that they would give in, as I am sure we never shall. I cannot give any details but the guns just keep going off for all they are worth, which usually means something.

The last three days have been very damp and one cannot get dry, all one's clothes get moist and remain so until we get good dry weather. Anyhow do not expect it will do us much harm, as we get well hardened to most things. The dugouts are very poor ones, and am not fixing it up, as we shall not be long on this spot. It is an old sunken road, and some very heavy fighting has taken place on it, but no, the Hun is a long way off it, and hope that he will be miles further by the time we have finished with him.

Am going to answer your dear letters tomorrow, as I have not the heart to do so after that news. Just heaps and heaps of love to you and God bless you both.

Your loving
Harold

P.S. Am sorry my letter writing has been so erratic, but moving has upset everything. The chair arrived safely. Just had a letter from Flurry, who has got his transfer to the 2nd Life Guards. Just long to be with you and share your grief. Tell your father why I did not write, but will do so as soon as I am certain of it.

29 September – Big movement of guns.

☆☆☆☆☆☆☆☆☆☆☆☆☆☆☆

6-10-16

30 September 1916

My own darling Con,
Well darling we have had a perfect day of it, but quite a touch of winter in the air. It is better so, as hot weather would be unbearable in this part, and want some fine weather as we are probably going into a new position, where we have not even got a dugout, and so will have to set to work and make them.

Yes, Kathy's letter does bring back the days one spent there, pity she has to work so hard and must want a real good rest now. We did not put Uncle Alfred on the list, I do not think that there is any need to.

I got a letter from Flurry, saying that he could not go to you, as all transfer papers had come, which kept him busy, but that he was going to you on Friday, so hope you had a good time, but am afraid your home is a very sad one, as that sad sad news brings things so near to one, and they are too.

Am glad to hear that Donald is so fit, and likes his battery, it is lucky hitting a decent lot of officers and a good battery, it makes a great difference. Personally I do not expect that he will come out before November, and then he may do so, so as to get ready for next spring offensive.

Curiously enough at a battery a few yards off ours, I was walking along and who should I come across but Mr Bruton, he is very fit and sent you recuerdos *(regards)*. He told me that Robin Le Begg had to undergo an operation, I believe something in his throat.

So you have at last had a letter from Winnie, you will have a race for it, I must try and be at home for it. By the way will you please send some envelopes and paper, they are very scarce, and have only one left. Now we are in action again the canteen has gone to pot.

Well pet, best of love, and just heaps of love to you. It is nearly 7 o'clock, so expect that Bindy is having a final chat to you before closing her shutters. Night night dear heart.

                            Your loving
                            Harold

Nelson
New Zealand
2017

Dear Harold,

You experienced so much loss during your year in the theatre of war – I am not sure why it is called that, maybe because war creates a spectacle for others to observe. I feel you are so right in your observations that it is the politicians and leaders that create wars, and not those that have to do the dirty work of fighting them. I can assure you that weapons have got worse and the potential of war hangs over the head of humankind. Sadly the majority of countries in the world are involved in some way or another in conflict. I do so hope that we learn to live in peace and harmony eventually, but your war was certainly not the war to end all wars. More than 38 million people from all sides had died by the end of it, you were just one of many who offered up their life.

It must have been so challenging for you to read in the paper that Con's younger brother Raymond had been killed in action. I know nothing about Raymond but I have a tiny bit of a letter he wrote to Con:

> *I was glad to hear D. was getting on so well and I hope Harold was pleased with himself. Well dotu I must fly now, this place is just the same old rush as ever but they have taken away half of my front which makes things a great deal easier. I don't see definite signs of being recognised yet, but as we are still in existence there is still hope.*
> *Love to you and all the people.*
> *R.B.W.*

Raymond was recognised for his work, he was a Captain in the 176th Tunnelling Company of the Royal Engineers. He was mentioned in dispatches and was awarded the Military Cross – this tells of his extraordinary bravery, something that so many of you found.

> Temporary Second Lieutenant Raymond Burke Williams, 176th Company, Royal Engineers.
>
> For conspicuous gallantry and devotion to duty at Givenchy on 25th August 1915, when in charge of a mine. He went down the gallery immediately after the end had been blown in and ordered the men out owing to gas fumes. He then endeavored to rescue the men till he was himself

overcome by fumes, and had to be dragged out; but as soon as he recovered again went halfway down the mine and directed further rescue operations.

Second Lieutenant Williams has been in charge of mines in the Givenchy area since 7th July, and has consistently shown the greatest coolness in difficult operations necessitating rapid charging and blowing up of mines in very close proximity to the enemy's counter mines.

London Gazette, 2nd October 2015

Raymond died in September 1916 and is remembered at Arras Memorial, in France, located in the Faubourg d'Amiens British Cemetery, in the western part of the town of Arras. The inscription simply states:

Here are recorded the names of 35942 officers and men of the forces of the British Empire who fell in the Battles of Arras or in air operations above the Western Front and who have no known grave.

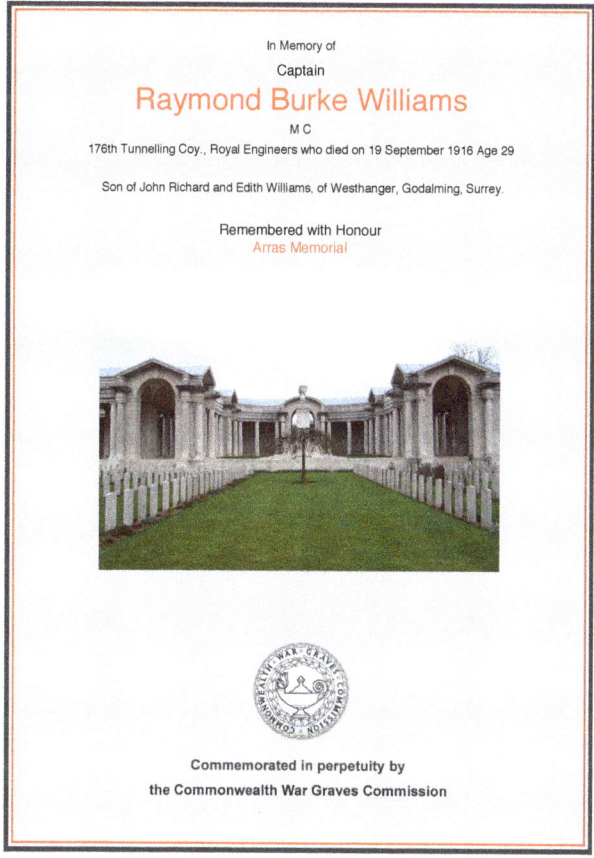

These memorials are cherished and well cared for. So many of you had no graves to lie in, instead the names of the fallen are carved in stone, to be fondly touched by family members for generations to come.

And so the family had their first taste of death by warfare. Raymond is also remembered on the war memorial in Godalming, his name also engraved in stone on there.
With love
Sheila x

OCTOBER 1916

Con and Bindy 1915

Silence before being born, silence after death;
Life is nothing but noise between two unfathomable silences.
Isabel Allende - *Paula*

9-10-16

1 October 1916

My own darling Con,

I am so so sorry that you have been 4 days without any letters. I have only once been two days without writing, so cannot understand why they have been delayed, and am truly sorry, as I have tried to make it a special point not to miss a day, and cause you as little worry as possible. I will do my very best not to miss a day, if only it be but a field postcard. It must have been all the moving about, as am sure that the post gets very upset on these occasions. Am afraid that everything will be upset for sometime, as we are very unsettled.

 Poor old girl, I do pity you having to break the news of Raymond to Helen, and darling do take care of yourself, as am sure that you are doing too much, and I do want to see you looking fit and well when I get home, which ought to be sometime next month. I wrote your Dad a short notita this evening, but am afraid it was a very poor one, am hopeless at writing such a letter.

 I have had a very exciting day, and seen a lot, you must remind me about it after the war and will give you an account of it.

 Please tell your father not to send any games at present as Uncle Fred has sent 3 or 4, which is quite enough for the present, in fact we will not be able to use them until we are out of this.

 Well my own, am off to bed, as have to be on the move at 2.30 a.m. So night night and just the best of love to you both, and God keep you and the wee one very fit.

Your loving
Harold

1 October –	Went to wagon line morning then to Observation Post and saw N.Z. advance, successful, took about 50 prisoners.
2 October –	Got into new position at Flers and started to dig in. Started raining midday, everything in a h… of a mess, did not shoot. Shelling in 59, not very near.

☆☆☆☆☆☆☆☆☆☆☆☆☆☆☆

6-10-16

3 October 1916

My own darling Con,

Just a very hurried one, as am just off out. It has rained a lot and I have never seen things in such a mess, it is awful and looks like keeping on.

Yes dear, you might send an occasional parcel and in it you might send some curried rabbit or chicken, they are very easy to cook and very good.

Glad to hear that you are all together, it will be a great comfort to you all, but you must not think about it too much.

We are very near where I first came into action, cannot say any more. We at present only have one dugout to eat and sleep in for 4 of us, and it is a mass of mud, but somehow one does not mind this.

Well goodbye and love to all.

Your loving
Harold

☆☆☆☆☆☆☆☆☆☆☆☆☆☆☆

9-10-16

3 October 1916

My own darling Con,
Am sorry I wrote such a short notita this morning, but I was in a great hurry, as the Captain was waiting for me, so had to push off.

That new horse of mine is an old ass at passing cars, but I have got him in hand now and will get him out of that trick, think that he must have been ridden by someone who let him do what he liked.

Am afraid that this is going to be another short letter as we are very busy and no time for anything. We have not had any outside news for a long time, 7 days, so do not know what is happening.

I got the cigs from the Emersons, but they are Turkish, which am not very keen on, but have finished the others, they will do for the time being. Will you send me some of my remedies as soon as possible as have run short, have got some for about 3 days.

It is just awful out here at present. I thought that I knew what mud was like but now find that I did not.

Well pet, just heaps of love and God bless you both.

Your loving
Harold

3 October – Very little shooting.
            Wretched day.

9-10-16

4 October 1916

My own darling Con,

Here we are and another day gone, and a wretched day too, very dull all day and a good many showers, it is just hopeless to try and keep dry. Anyway we are all cheery and the men are a fine lot and take everything with a smile, it does one good to work with them.

Fancy, we see crowds of partridges about here, I went over the ridge today and must have put up 60 or 70, and if only had had the gun, could have easily bagged a couple, that is if my eye was in, cannot make out why they stop here, as the ground is all torn up and very little for them to pick at. The Captain has a small walking stick shot gun so will have a try with it.

We have just had word that the French have honoured Captain Fraser-Tytler by decorating him with the Crois de Guerre.* Do not say anything about it to any of his people as he does not seem to like it, they first heard through you about the D.S.O. and he seemed rather sick about it, as he did not want them to know, but I told him not to be so greedy, and let his people enjoy it as well as himself. He deserves everything he gets, and I do not know why such a little was said about him, as he did very much more than MacLean, but the latter did very well too.

This is a wonderful part of the line and the more one sees of it, the more one wonders how the Bosch can stick it, he is a tough nut and no mistake.

I thought that Mabel was still in France, has she chucked her job, or is she going back to it? I expect that she wants a good rest, as it must be pretty hard work. I am glad that Flurry has at last got his transfer, and will be very bucked. Of course he is still in the cavalry and they are not doing much at present, just sitting and waiting.

Yes I think I am very fit, in fact quite sure as up to now I have not had any cold, and not even a headache, which is very bucking as there have been quite a number of light flu cases which last 2 or 3 days. My only trouble now is that I have got such a huge mop of hair, that it is quite hard to brush and gets full of mud, must try and get it cropped shortly.

Must close as have a lot of letters to write, so hasta mañana *(until tomorrow)* and tons of love and oh such a hug to you and Bindy.

Your loving
Harold

4 October –   Shot about 70 rounds.
              Miserable day.

---

* The Cross Of War, a French medal created in 1915.

☆☆☆☆☆☆☆☆☆☆☆☆☆☆☆☆

12-10-16

5 October 1916

My own darling Con,

Another day gone, we have now been 9 days in action, and in a way the time is passing fairly quickly, it will be 3 months on the 10th since I left you. Pet it will anyway be another 6 weeks before I get away, and that with luck, but will more likely be the end of November.

We have had quite a nice day, no rain but rather cold, the great thing is that is was dry, and a good wind to harden the ground.

I find it very hard to write anything tonight, my old head will not work. I have got very fond of my old fleabag, and can sleep in it wherever I chuck it down.

I expect that Bindy will soon be running all over the garden, and give you a great time of it chasing her about. I shall be quite shy of her, and expect she will wonder what sort of a person I am.

We have not had any mail for 2 days, but are in hopes of one coming tonight.

I got an old *Buenos Aires Standard* yesterday, it was fine having a look at the old rag, and I do believe that it is worse than it was before, absolutely no news in it, and seem to have done away with the old telephonicas (*telephone*).

One sees some fine sticks in the mud, and sometimes they are so bad that they just unhook the horses, and leave the vehicle there, and dig them out as the ground dries up.

6/10/16

No letter last night, so hope to get a huge one tonight and am looking forward to a good read. Luckily it has not rained more and there is a good strong wind to dry things up a bit.

I am going down to the wagon line the day after tomorrow for 8 or 9 days, they are about 2000 yards behind the guns and so will be in charge of that for that time. It will be interesting, and will gain some experience of how the munition is sent up for the guns.

Will you please order some more medicine and have it sent up as soon as possible, also my Gillette razor, as my batman has lost mine, or someone has gained it.

The guns are popping quite a lot today, which means that the Bosch is getting it in the neck. I see by the last paper that the Russians are hard at it, and hope that they will make a big push forward now, as the winter is very close on us, and we want to get a lot done before that comes on.

I hear that Aunt Janie is much better, Scotland does seem to agree with her and she has had a good spell of it.

I do not know when this letter will get away, no post in or out, unless some orderly by chance comes up.

I see in *The Times* that Lucy has been wounded, hope to goodness it is not serious, he had not long out here, and must have got hit right away. Will you try to find out where he is and how he is.

I have little time to write now, in fact next to none, but if we are not able to send the letters off this will be rather a long one and full of rubbish.

Well darling, have no news at all, so just tons of love to you and Bindy and a great big hug and kiss.

Your loving
Harold

5 October – Observing afternoon. Huns worrying us with 59. Fairly fine day.
6 October – Quiet. Showers.

13-10-16

7 October 1916

My own darling Con,

At last we have got a really fine day, so hope we will get a week or two of it.

I think that Ethel must have made some mistake the other day, that is about 3 weeks ago, as I received 2 cakes and a tin of biscuits, a few days after I got a letter addressed to me, but on opening it I found it was for Eric, and in it she mentioned that she had sent him the cakes and biscuits. Anyhow we gained, and had a good tuck into the cakes, so old Eric will have to wait. Have not heard for sometime from him and do not know where he is, should just love to come across him again.

Will you get me 2 pairs of really thick socks, and long in the leg, as it is beginning to get quite nippy here, and have just put my sweater on.

There have been several air fights today, but have not seen any come down.

9/10/15

Darling, so sorry to have missed two days, but have come down to the wagon lines for 10 days, but I ought to have got one off yesterday. The mail is very bad, but it is on account of the huge amount of traffic here, and as is very natural, war work comes before the mail. I got 2 letters from you last night dated 28th and 29th, so you see that they took 10 days to arrive.

It is dear of you to have thought of sending me a waistcoat, but I think it will be as well to wait, as I have enough warm clothes for the present, and have no more room to carry anything about, as in these days one must travel as light as possible. When I am at the guns I leave most of my clothes at the wagon line, just take a change with me and very little of that too. My hut is now composed of sandbag walls, and a large waterproof sheeting covers the roof, am really very comfortable and quite snug.

You girls are a terror when you get together, fancy talking to 1.45 a.m., what in the world do you talk about? I should be asleep long before that.

Sorry to hear about Monty being wounded, but as it is slight he is better there than here, and Kitty must be only too thankful to get him back. Hope he will get a real good rest.

That is great about Jessie Smith coming to stay with Aunt Janie, she will be a great companion to her, and think she will make a lot of difference to Aunt Janie, do not know if you have met her, she is very nice.

Yes pet, I am very fit, and do not get colds nearly so easily as before, I have been in wet clothes for the whole day, and a damp bed at night, but it has made no difference, and feel no bad effects from it. I am now messing with 6 other officers from other batteries, one or two of them are quite nice fellows and the messing is good, in fact the best I have been to out here.

Well darling, will close and just heaps of love to you both and God bless you.

Your loving
Harold

7 October –	Attack at 1.45 from east of Gueudecourt to Tovey Farm, partial success, about 500 prisoners. Fine day.
8 October –	Came to wagon line. Mac to guns. Rained hard.
9 October –	At wagon line, Montuban de Picardie. Dull no rain.

☆☆☆☆☆☆☆☆☆☆☆☆☆☆

15-10-16

10 October 1916

My own darling Con,

Fancy it is just three months since I left you at Woking, but it seems much more.

By *The Times* of the 7th I see that Jack Gordon has been wounded, it must have been very shortly after he wrote to you, they seem to be going through it, one after another, and can only hope that they are not serious, and that he will soon be well.

The guns are at it hard again, and is almost one continual roar.

Got 3 of your dear letters last night and also the enclosure from Beatie. Am afraid that Raymond's death has been a hard knock to you all, but you all must be very proud of him, and know that he died a fine death, and a painless one, and is now at peace. It is awful to think that so many fine lives are being given up, but one hopes that this war will be a lesson to all, and I do not think that anybody who has been actually in it will ever want to witness another, and in general, I do not think that the general public will ever allow one.

Aunt Janie has just sent me a fun parcel, Edinburgh rock, cake and chocolates, wish you could enjoy them with me. Also the cigs arrived and many thanks for them. Another notitia from you, you are just a darling at writing and bless you for it, glad you have at last received some of mine, as I was beginning to feel a wretch. Will you please send me 2 refills for the Tommies cooker, I asked you a long time ago, but that must have been one of the letters that went astray.

Would you like me to write and tell your Dad about the expected one, if so I will do so, as it will be quite easy for me to do so, then it will break the ice for you. So glad he is behaving himself. Dotu, they all write and tell me you are thin. I often wonder if you are taking Horlicks, do you remember that you said you would, and am sure it does you a lot of good, so like a dear try hard to do so. I shall be very disappointed if I find you looking thin when I arrive, how I wish I was there to look after you. Those social evenings must be a rotten affair and am sure that everybody would just as soon be at home by their own fireside.

The paintings are all of Dartmoor, and I really think they are quite good, and will look nice in our solita. (*sitting room*).

Q.F. means quick firing, so your guess is quite correct, as you say they are ugly, and are painted nondescript colours, yellow, red, blue, brown and Gray.

Well darling, will close now, with just heaps of love to you and wee Bindy and God bless you.

Your own loving
Harold

10 October –   At wagon line.
         Fine.

16-10-16

11 October 1916

My own darling Con,

I have now had a couple of very quiet days at wagon line, where there is not very much to do, but look after the horses and keep the guns supplied with ammunition. It is now 9 p.m. and am going to turn in, and have my Tommies cooker alongside heating some water. Have got your dear photo on my dressing table which consists of an ammunition box, quite a good substitute and very simple and plain.

Yes we did get an extra hour in bed, on account of putting the clock back an hour, I think that the French did this little wheeze before we did.

It is great bringing the 4 zeps down, and only hope that it will scare the Hun from going over, and if he does, hope he will have the lot knocked out.

I have a great deal of letter censoring here, about 50 a day, one gets fed up with it as there is nothing interesting in them, and if you read one you practically know what is in the rest.

Bindy will be comfortable in her wee cot by now and sound asleep, by the way, has she grown too big for it, if so where does she sleep? Also it will almost look as if she is taking the pram about, and not the pram her, by Jove I am longing to see her, and only hope it will be soon.

We are all just hoping and hoping that the weather will keep up, as such a lot depends on it. Wish I could give you the details but cannot, especially as there is so little else to talk about. What did you think of Lloyd George's* speech with America? We all think it was simple and straight and to the point, and it should show the Germans what the general mind is.

Well darling, night night and just tons of love to you both and bless you.
Your own loving
Harold

11 October –   At wagon line.
         Fine.

---

*   David Lloyd George, the Secretary of State for War, was interviewed by the United Press on September 28th 1916.

17-10-16

12 October 1916

My own darling Con,
Just got your notita of the 4th, and glad to hear that your Dad is taking a day off, he should not do so much, and take more care of himself.

We have just had another bit of a scrap this afternoon, the news so far is good. The canteen is going strong, and are making about 100 francs a day out of it, all this is good for the battery, and hope to give the boys a real good time at Xmas with it, a rare fine dinner, and they deserve it too.

The Germans are rotten, today 5 came over with a white flag, and behind them another creeping to see how strongly our trench was manned, we got all six, and they will never do it again.

Am very bucked to hear the Lucy is well and hope he will never have a narrower escape.

Bindy must be a great nut with her red slippers, and can quite imagine her eyes sparkling, she seems very fond of high colours.

Now I am the the wagon lines my canvas bath comes in fine and get one every 3 days, which is not too bad.

It will be nice for you all having Donald there for the weekend, he will be well into his work by now. The 60 pounders are doing good work here and getting good results.

I hear a fire crackling, which means that my bath will soon be ready and then my camita, I expect you will be going in about an hour's time, it is nearly 9 p.m.

Well darling, night night and just piles of love, and only wish I could give you a huge hug, and also the wee one.

Your own loving
Harold

12 October –   Attack 2.45 p.m. unsuccessful, about 200 prisoners. Objective taken and lost.

19-10-16

13 October 1916

My own darling Con,
Just a wee line tonight as I must write to Aunt Janie.

Another day without rain, but is trying very hard to do so. I went for a good walk with the doctor, all over the old ground where we used to fire, and have our last position, it was very interesting, but is now quite deserted, and getting quite green. Also went over the ground where we made the attack on, and where they used to try and snipe us from. The ground is all cleaned up, and baring old shell holes, looks quite respectable.

No dear, we are nowhere near 30 miles off Montauban, màs o menos 1 legua. *(more or less 1 league)*

Did you ever meet Lional Bingham in B.A. He came up to our mess yesterday, and has got into one of the batteries in our brigade. We used to call him the Rabbit as he had such a long run with a skip like a rabbit, when bowling at cricket. He saw Pancho Watson who is having a very easy time of it in the R.H.A. *(Royal Horse Artillery)*.

Glad the Miss Crofts turned up and must have been very nice seeing them again.

I never asked it you wanted any souvenirs of the battlefield, if you do let me know. I am collecting different kinds of bayonettes, but have not troubled about anything else. The infantry get most them them, but can easily get it from them.

8.30 p.m. and just finished dinner consisting of soup, lobster, roast beef, asparagus and peas, sago pudding and tea, so you see that we do not do so badly, and now I am eating chocolate. Your cake arrived this evening and looks very nice, will tell you all about it tomorrow.

Well my own darling, night night and tons and tons of love to you both, and God bless you both.

Your own loving
Harold

13 October – Went round Bernafy and Trone wood and toward Hardicourt with doctor.
14 October – Went up to guns morning. Revising canteen accounts now.
Fine and cold.

22-10-16

15 October 1916

My own darling Con,

Two letters from you and one from Eric, quite a post, and just think, I am sitting by a nice fire and in the chair which Ethel gave me, in other words I am very comfortable and only wish I had you with me.

I sent my servant out to try and get a grating or stove, so he hunted about and found an old worn out one in one of the famous woods where so much fighting took place at the start of the offensive. So with a few tins we packed it up and it is going famously. My hut from the outside looks like this:

The centre is 6 ft. high, the side 3 ft and the room 10 ft. x 7 ft. The pipe sticking out of the side is the stove pipe and just about that angle, the wall is of sandbags and the roof is a tarpaulin.

This is supposed to be how the furniture is placed:

The chairs are in the middle, really it is very comfortable, and only hope that they will leave me in it, but am afraid that they will not leave me here for more than 5 or 6 days.

About warm coats etc., I would rather not have any at present, until I see where I am going to spend the winter, as they take such a lot of room up, which we cannot afford.

The preserved fruit, medicine, and parcel of stores arrived safely, and are very good. Yes, the tinned rabbit and chicken are in too small tins, they usually come in about 3 times the size, but they do quite well, and also like the curried very much, warms me up more than the other.

Yes, it must be just grand out at *Lucero* and San Rafael now, the best part of the year and one can just imagine how the trees and everything are growing. I wonder how our giant ash is, and all the roses etc., but we will have a time of it when we get back.

Nobody in the Division is getting leave, and will not do so until we are out of action, then there are all the senior men before me, so quién sabe (*who knows*) when it will be, anyhow it will come sometime, and then we will appreciate it all the more, it will be grand.

Monty did have a squeaker and make no mistake, hope he will get a real good rest now. I had a long letter from Eric this evening, he seems cheery and well, but no sign of leave, he has had a good spell of it. So Ken Yarrow is on leave again, he was jolly lucky to have got a transfer, and has now got a cushy job. But somehow I do not think that I would have transferred, and the Black Watch have been through it since then.

I just love to write to you whenever I can, and now I am at the wagon line I have plenty of time, and plenty of sleep.

Well pet will close, just heaps and heaps of love to you and Bindy, and oh for a hug.

Your own loving
Harold

15 October –	Checked store account clear and proper. B.33.00. Small attack on right of Gueudecourt, partial success, Durham cut up. Captured 4 whizz-bangs.* Wretched old day, raining.
16 October –	Quiet. Lt. JM Bevan joined battery. Fine sunny day, cold.

21-10-16

17 October 1916

My own darling Con,

Our senior lieutenant Mr MacDonald has left us, and gone as 2nd in command of a 6 gun battery and yesterday Lieutenant Bevan joined up with us, he seems a decent sort, he is a full blown lieutenant. Am having a very quiet time of it here,

---

* German 77mm field gun, when it was fired the shells travelled faster than the speed of sound, making a whizz noise before the bang of the gun.

very little to do and the Hun does not worry us very much with shells. I go up to the guns about once every 4 days.

I got a letter from your Dad yesterday in answer to mine, will you thank him for it, I did not intend him to worry about answering it.

Glad to hear that Flurry has at last got away, even if it is to Salonika, he will see some good fighting, and more open than it is here. He will be very bucked especially as Hancock goes with him, it is a great thing to have a pal.

That account from Preston is a bit thick, he knows how to charge. I would certainly not pay him, especially as your stopping came out and my tooth has gone again. I will have a good talk to him when I get home.

It is a very still, sunny day and I feel sleepy and lazy, in fact almost like a siesta and will probably have one after lunch, so you had better join me in one, even if so far off.

Exactly 3 months yesterday since I joined the battery, in a way it seems a long time ago, but when one looks at different things that have happened it has flown.

Well no more today, just heaps and heaps of love to you both.

Your loving
Harold

17 October –   Quiet. Day fine, started rain 8 p.m.

22-10-16

18 October 1916

My own darling Con,

Your cake was very good, and by the way it disappeared I do not think that anything could have been wrong with it. You are an old dear ordering things from Harrods for my birthday, it is just like you to remember these things, wish I could remember them all.

I am off up to the guns tomorrow, have had 10 days of it here, and so it is Wilson's turn to come down, also MacLean. Anyway it has been a great rest and have been able to get all my clothes washed and everything properly dry. Will have a final bath tonight, which will carry me through until we come out of action. Am sorry to leave the tent as have made it quite comfortable and dry.

Am just off to lunch, so will finish this before the post goes. There is a great run on our canteen and we get rid of everything we buy in the day, about 800 francs worth.

Had a heavy rain last night and everything is in a fine old state again, nothing but mud and a general mess up.

So Bindy starts to ignore when she wants to, that is a bit thick, wonder how long she will carry on in that way.

Must close, sorry this is so short. Just heaps of love to you and Bindy.

Your loving
Harold

18 October –   Attack last night, good on Right and Centre, failed on left, about 400 prisoners.
Fine during day.

24-10-16

19 October 1916

My own darling Con,

Here I am up at the guns and a day it has been too. It started to rain about 3 a.m. and just poured until 4 p.m., everything is like a river, and one rolls into holes and out again, we are a great sight covered in dobs of sticky clay.

There is quite a good dugout here and can get quite cosy in it. Everything is very quiet at the present moment, and can hardly realise there is a war on.

Mr. Bruton has moved out, sorry to have missed him, expect he will be back for a good rest, and hope to follow suit shortly. Has Ken Curlish been posted anywhere lately? He has had a good holiday and now there is not nearly such a rest for artillery officers as when I came out.

Cannot think of any news or anything to write about, will try and write a better one tomorrow. Anyhow this will say that I am very well, so night night my own and God bless you and wee Bindy.

Your loving
Harold

19 October –   Came up to guns, Flers. Wilson to wagon line, generally quiet.
Rained all day.

26-10-16

20 October 1916
Harold's 33rd birthday

My own darling Con,

What a post arrived, your parcel with those two ripping bags, it is just dear of you to have made them and they are far too good to put muddy boots in, so will keep them until I can swank about again in my Sioy shoes. Also the socks came, they are just what I wanted so should like 2 more pairs. Ethel's toffee and also a parcel of honey from Aunt Janie and a box of cigs from the Emersons, so had a great haul.

That is a great photo of you and Bindy, but darling, I am afraid you are thin and the best birthday present I could possibly have is to see you a little fatter, but do not take Horlicks if you do not feel it is doing you any good, so do not worry about it.

It has now turned very cold here and froze last night, and is going to freeze harder tonight, but have a good warm bed, am going to get into it right away and will finish this tomorrow, so night night and heaps of love to you both, and just long for the day I can see you and the wee one.

21/10/16

There was a frost last night and no mistake, everything is ice and white, and underneath a mass of cold slush.

I had the first headache yesterday evening I have had since I came out, not so bad, 3½ months and only one, it was a beauty and today I feel very light in the head. Yes, I have given up my hot heart, only taking it about twice a month, and have had no attacks of indi for a long time, so it must be getting on alright.

Am very glad you told your Dad and am quite certain that he much preferred it coming from you, and very glad to hear that he knows. Will you give Beatie my best love and thank her for the lavender bag, it was ripping of her to have thought of it.

I got another pair of field boots from the Ordinance, they are issue and very good, so cost me nothing, the other I will keep as they will come in useful when I put 4 pairs of socks on. The men are well provided with socks, so do not send them out any.

When you write in future do not put the division on your letter, and tell the other people not to, it is prohibited.

What does John do up in the trenches? The Cavalry never come up, at least very seldom.

Well darling the post will soon be off, so just heaps of love to you and the wee one.

Your loving
Harold

Will you send me some cigarettes, in about 8 days time.

20 October –	Lazy day, fired 200 rds. 3 Hun planes brought down. Fine sunny day.
21 October –	Easy day, went up to Observation Post early. Cold, fine sunny day.

☆☆☆☆☆☆☆☆☆☆☆☆☆☆

Nelson
New Zealand
2017

Dear Harold,

Your letters told me very little about your past, your birth family and your growing years. I do know that you were very close to your sister Ethel and your brother Eric – he went on to play a large part in your children's lives, but again I can't tell you much more than that.

You were born in Montevideo in Uruguay on 20th October 1883 and you were christened in St Andrew's Church in Buenos Aires on 2nd February 1884 (the same church that bears your name on a plaque of remembrance). I don't know what kind of relationship you had with your parents, but I do have a letter written to you in 1908 by your mother, Kate, whilst travelling with your father, Christopher, to various exotic places in the Far East. At the time of writing they were in the Grand Oriental Hotel in Colombo, Ceylon (it is now called Sri Lanka). They obviously enjoyed their travels and adventures, I wonder if this photo was taken on their grand tour.

Christopher and Kate Musson – date unknown

I was amused at what appears to be an answer to your possible query about borrowing money to help with your estancia - you will be pleased to know that such requests are not something that has changed in this modern world, and parents continue to help their children.

SKY FULL OF STARS

"Also I've wondered much what has happened about that place down South that "Mac" told us about and he thought you would be sure to get. I think he said there were 10 leagues of campo to it and he thought you would be quite capable of managing it and I felt glad, for if you let your camp you might save money to help you with your own place later on, as Father says he cannot help you to stock and build a ranch on it at present. I am awfully sorry dearest, as I would have liked to build you boys a nice wee house and helped to stock the place for you, but Father says he cannot manage it, so I suppose there will not be any thing to do but rent the place for the present.

Ever Lovingly, Your Old Mother.

Sadly both your parents contracted Yellow Fever on their way to see Ethel in June 1909 and are buried in Bahia, Brazil.

I imagine they knew Con; she was also born in Montevideo two years after you on 27th February 1885 along with her twin sister, Beatie. She was christened Constance Mary Williams; she grew up in England, attending Cheltenham Ladies College with her sister. I know nothing about your courtship, but you were married in Holy Trinity Church in Upper Chelsea, London in 1913 and then returned to Argentina, to make Estancia *Lucero* your home. I have had the tiniest glimpse of life there through the diaries of Glynne Williams, I think a cousin to Con, who visited you for a couple of days in April 1914: -

> 24. Friday arrived Banderalo 7.30 a.m. Harold Musson's man met me with trap and I drove out to his estancia *Lucero* (3 leagues) in pouring rain. Harold and Constance and Crimmin there. Knowles and Waller came to breakfast and tea. After tea we went up to site of new house.
>
> 25. Saturday rode with Harold through the camp and to site of new house. Mr and Mrs Hoare arrived while we were at breakfast and remained till after tea. After they left we got ponies and knocked polo balls about.

Bindy was born on 6 September 1915, she was christened Renée Mary, although legend has it that she was a windy baby hence you called her Windy Bindy – she was known as Bindy all her life.

Your sense of duty obviously got the better of you and you returned to England to take up arms, arriving in 1916 and training for a commission with the Royal Field Artillery. That is where we meet and you share your dreams and visions for a life far better than the one you found yourself in. I wish it had a different ending for you.

Happy Birthday, Harold.
With love
Sheila x

27-10-16

22 October 1916

My own darling Con,

I got your letter, and am not a bit surprised that Bindy fell out of her cot, lucky it was on the right side, she must be sprawling over everything. How does the new corral suit her? I suppose she is boss of it.

Your parcels from Harrods arrived, and darling you have a great idea of things, they are just lovely.

Last night was a sneezer, I was out at 5 this morning, and the ground was just like a brick, it turned out a grand day and a noisy one too.

I do not know in the slightest who Mr Mallory is, but may come across him one of these days.

Bindy will be a great nut with her quilt, am afraid that she is really getting spoilt and we will have to charter a special boat to take her out with her luggage. I often wonder what she will say when her little brother arrives on the scene, she will think it a great joke, can quite imagine her looking and purring round.

We should soon have another letter from Johnnie, expect it will be full of news and all the camp looking fine and springy.

I cannot answer your questions about the wire, preguntar me dispues (*ask me later*). I often wonder if *L. & Co..* ever got that letter of mine about sending the £150 home, I think that I had better write again in case.

Today I saw a very fine sight, an aeroplane at a great height was hit by a shell and literally sent into small pieces, one saw bits of canvas etc. floating down quite 7 minutes after it had been hit.

Well darling, must close, just heaps and heaps of love to you two dears.
Your own loving
Harold

P.S. Please do not send out more food for a long time, as we have enough to keep us going for 3 weeks or a month.

22 October – 2 British planes down, one in pieces. Went up to front lines, saw lots of Bosch, could not shout or call on wire, telephone being out. Grand, dry cold.

☆☆☆☆☆☆☆☆☆☆☆☆☆☆

27-10-16

23 October 1916

My own darling Con,

The refills arrived safely and should keep me going until about the end of winter; that is at the rate I used the others up.

I had a letter from Ethel about the toffee which was very good, and another strong point of the Captain, must write and thank her, but it will not be for some days as I only wrote to her 2 or 3 days ago, so cannot spoil her, by letting her have another on the top of it. Should not like to get too famed as a letter writer, as it would spoil my reputation.

I am sure it will be a great relief to all of you to have got Raymond's affairs all wound up, and know that he must have had a great many friends, he well deserved them too.

I have had a great afternoon at it, fixing the mess up, I took off the whole roof and reconstructed it and strengthened it up, and then put a very fine ceiling up of green canvas, which has given it a very nutty appearance, and made it much warmer. I also put a thick row of sandbags on top, which makes it splinter proof.

This morning I had a good lie in till 8 a.m. and slept like a log the whole night, my bed is on a stretcher well off the ground and makes a very comfortable one.

Yesterday I was right up in the trench among a lot of Irish men, it was quite nice to hear their little expressions and funny way of putting things, they were as cheery as could be, in fact reminded me quite a lot of *Westhanger*.

Well darling, night night and just the very best of love to you and the cheery one.

Your own loving
Harold

23 October – Fired about 200 rds. Attack 2.30 p.m. successful. Fine day.

☆☆☆☆☆☆☆☆☆☆☆☆☆☆

30-10-16

24 October 1916

My own darling Con,

Yours with the snaps of Bindy came today, they look ripping, and it looks as if she cannot get out, but expect she has worn quite a path round the edge of the rug. She is getting quite an old look about her, and can quite imagine that she can understand most things in her baby way.

This is only going to be a tiny note as the post is just off. It would be great if Eric got leave the same time as I did, but it seems almost too good to be true. Anyhow would not see much of him, as am not going to move about much.

Must close, so just best of luck and God bless you both.

Your own loving
Harold

24 October – Fired about 200, quiet day. Cold and damp.
25 October – Fired 290 rds. Dull wet day. Battery shelling, one gun put out of action and officer. We blown in, no casualties, except Cox shell shock, Keely badly bruised when pick fell on him.

Near Flers. (24th October 1916)

A new subaltern came up to the guns that night, JM Bevan. He seems very capable and a good sort; it was a good evening for his arrival. The rations come up in a SAA limber, and although it was a light load for four horses, they managed to get finally stuck four hundred yards from the guns. Musson took some men down and unloaded it, but as bad luck would have it, soon after a close shell made the horses plunge, and the horses and empty limber capsized into a vast crater which was filled with liquid mud. After three hours' work they rescued the horses, but the vehicle had disappeared into the muddy depths of the crater. To make matters worse, while on their way back carrying contents of the cart, one of the men got stuck in the road, sinking up to the waist in a shell hole, and it needed a passing ammunition mule and a drag rope to 'yank' him out. Incidents like this are of daily or rather nightly occurrence.

Lt-Col Neil Fraser-Tytler, *Field Guns in France - Pg. 119-120*

30-10-16

26 October 1916

My own darling Con,

Here we are and a fairly fine day, anyway it is not raining but there is plenty of mud about, never thought one could get so used to it, and once it has gone I will quite miss it.

We had a very exciting time yesterday, and all went for a quiet stroll during lunch time, the Hun took quite a dislike to us and landed shells all round our mess, guns etc., and the wretch blew up our little house - you know what I mean, same as we had in the corner of the quinta (*house*) at *Lucero*. Wild applause from all, he did more damage and buried one of the guns, but soon put that straight, no casualties which is the chief thing.

Bindy does look ripping in those snaps and must be really entertaining by now. I will see a very big change in her, and we three will have great times of it when we are together, it will be a great pity that the days will be so short, but will have great times by the fireside.

Today I am putting up a new wash house, so far we have done without one, but on cold mornings it is quite nice having a cover to get under.

We were very bucked with the French news yesterday, Fort Douamont captured with 4000 prisoners, they are doing well and they deserve it too.

The refills arrived safely now, I told you this before so will say no more about it.

Well darling will close now, just heaps and heaps of love to you two dears and God bless you.

Your own loving
Harold

26 October – Position heavily shelled by Hun, 92 8 inch wiped out, no. 3 gun and half the dugout. Before this killed lots of Huns. Fine day.

27 October – Collecting odds and ends at position, handed gun one to D/148 and came to wagon line. Rained hard evening.

3-11-16

28 October 1916

My own darling Con,

Two days have gone since I last wrote, am truly sorry about it, but have really had no time for anything. Am now down at the wagon line for a few days, cannot really tell you the reason why, but you can ask me when we meet and the narrative will be interesting and exciting, and some very good work was done by all sides.

Here it has just rained and rained and the whole place is a sea of mud, and one never knows when one is going into some old shell hole or not, what it will be in another few days I don't know, but one will hardly be able to move. Now it looks as if it has cleared up a bit, and hope that it will chuck raining for some time.

This morning I went for a 15 mile ride and towards the end found that I had become very soft and tender and strongly objected to any contact with the saddle. That new horse does not take much notice of cars now and is much quieter, he is not much of a mount and am fed up with him.

Glad to hear that Donald was able to get down again. I should just love to get home for the winter, and then would be quite content to have another splutter at the Hun next spring. I hear that Monty will be in hospital for 2 to 3 months, it must have been a serious knock out, but even with that Kitty must be only too thankful to have him safely there.

We had Sybil and Isabel knocked clean out, the Huns put a few very fine rounds in and did fine work from his point of view, but not from ours. Sybil was the one which got it worst and Mary is as perky as ever, and we will one of the days return the compliment, with a little more to cheer them up.

I am getting a top coat our here, like the one I had at St John's Wood, they are very warm, and will be A1 for out here. I have heaps of winter clothing, so you must not worry about me feeling the cold. What you might do is to send me a couple of stars, not the bright ones, the bronze coloured ones, they are for the top coat.

Our battery consists of 4 guns, and the 18 pounders are 6 guns, the latter is quite a new scheme and a good one too, I don't think there is any harm in answering these questions, but cannot say any more about them.

Glad to hear that Bindy has quite got over her cold, she must be a strong wee lassie and throws these things off very quickly.

I have broken my watch glass again, would you send me a cheap watch out, about 5 to 10 bob,* a good one is not much use here, as they are always getting broken, just as soon not have a wrist watch. So when you send it, send a leather chain with it.

---

*   Shillings

Must close now and just heaps of love to you and Bindy.
Your own loving
Harold

28 October –   *Went to Méaulte morning, place thick with mud, afternoon nothing doing. Fine day.*
29 October –   *Captain and self went to Gueudecourt to look for position. Mac stayed at Flers position. Rained all day.*

☆☆☆☆☆☆☆☆☆☆☆☆☆☆

4-11-16

30 October 1916

My own darling Con,
Just a wee notita for this mail. Am very glad you did not send a wire as they take a long time getting here and would much rather have your letter.

By your description Helen sounds very comfortable, must be jolly glad to get out of the convent, it looked nearly as bad as the barracks.

I am sorry to hear that your Dad has not been well and so tired. I wish that he would take things a little easier, it is not good enough to overdo it, and also in the end it will mean that he gets much less done, as at the rate he is going he will have to take a good rest soon.

Yes, Aunt Janie seems to be having a great time of it, and it is the best thing that could have happened and will thoroughly rest her, and she will appear on the scenes like a girl of 25 once more. Hope she will not overdo it again, but am afraid she will.

Wee Bindy is coming on, what with a chicken bone and baked apple, she is getting a move on. She does look ripping in one of those last snaps, how she will relish rolling about on the lawn at *Lucero* with a nice hot sun and glorious day.

Here it gets worse and worse, today it is blowing for all it is worth, and rain every hour or so, how the gees stand it I do not know, they are one mass of clotted mud and cannot get it off on account of not having a dry moment to do so, their tails are awful – must weigh about a ton. The men slither and slop about and sometimes get so badly stuck one has to get 3 or 4 men with a rope to pull them out.

Must close, just heaps and heaps of love to you both.
Your loving
Harold

4-11-16

30 October 1916

My darling Con,

Just a wee notita as I wrote this morning, but as I will not have any time tomorrow or probably day after, must just get this in.

This afternoon it rained harder that it has done so far, and the place is not mud, it is a sea of water and the carts and men one can hardly recognise, they are a mass of running mud.

What a pity we could not have caught those 10 German destroyers, they are a daring lot and they got off very easy, in fact I should never have thought that they could have done it, and if they try it again, hope the Navy will be awake.

I think there has been a bad upset in the kitchen, and all our food is in the mud, there was a great clatter and then cheers from the batmen and a sizzling, so the whole stove must have gone over, and now they are puffing and blowing for all they are worth.

Some of the men I admire most in the battery are the drivers, the other night I came down from the guns on the limber,* it was pouring and took 5 pairs of horses tied in, the road full of shell holes and very dark, the way they wound their way down and missed all holes, except when impossible was extraordinary and their spirits never down. Sometimes the limber is on an angle like this,

but one clings on with both hands and teeth, and what with sticky mud remains on, my heart goes out to them and they deserve everything they can get.

Must close with just tons and tons of love to you and Bindy.

Your own loving

Harold

---

* A two-wheeled vehicle to which a gun or ammunition carrier may be attached, and pulled by a team of horses.

30 October – Quiet day at wagon line.
Rained a little.
31 October – Came to position in Delville Wood.
Rained a little.

☆☆☆☆☆☆☆☆☆☆☆☆☆☆☆

November 1916

Blood swept land and seas of red – poppy installation Tower of London - 2014

When the power of love overcomes
the love of power
the world will know peace.
Jimi Hendrix

9-11-16

1 November 1916

My own darling Con,

Just got yours, and glad to hear that Bindy has quite got over her cold, and is such a little ripper.

Yes, we got turned out of our mess again, and now I am by my lonesome for 2 or 3 days. The mess is in a famous wood which was taken and retaken 7 times, so no need to say that there is very little of it, it is quite chewed up, stumps here and there and huge shell holes all over the place. It is a very interesting spot as all the troops go past here, also transport, and quite often German prisoners, who look very dejected and miserable, and of course mud from head to foot. Should like to see them come by the thousands.

It is about time we had a letter from Johnnie, expect that his trip to Uruguay and the excitement of Mrs T Jeffries coming to see him must have bowled him over.

Am turning out a great cook, make my own tea and heat up all my food etc., that little Tommy cooker is a great thing and saves me a great deal of work. The men have their last meal at 5 p.m. so I take some of it and heat it up about 7 p.m., and with a cup of coffee have a fine old blow out.

I hear that there is a chance of Eric getting home about end of month, how bucked he will be.

Well pet must close, with just heaps and heaps of love, and God bless you both.
Your own loving
Harold

1 November – Went to Flers position with Captain, returned for lunch. Captain went out to wagon lines fixing up new position. Rained evening.

10-11-16

2 November 1916

My own darling Con,

I do not expect that I shall get a letter from you for a few days, as all our post is going to another part of the line, but when they do come will get about a week of them.

I have just come in from a walk around the wood, there is not a tree left whole in it, and about 5 only with branches. Trees of 50 years old are just rooted up and chewed to pieces. You stand in the middle and it makes one feel quite romantic, a bright ¼ moon, the sun just setting behind an angry sky, red with big blotches of cloud, and the remains of Longueval Village <u>silhouetted</u> against it all, do not know how to spell the underlined word, but yourself will understand. I stood quite a long time looking at it, and it really fascinated me, especially when one thinks of all the strife and loss of life which has had to be expended before we could claim the place, but now it is well in our hands, and the Hun will never set foot in it again, during this war. Probably at one time the wood was considered a great pheasant shoot of the year, wonder what the people would think of it if they saw it now, and the wretched owner of it to whom it will never be of any more use to.

I will finish this notita tomorrow as am just going to change my boots, as they are wet through, so night night and take care of yourself.

No more news, do not know why I say more as there is none in this except that it takes every bit of love to you both and your Dad.

Your loving
Harold

2 November – Went up to old position handed over ammunition, went to wagon line. Men fixing up new position. Rained morning.

3 November 1916

My own darling Con,

Just a wee line before I turn in, I do like that photo of you, and it is always in my dugout, the batman has begun to know where I like it, as soon as he unpacks it is one of the first things that he puts out, the other little one of you and Bindy never leaves me. It is just ripping to have something of you, and just long for your dear self.

I have not seen any papers for 5 days, and am longing for some of the other officers to come up, as at night it is very dreary here, and so occasionally I have to talk to my servant, and during the day I work with the men, and stir the Corporal up and grouse at nothing just to fill the time up.

Today has been quite a decent day and things have dried up a bit, which is a change. The Captain came for an hour, but had no news. This is a rotten flat letter and feel I could make nothing interesting.

What sort of course did Donald have to do at Lark Hill? I suppose a few field days and maybe a little firing, it should be interesting, suppose the whole battery went with him, or was it a course for his own personal instruction?

The Army have supplied us with fine warm cardigan jackets, they are excellent things and keep one warm as toast, (maybe not quite so hot).

It is quite funny to hear an old train puffing in the distance, between the shots that are fired, one hears it quite distinctly and reminds one very much of the outside world, hurrah for the day I step in the train at Southampton.

My leg has just gone to sleep, so will follow its example, so night night my own and God bless you both very very much, will finish this mañana.

4/11/16

Darling, I thought that this had gone this morning, and here I find it still in my writing pad, but never mind it will be 2 days combined into one.

I have had a lovely cold the last 4 days, but it is now going, and by the day after tomorrow ought to be quite gone.

We have just had a very exciting rumour that the Russians have had a great victory over Mackensen, taken him and 4,500 prisoners, it sounds much too good to be true, but if it is I reckon it is one of the finest victories won since the war started, and will buck everybody up enormously. At present I take it with a very large spoon of salt, but hope the salt will have to tipple over. It will give the Germans a fine old shock to lose Mackensen, should think probably one of their finest soldiers, I am longing for the news tomorrow about it all.

I wonder what you are doing tonight, expect sitting comfortably by the fireside, and having a good old chat with your Dad, wee Bindy sound asleep in her new cot. Here I am quite comfortable, a good tin hut over me and have had a fire going all evening. The fireplace is made out of a fluid tin and home made tin chimney to it, and draws like a good one, an occasional puff of smoke comes out, but that is good for one.

It has cleared up and is blowing hard, so hope it means fine weather as I think we deserve a little before winter really settles in. I am going down to join the others tomorrow, and one of them comes up to relieve me, it is very lonesome here, I did not mind it for the first two days, but after that one gets fed up with it.

Am going to turn in now, so night night my own, and just heaps of love and a huge hug to you both.

Your own loving
Harold

3 November – At position all day making new dugouts and fixing up pits. Quiet and fine day.

4 November – Went to 104 battery alone, ammunitions and then to old Observation Post, put up dugout new position all afternoon. Quiet day. Fine.

5 November – Bevan relieved, men at gun position. Wet day.

14-11-16

6 November 1916

My own darling Con,
Yesterday I had a great post, only <u>6</u> of your letters arrived, so had a great read.

I am now down with the wagon and had a very peaceful night last night, no noise of guns or anything to worry one.

I really do not know what you could send Flurry, excepting some cigarettes, a good plum pudding and a few little odd and ends for Xmas, poor old Flurry, in a way I am very glad that he has gone to Salonika. I am in the middle of a letter to him and suddenly found that I had lost his address, so will send it on to you for addressing. He seems to have hit a great lad in Hancock, and am sure will have one or two great pals before the war is over. I wish he would not worry about those little money affairs, he thinks too much about them, he is too honest and deserves a better fate than he has had.

I wonder if Lucy is out again, I am going over tomorrow to find out, hardly expect so as it is such a short time since he went home.

Am very glad you gave your Dad that enlarged snap of Bindy. I think we ought to have a good one taken, or else have her best snap enlarged, have several of them done, and we could send one to Ethel, Aunt Janie and some of your favourite relations. Do just as you think best, as you know much better than I do. It is very funny her beginning to rub her ear, but I sympathise with her and know how good it is. I had a funny dream about her, that she had huge ears and fairly flapped, was very glad to wake up and find all was well.

I did not see about Daisy having a little girl, pity it was not a boy and hope that we have better luck, although I would not object to another little Bindy. Peter must be a great boy, and doing very well. I can imagine him beating Bindy as he was always a big baby, and probably boys weigh heavier than girls. I think that you are quite right about covering Bindy's head, personally I should not care to go about in the very cold weather with a bare head, although I do not think that it would do her any harm.

When you acknowledge the £150 to *L. & Co.* it will be as well for them to send the remittances direct to the bank, it will save the trouble of them collecting etc. About *Land and Water*, do not send it anymore as we have it sent weekly to the mess.

That must have been Pollard, it does make one sick to see all the lads one knows gradually going. I often wonder why they should be killed, in a way it does no good, and only causes grief and sorrow to those who are left behind. One wonders when it will end.

We get both the *Punch* and *Tatler*, so do not worry to send them. This winter we will want a lot of papers for the men during the winter, and are going to have a lot of wrappers printed and sent to different people, so that they can send old papers and not have the worry of addressing them. So you will probably get 100 of them, which you might distribute round to people who care to send any. Papers, magazines and books will be the thing, but do not send them yet.

Must close, so goodnight my own and a huge hug to you and Bindy and God bless you both. Remember me to Alice, should not like her to forget me.

Your own loving
Harold

6 November – Quiet day.
Rained hard and showers.
7 November – Went to Méaulte and Heilly for stores and cash.
Rained hard all day.

15-11-16

8 November 1916

My darling Con,

Afraid that I missed writing yesterday, but had a fairly big day of it. I started out 8 a.m. to get stores and cash, had a ride of 30 miles and got back here at 5.30 p.m.

It rained hard all day, just like a heavy day of rain in Buenos Aires, only colder. Am glad to say that the mackintosh is a ripper, and thanks to it I arrived back quite dry. In a way I enjoyed it as I saw a lot of life, and at the other end had a swagger lunch, consisting of 2 omelettes beautifully cooked, and a real good cup of coffee, and some chocolate. I did not see anybody that I knew, one usually does on those long journeys.

When I got back I found your cartita, but covered in mud, the wagon had fallen over and deposited the mail in about 2 ft. of mud, but luckily we retrieved all excepting 2 parcels, hope my socks and cigs were not among them.

That servant of mine burnt two holes in that nice pair of trench socks you sent me, so tomorrow he will have a good day at mending them, and expect he will make a rare old mess of them, am very sorry as they are rippers and just suited those boots you sent from Manfields.

If I were you I should be very careful about wanting to share your Horlicks etc. with me, as I shall probably have it all when I get home, so take it while you have the chance.

By the way do you know what Mr Begg got his Military Cross for, and also the Bar to it? I should like to know also what squadron he is attached to. He must have done very well, and good luck to him. Probably he has often flown over my head many a time, may have seen him have a real old fight, and the Bosch come down with a run.

Two more of your letters have just arrived and this time without the mud. You must not worry or think that the mud troubles us much, it does not make any difference as long as we have a fire to come into in the evening, and a dry bed, and these we have. What it does upset is the infantry and horses, and these I am truly sorry for, the infantry have to go through it and my heart goes out to them. We are very comfortable at present and am not worried at all.

By yours of the 2nd it appears that you have not had any of my letters for some days, expect several must go astray. The stars arrived quite safely, y muchos gracias. About the watch, I will not trouble to send it, but will take it when I go off on leave, it would probably only get lost on the way. I thought that I had paid Negretti and Zambra, so if I did you will find the folio of cheques in the bank book, if not you might as well pay them.

It is just lovely to hear the great accounts you write of Bindy, and long more and more to be with you both. When next we meet I will give you my opinion of the war, it is not worth much, but may be a little interesting. If Bindy has such a good memory she will be picking me up, as mine is very bad. Am afraid that you must not expect me this month, but with any luck might be next, but one never knows.

You were quite right in telling Ethel and the others about the future little one, and if you want to tell anyone else do as by all means, as in any case the news will soon spread, and it is more satisfactory to tell them your own self. Also I think that it will be just as well to book a nurse as soon as possible unless you would rather go to a home. Have a good talk to your Dad, and if he would like to have you at *Westhanger,* I think that you should remain there, as it would be much nicer for you to be among your own people. If things are not busy here I think that I could manage to get home for it, so if you would rather have me then than after will do my very best. Anyhow we can have a good talk over it when on leave.

That was quite a good letter from Philip for him, and on the whole the news is fairly alright, but of course many things may happen before they get the crop in. There will be quite a merry party with the Johnsons and the Broughmans, they all know how to enjoy themselves. It will be ripping at San Rafael now, when I shut my eyes I can quite imagine the place around me, almost to a tree, anyhow we shall one of these days have a great time of it there, and will enjoy it more than ever.

Must close as this has got into rather a long talk and may spoil you, remember what Aunt Bella said, "not much" but will have nothing to write about tomorrow, but better write when one feels like it.

Just tons and tons of love to you and wee Bindy, and God bless you more and more.

Your own loving
Harold

8 November – Orderly Officer, general work in the lines, mail got upset in the mud, lost 2 or 3 packets.
Fairly fine, showery.

9 November – Quiet day, general duties.
Showery.

15-11-16

10 November 1916

My own darling Con,

Just a hurried wee note before the post goes. It is a lovely day again and excepting for the mud is perfect. It has been grand for aeroplanes, and so one or two fine fights, and a Hun came down.

Last night was fine moonlight and looking across the country one could see one huge camp, lines and lines of horses, huts and dugouts made of any material one could find, chiefly sand bags, corrugated iron and canvas. All the roads one could plainly see being much more shiny than the rest, so were one silvery stretch of sloshy mud, with an occasional limber stuck here and there.

Post just off, so night night and just heaps and heaps of love.

Your own loving
Harold

10 November – Went to Méaulte for stores.
Fine day.

16-11-16

11 November 1916

My own darling Con,
Have had a great morning of it in the stores and looks like being a hard afternoon's work too, it is not really hard work, but we get through a lot of goods.

We have had 4 fine days running and has cheered and warmed men and horses up a lot, and given quite a different appearance to things in general. The only trouble now is the mud, which is getting very sticky and when you get one foot well in, you have to stop and dig yourself out.

I can quite imagine that you had a really bad storm, as I have never seen it rain so much in Europe before, hope it did not do much damage, luckily it came when all the crops were in.

Wonder if Kenneth is coming out to a battery or with one, expect the latter, and whether he comes out here, or to Salonika.

Sorry to hear that Kenneth Williams had got wounded, but hope it is not anything very serious, and that he will get a good rest at home. Pity he did not go where Kathleen is, personally I do not think that he will stop long there.

The other day I went past the first place the train dropped me at the front, and it looked quiet and peaceful, and very few people about; nothing like the bustle that there used to be.

Well will stop as letter writing has disappeared from me today, so with just tons and tons of love, and keep well, and love to your Dad.
Your own loving
Harold

11 November – General duties. Fine day. Air activity great, 2 Hun and 1
British brought down. Chinese bombards 2 hours.*
12 November – At canteen all day.
Fine day.

---

*   Shelling an area as a diversion

19-11-16

13 November 1916

My own darling Con,

Have been for another good ride today searching for canteen stores, they are very difficult to get, as there is such a huge demand for them, but with all these drawbacks our canteen has done very well and have quite a sum to our credit, roughly 5,000 francs which will do the battery well this winter. We had a great committee meeting last night to find out the most suitable way to spend it, and are getting quite a lot of comforts etc. for the men.

Mail will be very erratic for the next several days as we will be on the move again and do not know where our wanderings will take us. Have just had a letter from Patsy, he is somewhere down here, and is now posted to a battery, at which he is very bucked, and much prefers it to the D.A.C. (*Divisional Ammunition Column*), am not surprised as it is very slow work and not much variation in it.

Well darling, will finish this tomorrow, so night night, and just heaps and heaps of love to you and Bindy and sleep well.

14/11/16

After all this never went, so will finish it now. The watch and socks arrived safely and the former is just the thing. The socks are a bit short in the leg, and not quite thick enough, but will do very well, so please do not send anymore out.

The news today is good, another 3,200 prisoners just the north of us, and a few on our front, and also semi-official news that there has been a good move at Salonika, any news on this front is good enough, and hope that it will lead to a lot more such moves.

Flurry's letter is interesting and there is nothing the censor could object to in it. I did not know that they had it so cold there, wonder what he has got posted to, and will be a fine thing for him if he gets taken into the Devons again.

Poor wee Bindy, wonder what was the matter with her. It is hard luck on them so young as they cannot help one in anyway, I do hope that she is quite herself by now, and had no need to call the Doctor in, probably a little cold in her bowels and will soon pass away.

That is great news of Hugh getting his Captaincy and well deserves it, he will be very bucked. It is a curious thing, but promotions are given at home much easier than out here, and from the artillery point of view to much less expereinced.

Flurry gives a very good account of things, and wish I were able to use the pen in the same way, what he says is quite alright. Personally I will not risk anything as some unfortunates have had their leave stopped for saying too much.

Will close now, just heaps and heaps of love to you and wee Bindy and longing to hear that she is quite fit again.

Your loving
Harold

13 November – Went to Méaulte and Heilly. Attack near Beaumont very successful, 3200 prisoners.
14 November – Small attack at Gueudecourt successful, few prisoners. Heavy firing. Fine dull day.
15 November – At Montauban-de-Picardie all day preparing for march. Fine day.
16 November – Out of action. Marched to Morlancourt. Fine day, froze during night.
Fine dull day.

☆☆☆☆☆☆☆☆☆☆☆☆☆☆☆

17 November 1916

My own darling Con,

Two days have gone and no letter written, so hope you did not expect one, as I mentioned in my last letter that you would probably not. We have been on the move for those two days, and at the present moment am comfortably seated on the chair Ethel gave me, in a comfortable room, with a good fire going, the first night I have slept in a house for close on 2 months, and I must say that one appreciates it very much. Tomorrow I am off for a day bust with the Captain to quite a nice town close by.

Last night we had a tremendous frost and the ground is as hard as bricks, and has frozen the whole day, but this is a great relief after the wet and mud, and now we move on good roads. The men are cheered as could be, and are all quartered in a galpón *(shed)* with a roaring fire, and a good stew for their suppers. We have also had a good supper, and am very soon going to turn in and have a good night of it.

Before I forget will you please send me out a dose of my remedies as soon as possible, have got enough to last 10 days.

Well dearest will close up now, and write you a long one tomorrow, my little brain will not work, so night night and God bless you, and just heaps of love to you and Bindy, and am longing to hear that Bindy is quite well again.

Your own loving
Harold

18/11/16

This morning I woke up and found the ground covered in snow, and so there is a fine old winter appearance about everything, it is very cold, but still it is not going to stop us from going on this spree, and only wish you were here to come with us.

Well dear, we have had a great day of it, I weighed myself and got a terrible shock, so will you guess my weight before you get to the end of this letter? I only had a thick cardigan on, at the most 1 kilo.

Our day consisted of a big lunch, a little shopping and tea, which we thoroughly enjoyed. By the way I sent you and also Joan a box of chocolates, so let me know if you get them, I should say very doubtful.

Will close now, just tons and tons of love to you both, bless you.

Your loving
Harold

P.S. I only weigh 95.6 kilos, almost 15 stone (cheer ho).

17 November – Marched to Bussy-lès-Daours through Buire, Corbie, and Heilly. Hard frost and very fine cold day.
18 November – Captain and self to Amiens. Snowed during night and rained during day. Bussy-lès-Daours.

26-11-16

19 November 1916

My own darling Con,

Well the snow turned to a good old rain, and went on solidly for 24 hours, and has made a rare old mess of things again.

The other day our Prince passed us looking very cheery and well, just riding along as one of us with a groom behind him, it was nice seeing him among all the traffic and in that simple way.

I got your 3 letters yesterday. Dennis seems to have suddenly taken to writing, and fancy both of them being in the same box, and all the same time, there will be some excitement about that time and rare old race for it, Bee and Brush want exactly the same as we do, and hope they will not be disappointed.

Was very bucked to hear that Bindy was quite well again and as cheery as ever.

Poor Susan, it is just rotten luck, and wish Mrs Runciman would make up her mind and do something definite and settle down, but am afraid she never will.

Also the asthma, am very sorry about it and afraid Susan will always have it. I often wonder if Eric knows about it, I did not like to tell him when I saw him, but expect that she has told him something about it. Am in great hopes of seeing Eric, but he may have moved up by now.

We are all off to have dinner with the Colonel, and expect we will have a great night of it, will give you a description of this tomorrow, as I do not expect that I shall be able to post this till 3 days time, as everything is upside down at present.

21/11/16

We have moved quite a long way since I started this, and no chance to post it, but hope to get it off tomorrow. We have had grand weather for the move, and are now comfortably settled for a few days. We have now started to play 21 in the evening and having great gambles, which pass these long evenings quite well.

We have just had the news of the capture of Monaster, it is good and only hope that they will hold onto it for good. Expect that Flurry will now be forward and seeing a bit of fighting, and is liking it as much as he expected.

22/11/16

The Captain and 2 other officers have just gone into town for the afternoon to get a good tea, Wilson and I go in tomorrow. We have very comfortable billets here and hope to remain for some days, and then into it again. We are just close to a town where Eric was when we were last on the march, at least that is where I think he was. I must write to him now, as have not done so for a long time.

We had great weather for the march and looks like keeping up, it does make such a difference to one, being away from the mud and slush, the horses have got quite a different appearance.

We have not had a mail for 4 days and are living in hopes of getting one tomorrow, papers we can get in the town, which keeps us informed of any excitement that might be going on.

Afraid this is a very poor letter as am not in a letter writing frame, so will close until tomorrow, so night night my own and a big hug to you and Bindy, and love to your Dad.

Your loving
Harold

19 November – Bussy-lès-Daours.
Fine day.

20 November – *Marched to Villeirs Bretonneux.*
  Fine day.
21 November – *Marched to Grouches-Luchuel.*
  Fine day.
22 November – *At Grouches-Luchuel.*
  Grand day.

Doullens. (19th November 1916)

Our Colonel also came in late, as he had some trouble in finding anyone to take over his Headquarters. However, he arrived and went to bed. He had just got to sleep when a lost and wandering "Sausage" bumped up against his tent and enveloped it completely. In the darkness nobody could find a vent to let the gas out until a small army of panting French balloonists turned up and gralloched the beast. It had broken loose from its moorings, and they had been chasing it for miles as it trundled across country.

I had a dim recollection of a crisis outside my tent, but each night has its crisis. I certainly heard someone crying for help, but did not realise it was the Colonel and, being half asleep, paid no attention to the frantic yells of the strugglers in the night.

Next day we marched 20 kilometres to Bussy-Les-Daours, and the day after I rode to Amiens with Musson – a ride of about three-quarters of an hour. The Colonel was coming with us, but a comfortable bed and blizzards of snow outside made him change his mind.

The Head-Quarters Staff are billeted in a chateau with a fine ballroom, so the Colonel gave a great dinner there to the Brigade the night before we marched away. We are now resting in a rather dirty village (Grouches), about five miles from Doullens, so we pass the time cleaning up and straightening things generally, ending up with Poker every night.

Lt-Col Neil Fraser-Tytler, *Field Guns in France - Pg. 137*

Nelson
New Zealand
2017

Dear Harold,

Just a short notita, as you would say, as I simply can't resist giving you a soupçon of gossip about the Prince you saw riding past. I am certain you were referring to the Prince of Wales, Edward, as he had joined the army and toured on behalf of his father, King George V. Despite objections he did also serve on the front lines and was awarded the Military Cross.

Things did not go quite so well for him when he became King in 1936, as he was smitten with an American lady, Wallace Simpson who had already divorced one husband and was in the process of divorcing a second one. He was unable to marry her and be the King; he chose love over a kingdom, abdicating less than 11 months later. He married Wallace and became the Duke of Windsor. I wonder how Con and the girls viewed the scandal it created, it must have been a huge talking point, I can picture shaking heads and tut tutting going on over cups of tea or pints of beer across the nation.

In his abdication speech he summed up his difficult decision with these words:

> "I have found it impossible to carry the heavy burden of responsibility and to discharge my duties as King as I would wish to do without the help and support of the woman I love. I now quit altogether public affairs, and I lay down my burden."

Edward's brother George stepped into the king's shoes. King George VI took the country through the next war, he died in 1952, his daughter Elizabeth became Queen, and as I write this she still is. She is now a grand old lady of 91 and is the longest serving monarch, I have never known anything different.

Life goes on whether we are present or not, it just seems a shame that there are some moments that are missed.

With love
Sheila x

23 November 1916

My own darling Con,

Fancy I got a letter of yours yesterday dated the 18th, and the one before was the 11th, so it just shows how letters fly about, and very often never turn up.

Glad to hear that Donald likes Aldershot, is he there with his battery? If so I expect that he will be doing a lot of out of doors work; is that 6 days leave his final before coming out?

You seem to be having rotten weather lately, and about the same time we did, but since then it has been grand and makes one feel quite comfortable once more, especially as we have got beds to sleep in.

The socks you sent me are A1 and are just the thing. My servant did a great turn the other day, he managed with a great deal of skill to burn the Mansfield field boots you sent me. I was very sick about it, as with the thick pair of socks you sent they were just the thing, but do not send anymore out as I can get along quite well enough, and will write when I want more, which I hope I will have no need to. I do not know if I wrote for more medicine, if not will you please send me another lot, somehow think I did about 10 days ago.

The mitts arrived quite safely, and give Bindy a great hug, and thank her very much for them, I wore them this morning and they are great. Does she suffer very much from cold hands, they always used to turn quite blue? Will you thank your Dad very much for his letter, and will answer it in a day or two.

Lucy is very lucky to be at Wellington Barracks for the winter, I came across the Scots Guards the other day and enquired for him, in case he had got back, but no sign of him. Hope I will be able to see him when I get home, cuando no puedo desir (*when I don't know.*)

Just off into town, so hasta mañana and just heaps of love to you and Bindy.

Your loving
Harold

23 November – General harness cleaning etc. Went to Doullens with Wilson afternoon and saw cinema – rotten.
Fine day.

30-11-16

24 November 1916

My own darling Con,

Another great pile of 5 letters from you, with Johnnie's enclosed, it was just ripping to get them. Also one from Lucy with nothing in it, he is a rotten letter writer, and I will tell him so, with a very short letter to the point.

They are having a poor time of it in the camps, and is one of the longest secas (*droughts*) we have had for a long time, only hope they have had rain by now, and so have plenty of grass, the only trouble is that the locust will soon be down on us, unless the drought drives them away.*

It is great news about the capataz and his wife, she may turn out a great treaure to us later on. We have got a very decent lot of people on the place, although they are such a crowd. That hay we cut just before we left has turned out very successful and should pull through the cattle safely. He never says very much about your mares, but hope they are flourishing. I often wonder how the old car is getting along and hope it is not rusting up too much. I wrote out and asked Johnnie to get a good man to overhaul it, and grease it well up, so hope he has been able to do so.

Fancy Bindy bullying, I expect that she is so big and full of life that she hardly knows what to do with her spirits. Does she like to have her baby visitors? If she is on her feet she will be soon giving them a rare old time of it and pulling their legs. I am surprised that she had not got fed up with my photo, and will soon be wearing it out. Your Dad writes good accounts of her and seems to be a great pal of hers, and expect helps to keep him thinking too much of other things.

Kenneth C has got a very cushy job and expect he will be in moderate comfort during the winter. Fancy, St John's Wood has taken over Lords and now have 800 cadets training, it must be a huge place, but they now have an easier time than before. I got all this from a chap who has just arrived out, and knew Kenneth well.

Helen seems to be very comfortable at Grayshot, and must find it a great change from the dull old convent. How is Kathleen getting along? Send me her address, as I have lost it, and one of these days hope to call on her.

This morning the Captain, Wilson and self went for a ripping ride, first over open country and then into a forest, which reminded me very much of our hunting days. We stopped on one of the paths and put up a jump which we had great sport over, then the Captain got wild and gave a hunting cry and off we went for all we

---

* Argentina experienced a severe drought in 1916, this would have been of concern to Harold as he needed grass and feed for his cattle. In times of drought locusts become more active in search of food, and can destroy crops in a short space of time.

were worth, oh how I wish you could have been with us on old Rio Negro, you would have thoroughly enjoyed it. It was a ripping morning for it, but has now turned to drizzle but hope it will not be much.

Well dear will close now, with just heaps and heaps of love to you both.
Your own loving
Harold

24 November – Captain and Wilson and self fine ride during morning.
Fine during morning.
25 November – Grouches-Luchuel
Rainy.

☆☆☆☆☆☆☆☆☆☆☆☆☆☆☆☆

28-11-16

26 November 1916

My own darling Con,
Another wet day gone, a real wet one too, but as we are in comfy billets it does not make much difference. We will most likely be here for 10 days, and then go into the line again a little south of Arras, which I believe is a very quiet part of the line, and hope that they leave us there for a good long time.

The senior officer Wilson goes on leave tonight and so takes this over, and as I have mentioned where we will be, be careful who gets hold of this letter.

We have had our photos taken this morning, so will send you them as soon as possible, that is if they turn out any good, as they were taken in the rain, but the photographer did not seem to mind that.

I have a new pony now, and quite a nice one, he is the one I went for a ride on yesterday, quite a good jumper and comfortable hack.

The country round here is very like the Somme but much more undulating, and on the tip of very bleak. We are 2 miles from Doulous, where we occasionally go for a little spree. When we were on the Somme our position was up at Flers, so now you will know exactly where we were, it was quite a warm place at times, but saw some very fine sights, which will give you a description of a few of the struggles I saw.

I am living in the hopes of getting leave about the 1st January, but do not put too much hope in it, as one never knows what may turn up. Bingham went home the other day, and was going to see Aunt Flora, who is a great friend of his, so if you would like to see him, try and meet him there, and he will tell you how I look.

Must close now, just tons and tons of love and a great big hug to you both.
Your Loving
Harold

26 November – Wilson left for Blighty, Jones and Sgt. Cox.

6-12-16

27 November 1916
Third wedding anniversery

My own darling Con,
I wrote you a notita last night which I hope you will receive, as you will know why by it.

This evening we are having a little dinner party, 2 officers from another battery are coming and afterwards have a game of cards, or something after that style.

We are also in the throes of trying to get all the men a bath, which is rather a job, as we have only one small tub, and have 140 men to bathe, so you can imagine what it is like.

You mentioned in one of yours some days ago that you told Harrods to send a mixed parcel, up to now it has not arrived, I am telling you this in case you paid for it. Where we are now we get lots of provisions, so at present please do not send any more, but could do with more cigarettes, as am beginning to get on the short side.

That must have been a great tea you and Bindy had of syrup etc., we eat quite a lot of it here, and on the whole it is not bad stuff, but one gets rather fed up with it.

Glad to hear you are looking after a prisoner of war in Germany, I think by all accounts that they are having a much better time than they did, and better looked after, it is a great scheme and wonder if you will ever hear from him.

It is a bad bust on Kathleen being separated from her pal, and I bet it is cold in the tents, and the night she had her sponge etc. frozen. I was sleeping in a tent and when I got to putting my boots on they were frozen hard, and as that was they case I did not attempt to wash, and that morning we were on the march and so walked until we got thoroughly warm, luckily it was a lovely day, so enjoyed the march.

If she is going to sleep in tents for sometime, a sleeping bag like the one I got would be a great comfort, as they are very soft, and if she does not like sleeping between blankets she could have a sheet in. So if you think it would do, why not send her one. Just the woollen sleeping bag. I never sleep in anything else, if there are sheets in the bed I put this in between.

It has turned out a grand afternoon and we are going to have another photo taken.

Well dearie will close, just heaps of love to you and Bindy and keep well and fit.

Your loving
Harold

27 November – Johnson and Phillips came for dinner, played 21. Fine day.

4-12-16

28 November 1916

My own darling Con,

Our dinner party the night before last was a great success, and we had a great spread. To start with our tablecloth was a sheet, which was quite good, and then we had to wrack our brains for a table centre, and eventually we had those two bags you sent me, which looked very nutty, and placed them in this way, with a candle stick on each side.

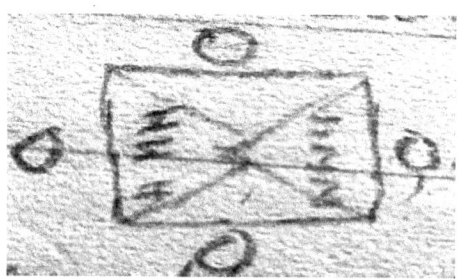

For cutlery we were very swagger as a canteen we ordered had just arrived from the goldsmith & silversmith a few days before. Our menu was tomato soup, pork chops, apple sauce and potatoes followed by sago pudding, apricots, a savoury, fruit, coffee, nuts and port. This lasted for about 1½ hours and then we settled down to 21, we played for about 2 hours in which time I dropped 41 francs. Anyhow we all enjoyed the evening very much, and is quite the talk of the brigade, especially as we had all the walls pictured by Herchness sketches, and menu cards of the same, which were all on the breezy side.

Will you please send my camera (the small one) to G.F. Wilson, The Rise, Penarth, S. Wales, with a note inside from whom it is sent, also 6 rolls of 6 exposures each, I promised to lend it to him, so send it as soon as possible.

It is bad luck on Adrian having to go straight to Salonika, which means he will not get home for a long time to come, but still let us hope that all will be over long before we expect it.

We had our photos taken again this morning, so hope that they will turn out well and will send them as soon as we get them, which will probably be 4 or 5 days. Halfway through them being taken I felt awfully sick and rotten, so as soon as it was done I retired to bed and slept for 5 hours, and woke up quite fit.

Will you please send me that thick pair of black shooting boots as soon as possible. The ones with the nails in, they may be at the flat.

I feel A1 again, luckily I have now got a good room and bed, so am very well off. It is in the Padre's house, but he does not live there, it is the best house in the village.

Just fancy Bindy being able to walk round the room, with the assistance of chairs etc. I can quite imagine it, also her when she gently topples over and her peals of laughter, oh we will have a time of it together.

Well dear will close, so just heaps and heaps of love to you and Bindy.

Your own loving
Harold

P.S. The medicine and cake from Harrods just arrived, many thanks.

28 November – Had photo taken of subsection.
29 November – MacLean and self to Doullens. Almond and Hart to dinner.

4-12-16

30 November 1916

My own darling Con,

2 of yours arrived today, and was very sorry to hear that Bindy has been seedy again, but as you say, expect it is nothing and all kiddies are liable to it, and hope that she will be quite fit by the time that this reaches you.

You seem to be doing a great deal of work at the depot, but hope that you are not overdoing it, but know that it keeps you busy – probably you prefer it.

My sergeant is going home tonight and is going to get married, so will you be a dear and get a present for him, about 30/- and send it to him, will enclose his address. Do not quite know what would be suitable, but should think some kind of home comfort that would be useful in their house, you could find out from someone at home that is more or less of his standing. I am also sending a small parcel home, with some spare clothes etc. which I do not require.

We are on the move again tomorrow up to our new position. Must close as he is just off.

Heaps and heaps of love to you and Bindy.
Your loving
Harold

P.S. Address for Sgt. Porter, 287 Ormskirk Road, Wigam, Lancs.

30 November – Quiet day.

Nelson
New Zealand
2017

Dear Harold,

There is so much that has changed since your day, the world has moved on at an alarming pace, especially with technology that would appear so advanced to your 1917 eyes. The world, although nowhere near having achieved peace, has become very connected through a marvelous thing called the Internet. I am writing to you on a small machine called a computer – imagine the Captain's noisy typewriter with a tiny cinema screen attached and you will get some idea of a computer. All I need to do, to find out any information I choose, is to press some buttons and hey presto I am on the World Wide Web, I ask a question and get multiple pages to wander through to find my answer.

Imagine my delight when one day I typed in your name – Harold Methven Musson – and up popped various bits of information about you. It truly is magical. There were things about your family tree that Jim had created, things about your war and perhaps best of all about your school days. The school that you were sent "home" to as a boarder still exists, Oakham School in the

Harold aged 17

county of Rutland. This county was taking the centenary of the Great War very seriously, and finding all their dead and their graves. There you were, in all your teenage glory looking at me from your photo, bearing such a similarity to my son when he was the same age. Your genes have certainly travelled well through the generations. My son is now older than the age you got to, and I wonder if you would have looked like him! I have to tell you that I felt totally overwhelmed when I saw this photo, it was absolute confirmation that I needed to create your letters into a book. Thank you, Harold, for this opportunity that you placed before me.

These words are written about you on this site:

Harold Methven MUSSON   MC
Second Lieutenant, D Battery, 149 Brigade, Royal Field Artillery, 30th Division.
He died of his wounds on 26 September 1917. He was 33.
He was the son of Christopher J and Kate Musson and the husband of Constance M Musson, 79 Belsize Park Gardens, Hampstead
He is buried in grave XXVIII A9 Étaples Military Cemetery, France.

You are remembered on a plaque in the school chapel, and I know that on the 100th anniversary of your death that they will hold a ceremony for you – you are gone but not forgotten. Your name will be at the top of the School Red Book, a member of the School Combined Cadet Force lowers the School flag, a candle is lit in your honour and your name read out, followed by a prayer. I rather like the school motto, especially as it seems to be very apt for you. Like most mottos it is in Latin, which I confess to never having to learn, but I imagine you did. "Et quasi cursores vitai lampada tradunt." It translates to a delightfully easy,

"And, like runners, they pass on the torch of life."

I have some reminders for you regarding your sporting skills; maybe you were keener on it then than when we met, where you seemed to be happier as an observer. You were probably far happier on a horse and a keen polo player – more of that later.

It seems you were in the rugby and cricket teams and your school magazines tell of your prowess in these games. The 1900 magazine comments on both your football skills – I imagine this was rugby as it lists you amongst the 15 players, which make up a rugby team, I know this as I live in a country obsessed with rugby.

> H.M. MUSSON: worked well as a forward for the first part of the season; has latterly greatly fallen off, showing a distinct tendency to shirk the scrimmage.
>
> Football - *Oakham School Magazine 1900*

You fared a little better in cricket, showing more enthusiasm in your first year of playing.

> MUSSON certainly had the best batting style of all the 2nd XI; he plays with freedom, and he hits hard along the ground; with improved defense and better fielding he may be looked upon as a likely candidate for next year's XI.
>
> Cricket – *Oakham School Magazine 1900*

> H.M. MUSSON: came on wonderfully towards the end of the season; should prove very useful next year, both with bat and ball; not a good field.
>
> Cricket – *Oakham School 1900*

However the next year it was noted "Musson can hit hard but is too slack." It would seem that you did not quite fulfill the promise you had shown in the previous year.

> H.M. MUSSON: a disappointing player; he bowled occasionally with success.
>
> Cricket – *Oakham School magazine 1901*

It is amazing to think that the archivist of Oakham School sent these little notices of your sporting prowess to me, he would have scanned them into his computer in order to send them to me on the other side of the world, but as they were a bit wobbly I have typed them out for you. He also sent me photos of your cricket team for both years, but as the individual photo of you is from the 1900 team I have the latter one for you. You are certainly the tallest member of the team; being tall with big feet is another strong gene passed down the generations.

I have no idea if school was a happy place for you, but it was probably hard being so far away from the place you considered home. I have no comments

Cricket Team – Oakham School 1901

on your academic life, the school put great emphasis on the classics, maybe not everyone's cup of tea. You mention often in the letters that writing is not your strong point, but you tell a story that is important to share.

I wonder if you were to wander the corridors of Oakham if you would recognise anything, I suspect you would be extremely surprised to find that a large amount of pupils are girls. Times have certainly changed since your day.
With love
Sheila x

DECEMBER 1916

Portrait of Harold by Frederick Purvis
– commissioned by Con

'But there was a dead silence that morning, right across the land as far as you could see. We shouted "Merry Christmas", even though nobody felt merry. The silence ended early in the afternoon and the killing started again. It was a short peace in a terrible war.'

Alfred Anderson on the Christmas Truce of 1914

7-12-16

2 December 1916

My own darling Con,

We had a hard frost last night, and during the day still freezing but it is a nice dry cold, and one does not feel it much.

Am going into action tomorrow night, but a very peaceable one, and what we call peace warfare. We have had about 12 days rest, and have all enjoyed it very much, and now feel quite ready for it again.

What happened to MG Williams? Having to put back as many times, he must have got thoroughly fed up with it, and glad he got to his destination.

I got your letter with Flurry's enclosed, not much in it except that he seems rather fed up with the battalion he is in, but will soon get used to that.

The Romanian news seems to be very poor, and they are getting it into the neck properly. I do not think that they will prolong the war, but have no reason for saying this except that it is such a small victory compared to what is going on. I would not be surprised if they received a severe check shortly; but it depends greatly on how the Romanians have left the country, and the amount of stores they have left behind, that is in the region they have evacuated.

Mr Jenns is somewhere very close to here, but cannot find out exactly where, should like to see him again, he is in the Field Artillery.

It has quite begun to freeze hard again, and ought to be skating tomorrow instead of popping an old blunderbus off.

Wonder how you all are on that side, and hope your Dad and Bindy are quite well again.

Must close as post is just off. Just heaps and heaps of love to you and Bindy and God bless you.

                Your loving
                Harold

1 December –   *Sgt. Porter to Blighty. Captain and Mac to position. Not well, cold in stomach. Right section into action.*
                Dull day.
2 December –   *Preparing for march to Bavincourt.*
                Fine day, frozen hard.

8-12-16

3 December 1916

My own darling Con,

Well here we are at our destination, and a very agreeable surprise too, all our dugouts are very comfortable and the mess is quite a fine place, a good stove in it which makes all the difference in these wintry nights.

I also have a little shopping for you to do, one thing is to get a common tablecloth, 5 foot by 5 foot, or as near as possible to this measurement. Also the following curtains: One 140 cms long by 96 cms deep. Two 90 cms long by 96 cms deep. The length is the actual on a tape measure, but we should like to have them long enough so as to make them look loose, in other words not tightly stretched, so will you please allow for this. Also we want small brass rings along the top, so as we can make a string through, as it has to be pulled backwards and forwards. Here is more or less a drawing, am not going to try to explain any more as you know a jolly sight better what we want than I do.

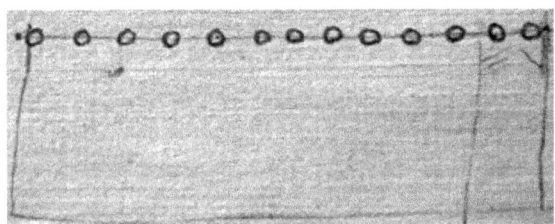

Will just give you an idea of the room, the walls are white, the ceiling also, but it is a slight cream colour on account of the smoke. There is a handsome wooden table in the centre of the banqueting room, and a few war worn chairs round. We thought some kind of chintz would be very much to our liking, so get what you think best. It wants a kind of frill above to hide the rings. Also we think a dark red curtain for the door, the same stuff we got for our curtains at *Lucero*, length 200 x 110. The curtains will either want rings on the top or a strong tape running through. We are very keen to get these as soon as possible, as we want to get it all fixed up for Xmas. Let me have the account as this all goes to the officers' mess. I only wish that I could be with you to have a rag buy, but this will have to be another time.

We ordered a gramophone about a month ago, but up to the present nothing has arrived so far, but should turn up soon.

I expect you have been to Eastbourne by now, and hope you have had a good time of it, I am sure it will do you a lot of good, and that you have gone for at least a week.

Poor wee Bindy, I do not expect that she can understand at all why she should be so seedy, this is the longest bout she has had, but hope she is quite over it by now.

Must close as this is just off by a very quick post I hope, so night night and God bless you both always.

Your loving
Harold

3 December – Marched to Bavincourt, wagon lines very bad, went onto guns at Basseux. Fine cold day.

☆☆☆☆☆☆☆☆☆☆☆☆☆☆

4 December 1916

My own darling Con,

Just a wee notita before I turn in, as am afraid that I have missed a lot of days lately, and must now try and make up for them.

It is a very different life we lead here compared with the Somme, gunnery once more becomes an art, and a general confusion of figures, glasses and red tape, but with all this we will do good work, and wipe out a few of the Hun breed.

The parcels arrived alright from Harrods, and just come in fine.

Up here it is peace warfare and no mistake, it will suit us for sometime to come. In this part they are great at sending one to gunnery schools, so do not be a bit surprised if you find that I am there one of these fine days, it does one a lot of good as one gets some very good lectures and practical knowledge. One can hardly realise without one seeing it how different one part of the line is to another, in every way.

Dotu, I feel an awful wretch at never saying anything in my letters of the day we were married, must own that my wretched head clean forgot the day, and am very sick about it. Fancy, what a change, things could have not been more opposite to what they were then, and just long for the day when it will be the same again, with the addition of the kiddies, bless you and them. Never mind, it must come sometime, if not next year, the year after. We had that dinner on the 27th, and had quite a cheery little evening, but no cards.

I never heard that Mabel intended going to Romania, what a girl she is for new ideas and excitement, she will never stick to one thing, and so spoil herself, but of course gain a lot of experience, which is most interesting. Monty has recovered very quickly and hope he will not have to come out for sometime to come. I must write and congratulate Lucy on his decoration, he was very quick about it, and must have done some good work to gain it.

Here we have to give up the idea of a canteen as the villages are full of them, and one can almost get whatever one wants, but as we had a good innings down in the Somme must not complain.

My batman is now ill with flu, but do not think it is that bad, hope not for his and my sake, as one misses them very much, especially as up to now he does everything for me, and so now when I want a thing I have to turn everything upside down.

Well sweetheart, must close, with tons of love to you and Bindy.

Your loving
Harold

4 December – At guns all day.
Fine day.
5 December – In front lines all day at observation post. Quiet.
Dull cold day.
6 December – At guns, fired one round.
Dull cold day.

12-12-16

7 December 1916

My own darling Con,
Just a wee notita as post is just off. There is absolutely no news.

Sorry to hear that Eric doesn't see any prospect of leave, but hope it will come sooner than be expected.

When you last wrote you had just got down to Eastbourne, and now you are there, I hope you will have a real good rest, and stop at least a week, as it will do you any amount of good. I am sure Bindy will flourish and thoroughly enjoy it, although the other kiddies must be too old for her. Jack must be a great nut at school and expect he leads a rare old life of it.

This is indeed a very quiet spot, and hope it remains so for sometime to come, it is quite curious to wake up every morning and see a civilian knocking round, instead of the eternal khaki.

Has Beatie come to Godalming for a holiday, or has she chucked her nursing home? It seems to have agreed with her, and one never hears of her being seedy or anything of that sort, so hope she has quite got over everything and feels as fit as a fiddle.

Wonder how many of you will be home for Xmas, one can hardly realise that it is so near and only wish we could be together.

Well dearest, must close, with just heaps and heaps of love to you both.

Your loving
Harold

7 December – At guns all day. Gen. Ross Johnson inspected guns. Fired 48 rounds. Fine day.

12-12-16

8 December 1916

My own darling Con,

Another day gone and it will soon be the middle of the month. I must say when one is in action the time goes very much quicker, as one has so much more to do and think about, and more to talk about.

I very nearly had an exciting time this afternoon; I was in the front lines early, and had conversations with a sergeant and then an officer, the latter I had a long talk to, and then he asked me if I had been round yesterday, on which I said no, and so was looked at suspiciously, me not taking any notice. Also I told the sergeant to ring me up with one name, and when the officer asked me I gave my own, this must have caused great confusion, of which I did not know until later. Anyhow I went away and after about 2 hours I met another officer in another part of the lines, he immediately asked if I was the officer who was nearly shot, naturally I said no, and could not make it out. I went back to interview the officer and the sergeant, and found out that they had covered me and very nearly collaring me and taking me off, but eventually were satisfied with my conversation and let me go. We had a good old laugh about the whole thing and parted friends, with an invite to go for a feed with them, which I will do one of these days. Afraid the narrative is not very well put, but will explain it to you when we meet.

I got your letter from Eastbourne and it is ripping to hear that you are enjoying it and is bound to do you a lot of good. Bindy will have great rags with all the children, what does she think of Peter? Am awfully bucked that he is so fit and such a fine laddie, he will soon be a year old and getting quite talkative. By the way when is his birthday, is it in Jan or Feb?

That cold seems to have hung a long time on Bindy, but one cannot expect them to go very quickly in the changeable weather. Anyhow she appears to have had a good sleep which will have done her a lot of good.

You ask whether I want cigarettes, I wrote about 10 or 12 days ago asking for more, so hope you have received that letter, if not please send them along as soon as possible as have only 2 packets left.

I see in the papers that they are going to restrict all foods and only three course dinners at restaurants etc. They are the same with everything; too late and then one wonders why we do not win the war, but still it will come, and the sooner the better for everybody.

Wonder what will happen now and who will compose the new Cabinet, personally I think Lloyd George is the best man of the lot, and should like to see him holding the reins.*

Must close as am writing to your Dad. Just heaps and heaps of love to you and give my love to all the others.

      Your loving
      Harold

8 December –   At observation post all day, very quiet. Fired 5 rds. on Beauvilliers
9 December –   At guns.
      Cold dull day.
10 December –   At observation post. Huns firing on trucks and valley Bellancourt. All day with No. 577 heavy Trench Mortar. Fired 36 rds.

15-12-16

                11 December 1916

My own darling Con,

I got yours written just after you had made the toffee, which has also arrived and we are all enjoying it very much. Mr. MacLean goes on leave tomorrow, and so if all goes well I will get away about Jan 1st, which won't be long in coming round now, so cheer ho, the sooner the better. It has been a long time coming.

We are in action at a place called Bellancourt about 10 miles south of Arras. You will see Rancourt named occasionally; it is in the Hun lines and straight in front of us. The life here is almost more strenuous than in the Somme, and the gunnery much more scientific. The reason is that we have more time to fire, as we

---

*   David Lloyd George was now Prime Minister of Great Britain.

know sometime beforehand what we are going to fire at, whereas on the Somme we had what we call fleeting opportunities, which means very quick work. The artillery fire here is very mild and does not worry us very much, the chief objection is trench mortars which kick up a din occasionally, otherwise the front lines are palaces compared to the other place. One also gets to know all the officers of the infantry and engineers well as you are always among them, and this makes the combination between us much more effective.

Our dugouts are built into the side of a high bank and are very comfortable. The mess is lined with wood and painted white and has a good stove in it, which gets lighted at 7 a.m. so we have a fire going all day. It is 5 yards by 3 broad and one end of it is the office, the remainder dining and lounge. I have a bedroom to myself and quite a fair sized one too, so I am very comfortable.

The country here is very much of the same formation as the Somme, good fighting country, very open and fairly undulating, and not many trees or forests about. The most extraordinary thing is that the civilians live in the village 700 yards behind the front line, they take no notice of the fighting, they are hardly ever shelled, in the evening bullets come whizzing into the village but hardly ever get anybody.

The Romanians have got it in the neck and no mistake, what do they think of it in England? I won't say what I do, as the paper might turn a different colour, it does not only show how badly Romania was prepared for it, but to my mind shows how shortsighted England are, and should never have let them declare war. Now they are broken and no use to anybody and we have lost thousands of tons of wheat and gold. It makes me wild and sick of the whole thing. Only hope to goodness that the new ministry will show a little common sense, and try and manage the country and affairs like a man, and not squabble and fight among their wretched selves. I think we have now got the best man at the head of affairs and quite a good backing, so I hope that they prove so, and pick the country out of the very deep mud hole it is *in*. You can count their muddles by the dozens, and Greece is the first prize one, it makes me long for the Argentine, and not to see England until they have a little more sense knocked into them, and not be such muddlers, enough of this.

Glad to hear you took Bindy and Peter to be photographed, it will be great and hope that they will turn out good. Those Ethel had taken of the kiddies were A1. Fancy Peter being bigger than Bindy, he will be a fine big lad and keep Eric in order. Wonder if you have gone back to *Westhanger*.

The boots arrived safely and will you please thank Beatie very much for them and say I will not write, as there is only the Captain and self here, so very little time for it.

Will close as there are a whole pile of letters to censor. So night night my own and just heaps and heaps of love to you both.

Your loving
Harold

11 December – At guns fixing up pits etc.
      Dull day and cold.
12 December – At observation post all day. Very quiet.
      Snow and rain, rotten day.
13 December – At guns, bombardment of Monchy-le-Preux 11 a.m.
      Dull day.

☆☆☆☆☆☆☆☆☆☆☆☆☆☆☆

23-12-16

14 December 1916

My own darling Con,

Just received yours, with Bindy enclosed, on your return to *Westhanger,* and so bucked to hear that the wee one is quite fit again, and hope the change has done you a lot of good and that I shall find you blooming when I come home.

No pet, our clothes are usually quite dry, anyhow if they are not do not seem to do me any harm.

Have been o-pipping the whole day, and had one of the most quiet days I have ever had at it, and only heard a few bursts in the distance (quite disappointing). Yesterday there was a great bombardment of a village close to here by us, nothing left of the place, houses, trees, roads etc. all went into the air, in fact the Hun must have had a rare old shock.

We are now getting ready for Xmas and are buying all sorts of things for the men, and hope to give them a real good blow out.

Am afraid that you will think me a very poor writer during the last 2 or 3 weeks as I have missed so many days lately, but to tell the truth have been very busy as we have one officer acting as adjutant and another away on leave, it makes rather a hole, and so have to do all their work. The Captain is a brick and does all he can, in fact does too much, but we are only too willing to do it so as to let anyone have his leave. The men are also top-hole and do all that they can to help one.

It does not matter about the camera, so keep it. The torch I do not require as have got an issue one, but you might as well get a cell for it and use it, it gives quite a good light and will help you down the hill etc.

The seca (*drought*) and locust seem to be very bad, and I fear very much for our monte (*woodland,*) I only hope that they will be able to save the trees etc., it is hard luck and will put them back a lot. Even with all this I would not mind being out there and be able to look after the old place.

The M. Luna races did turn out well, 5000 pesos is a big sum, old Argentina has done well and no other place has done better.

Lord Farnham came and stopped with us for 3 days, he is an Irish man and in the Irish Horse, most excellent person and would not mind serving under him. Do you remember Mr. Adair? He used to play polo at Villegas, red haired fellow; he is also with Major Farnham and is coming over to see me one of these days.

Hope Donald will not have left Blighty before I get home, should like to have a chat and probably put him up one or two tips. His guns do very good work and in the Somme have exciting times, and always fairly well up.

The cigs have arrived. Well night night sweetheart and just tons of love to you and Bindy.

Your loving
Harold

14 December – At observation post. 30 rds. fired. Counter-battery fire.* Wretched day.

15 December – At guns, 50 rds. Counter-battery fire. 10 rounds retaliation. Dull damp day.

22-12-16

16 December 1916

My own darling Con,

Just a wee notita, as shall not have very much time tomorrow. It has been a cold fine day, and it is a treat to see the sun, if only for a short time.

The Captain has been away all day at the wagon lines, so have had a day of it, reforming gun pits, and had one little shoot, so hope livened the Hun up at its destination.

We have just received the great news from the French at Verdun breaking through on a 10-mile front, and penetrating 3 miles. 8000 prisoners and a quantity

---

* Counter-battery fire (sometimes called counter-fire) is a battlefield military activity to defeat the enemy's indirect fire elements (guns, rocket launchers, artillery and mortars), including their target acquisition, command and control components. Source Wikipedia

of guns, it is good hearing it, and hope that it will develop into something big, and fairly stagger the Hun. It comes as a bit of relief after the Romanian set back, and will cheer the French troops up tremendously.

I wonder what the German peace terms are going to be, something laughable I expect, as they are very much on their high horse at present and will have to be pulled down, and this time properly and thoroughly, veremos (*we will see*).

There is absolutely no news so will close and will try to write you a better one from the observation post tomorrow. Just heaps and heaps of love to you both and take great care of yourselves.

Your loving
Harold

16 December – At guns, very quiet day, 55 rds. Counter-battery fire. Fine.

17 December – French victory Verdun, 9000 prisoners and 80 guns. In trenches all day, very quiet, 30 rds. C battery. Fine, dull.

22-12-16

18 December 1916

My own darling Con,

Another hurried note, time seems to just fly by and have very little time for anything.

Sgt. Porter has come back, but I do not know if he got the set, as I have not seen him. He had back luck, and was in bed for 5 days out of his leave.

By the way do not trouble to write after the 24th for some days, as I shall not get them before I see someone that I am longing to see, that is if all goes well, so cheery ho. I am enclosing an Xmas card, special battery ones, which are very simple but nice.

It is just ripping of your Dad to send games out for the men, and will thank him when I can, he may rest quite content that the men appreciate these things very much.

Must close, so night night and God bless you all. Please ask all to excuse me not writing for Xmas, but cannot possibly do so.

Your loving
Harold

18 December – At guns, fired about 50 rds., various targets, Hun noisy. Fine, dull.

27-12-16

19 December 1916

My own darling Con,

The tablecloths have just arrived and are A1, many thanks sweetheart for sending them so soon. You must have had a very busy day of it in London, and very nice to have seen some of your old pals, and expect that you will have enjoyed your lunch with Myra, and only wish we could have gone out with them. It is luck, and no mistake, but do not think that any other unit would have let him go.

I often wonder if there is such a place as *Lucero*. Johnnie's letter was not very cheery and they must be going through a very bad time of it, the fact of them having to give hay out in November shows what it must be like. If they do not get several good rains before the really hot weather comes we will be in a very bad way, as there is much too much stock on the place, as on top of the count he gave there will be all the young calves. I am afraid he will have a hard job to save the monte (*woodland*); it will be very sickening if it gets badly eaten down after all we have put into it, and the labour it has cost, but when we get out will have a good shot at putting it straight again and forget about this last year or two.

Gordon Taylor seems to have recovered very quickly, and is a fine recovery after all he has gone through.

I have written several letters to Aunt Bella saying that I received her parcels, but cannot write every time and do not intend to. She is a dear and always thinks of one, and only wish I could write more often, but as everyone knows my writing is not my great point and will never be.

Expect the curtains will be great, but am afraid we will not use them much here, as are likely to stop a very short time, but all about this when I see you.

Glad to hear that Donald will not be coming out soon and will see him when I get home, he must try and get a weekend during that time. Try and get him for New Year, as with any luck I will arrive in Blighty on 28th or 29th, so don't forget to have my slacks out.

What about making an appointment with the dentist? If you think that it ought to be done soon, do so whenever you think best, and arrange to stop at Northgate or Milford for the night, including some theatre. I am not keen on going up more than once and will be sure to require the dentist for two goes. Mr. Lockwood will be at home then, so will you try and find out where he is, as I must see him if possible. Expect that John Venn will know his whereabouts; your Dad will give you his address.

Any news of Eric's leave? It will not be much use answering these questions, as they will be too late to catch me.

Well dearest must close now, just heaps and heaps of love to you and Bindy and be very fit and well. Love to Beatie.

Your loving
Harold

19 December – At observation post morning constructing new observation post. Quiet day, came to battery midday.
Very cold, snowed and icy.
20 December – At guns, fired 70 rds.
Fine dry and cold.

28-12-16

21 December 1916

My own darling Con,
A perfect gale blowing and an occasional shower with it, perfectly rotten, so have been inside most of the day, luckily it was not my day for the O.P. but expect tomorrow will be just as bad. About 7 p.m. last night it was freezing very hard and expected to see inches of ice this morning, instead of that it had thawed and a grand slush everywhere.

The mail has gone to blazes again and no letter for 3 days, but must expect this now we are so near Xmas and they must have a rare amount of mail to handle.

Had a letter from Jean the other day, and quite a shock, as I really believe she is worse than I am at writing. Am afraid that Uncle Bob will feel the winter very much and he most certainly should go away for it, but nothing will move him unless he takes it into his own head to do so.

By the time that this reaches you I expect Xmas will be over, but in case it is not it takes just tons of love and greetings, I hope you are all together and having a jolly time of it.

There is a huge rumble from down south, which one knows very well what it means, and also that the lads there will have a dirty time of it. I hope it will bring good results and more victory, but the cost of life is heavy and will never stop until the end, and peace is declared. What do you think of the German peace proposals? I am longing to hear them, but know jolly well that the end is a long way off.

Will you please order some of my remedy and keep it, do not send it out and will enjoy it with you. A notita from you, and the table centre has just arrived. Please thank Beatie very much for it and never knew that such fine things existed and will christen it at Xmas. It is ripping of her to have sent it.

Yes, it is now over a year since we left our wee home and hope that it will not be another before we are back again. Must close, just tons of love to you both.

>Your loving
>Harold

21 December – At guns, easy day. No 1 guns up to forward position at Bellancourt. Dull day.
22 December – At observation post, fired 30 rds. Hun attention about 90 rds. Cold rain all day.

29-12-16

23 December 1916

My own darling Con,

Here we are very close to Xmas and we (that is the officers) are going to have our little Xmas dinner tomorrow, and the day after the men will have it, and so reserve ourselves to be with them, and see that they get a real good feed.

Great news, the gramophone has just arrived and is going full swing now. The Capelin March is on now; do you remember it from out there? Plenty of go in it and makes me feel rather perky and long to jump on the boat and be with you. Hurrah, it will now be soon.

All the accounts have just arrived from *L. & Co.*, such a mass of them that I do not know which end to begin, but must try and get them all done before my leave, or else will have to have a day of it when I am with you, which will not suit me at all. It has turned out a fairly good year, but at present have not looked at the valuation, and think that Johnnie must have put a low valuation on the stock. I am in the middle of writing him a long letter and told him that if anything goes wrong with the quinta (*house*) he will have to deal with you and I will not be responsible for the consequences, and his best plan would be to take a hurried trip to the hills.

This has been the worst day we have had since we have been out here, blowing and raining for all it is worth, the wind so strong that you can hardly walk against it. Yesterday was nearly as bad, hoping to have a decent day of it tomorrow, as shall be among the infantry lads the whole day. In muddy weather we are pictures when we return, a ball of mud and have to undergo a good scraping, but it is extraordinary how one gets used to it, and sometimes sit the whole evening in it.

Pity those 2 photos were underexposed as they would have been quite good ones. I quite expected to see her standing up; she fairly swamps your back and will soon be carrying you about!!!

No news at all so will close, good night my own, God bless you both and keep very fit.

Your loving
Harold

P.S. I never came across Malony, but may have been quite close to him, I wonder what siege, you might find out and let me know.

23 December – At guns, very quiet. Fired 40 rds.
Gale all day and rain.

25 December 1916

Nelson
New Zealand
2017

Dear Harold,

I wonder what made you decide that you needed to leave your beloved Argentina to fight in a war – I guess you simply felt it your duty to return to England and do your bit for king and country. Your letters to Con created the 'mystery of you' for me to piece together, there are many missing bits but I have so enjoyed my detective work and all that has happened for me on our journey together. Writing this book has brought me more than I could have possibly imagined, at times I was not sure if I was writing it, or it was writing me.

You are probably wondering why I called our book *Sky Full of Stars*; it was not my original title, nor was the cover of the book, it all changed because of a recurring dream. I had several nights of dreams where I would hear a song called A Sky Full of Stars sung by a favourite group of mine named Coldplay. It seemed to be on the radio every time I switched it on, and was playing in shops that I went into. Eventually I understood that this was to be our title, especially as you had named your home *Lucero*, which translates to bright star, and filled you dreams throughout your last year. Jim created the cover photo for me of Étaples C*emetery*, where you now lie, but instead of the northern sky is has the Southern Cross above it, which you would see in the night sky of Argentina. I see it too in my New Zealand skies, which are so often awash with stars. I also see that stars may represent loved ones who have departed this world, offering comfort to those left behind. With so many lost in your war it is no wonder that the sky is full of stars. When my sister died I was so touched by my son finding a star that represented his much-admired aunt. Another star connection is that every couple of years my family are part of a team that walks in an event called Relay For Life. It is a night-time event to raise awareness of cancer, we take it in turns to walk through the night to honour both poorly and departed souls, our team name is The Stars, making us the stars that walk under the night sky.

There have been a few odd things happen to me as I have written this book. I often found my dreams full of you and your comrades; it did not make for a good night of sleep, but I felt that you were all nudging me to tell your stories. One particular night I was dreaming of the trenches and the rats, only to find that my darling three-legged cat, Mystic, had brought me a gift of a mouse that was running around my bed. Suffice to say the cat and mouse spent the night in my room, and I slept as best I could in the spare room.

This morning I also had an odd moment. I had it in my mind to write of your polo prowess, after I had taken the dogs for our usual walk, which is a short car ride away. On opening my door I saw a cardboard designer clothes label, that simply said POLO, and when I got back to the car it was hanging on my door handle. It felt like a nudge to get on with this part of your tale.

I was aware that you were a polo player, your team called the Borderers. Another of those wonderful Google searches produced a couple of books on the History of Polo in Argentina by Horace Laffaye. I was able to track him down and exchange information with him, another of my adventures set up by you. He was also helpful in helping me to track both Flurry and John Campbell.

The Borderers played competitive polo within the Polo Association of the River Plate. Each year an extra trophy, the Lady Susan Townley Cup, was given to the best pony of the season, your friend John Campbell won this 1909 and Luis Lacey of the Borderers won it in 1913, a year you did not play as you were on your way to England to marry Con. You played in the Borderers for two seasons and were in the final in 1912.

Although you and Flurry were not the only ones to die in the war, Horace mentions both you and Flurry in this little snippet: -

> "The Great War exacted its toll from members of the participating teams, both Musson and Crimmin were killed during the war. Harold Methven Musson, a 33 year old second-lieutenant in the Royal Field Artillery, decorated with the Military Cross died September 1917."
>
> Horace Laffaye, *Polo in Argentina – A History 2014 pg. 77*

Amongst the few treasures we have of you is a lovely silver Bridge box that you won, complete with playing cards, score book with pencils attached and the instructions for play. The inscription on the box, which I have copied exactly, tells us:

CALILEGUA RACES
JUJUY POLO CLUB
POLO BALL RACE
OCTOBER 21St 1911
WON BY RIO NEGRO
RIDDEN BY H.M. MUSSON

I can't find out anything about this race, but imagine it was thrilling to win and I know that Rio Negro was a much-loved horse as you mention him a few times. I think Con probably used to ride him as well. She obviously bred horses and they were a huge part of your lives.

I do have one little gripe with you about the horses, you never told us what your mounts in France were called. A minor detail of course, maybe it was easier not to name them, as you never knew what hand fate would deal them, and I know you saw some dreadful sights.

Horses remained a part of your family; these days Jim enjoys working with Riding for the Disabled as it keeps him in touch with these gorgeous creatures, with their soft velvet-like noses, big eyes and listening ears. I too rode as a young girl, and had many a wild ride in Hong Kong on the polo ponies, trekking through the hills of the New Territories, and have even managed to hit a polo ball at a slow pace. I am sure you would think that was A1 or top-hole.

Merry Christmas, Harold.
With love
Sheila x

JANUARY 1917

Harold and Bindy 1916

Let's remember that our children's spirits are more important
than any material things.
When we do, self-esteem and love blossoms and grows more beautifully
than any bed of flowers ever could.
Jack Canfield

18-1-17

12 January 1917*

My own darling Con,

Here I am safely over, and quite a good crossing. This time I went below and had a slack on a very comfortable couch, and was half asleep most the time, luckily the boat was not very crowded. When I got off the boat I met Bowen and had a long talk with him. Am stopping here the night, and leave about 8 a.m. tomorrow morning.

What a rush our parting was, and now feel that I had such a lot to say and did not, but the time must pass quickly, and the war end very soon, and will all be off to the old Argentine. I felt just horrid leaving you all alone, and not even wee Bindy to keep you company, but within two hours you will be together and I can see it all, and may she be just great comfort to you.

We had a great rush for the train, no taxi so we went to the underground, waited 10 minutes and then rushed up and luckily found a taxi, so flew back and got Ethel, jumped in and got to Victoria at 7.40 p.m. which gave us good time to catch the train. If we had not got the taxi I am sure we would have missed the train, which I did not wish to do, as it might get one into rather a mess. (But expect that Ethel told you all about it.)

Bowen is coming to dine with me this evening, and so will have a good talk with him about old times. There was nobody on board that I knew and it is extraordinary how few people one sees that you know. Just as I left the dock the boat that brought me left for Blighty, full of troops and V.A.D.s, (*Voluntary Aid Detachment*)† so looked to see if Kathleen was among them, but could not see her cheery face. It made me long to jump on again and get back to you, but we cannot complain as we were very lucky in getting the 14 days together and how ripping they were, and all so dear and kind to us, they are one bright spark in the last 6 months and will help to carry me on till I next see your dear self.

I hope that Eric will able to get a good extension, it will do them both a lot of good, 10 days does seem short and just flies along.

Well darling I hope you met your Dad and had a comfortable journey to *Westhanger*, take great care of you dear dear self and bless you both. I am a lucky beggar to have you both. Night night sweetheart and will write as soon as I can,

---

* Harold sent a telegram dated 12th January from Folkstone, which simply said "Best of luck and love, Harold."

† This service provided volunteer nurses, ambulance drivers and cooks.

which will probably be when I get to the battery, but hope to get a good chance of a semi-table on the train.

Your own loving
Harold

12 January – Left for front 7.50 a.m., good journey and fair crossing from Calais to Doullens, very slow and rotten journey. Cold and showery.
13 January – Calais to Doullens.

☆☆☆☆☆☆☆☆☆☆☆☆☆☆☆

19-1-17

14 January 1917

My own darling Con,

Here I am, have not reached my battery yet, and am so fed up that I do not care how long it will be. When I arrived here I found that our battery had been split up and a section handed over to another battery. It is just the rottenest thing that could have happened, and now I lose all my fellow officers and have to start in with a new lot, but the worst of all is that I lose my old Captain. The only bright spot in it is that I have got my own men with me, but nothing will be settled for a few days, and I may be pushed off anywhere. My address until further notice will be D/149 Brigade. Never mind I hope to cheer up one of these days, but at present do not feel like trying to please anyone. Just as you get to know everyone and their ways, you are shunted about like a goods train. I feel like scragging somebody. It can't be helped and will just make the best of a bad job. The Captain will feel it very much, and only wish that I had seen him in London. I met two of the men today just off leave, and they say that the men are broken up with it, they have worked 1½ years together, and their best pals are now parted from them. I think I feel more for them than anybody.

It has rained a great deal over here, and everything is just a swamp. Last night we had about 2 inches of snow, so you can imagine what the slush is like. From the port we landed at we had a very slow journey, 14 hours in the train, when it should have taken 6, we passed through Étaples and it looks a very cheery spot and is mostly composed of huge sand hills and fir trees and right on the river. I kept my eyes open in the hopes of seeing Kathleen, I saw a lot of V.A.D.s, but not a sign of her. We arrived here at 11 p.m. and had nothing to eat on the way, bar a few dried figs, which I luckily bought at the port when we arrived here. It took us 2 hours to get anything to eat, and then slept on the floor, which I found quite good. Anyhow, for tonight we have got a good bed in a hotel, and will make the most of it.

Well darling, the more I think of those 12 days, the more I think that it was all a glorious dream, that day we had together with Bindy and the night alone at the theatre stand out above everything. It was all just ripping and hope we shall soon have it over again, and will make a jolly good try to have it so. Somehow I cannot write what I feel about it, but there it is, sort of stuck inside me, and will not come out, and will remain there until we meet again.

I had a long talk with Bowen, he is very involved with his job as R.S.O. *(Railhead Supply Officer)* and lucky to have it and also very interesting, as he sees such a lot of movement etc. As the floor was so full, he gave me a bed in his rooms.

Luckily I hit a good compartment in the train, doors and windows whole, some are in an awful state, windows smashed in and doors wrenched out and on a cold night must be very difficult.

Our battery is at present resting, and expect we will be for sometime, do not know any of the officers in it, but it is the same division.

Hope that you got out to Godalming safely that evening and met your Dad, and found Bindy in great form. I wonder if she will have changed as much again when I next see her, I somehow hope not as I think that she is just ripping at that age. When she gets older she will probably be too clever for me, and be up to all sorts of tricks.

Well darling will now close, with just tons and tons of love to you both, and keep yourselves fit and well.

     Your loving
     Harold

14 January –	At Doullens all day. Heard that D/150 had been split up, sickening and fed up with it. Snowed.
15 January –	Joined Battery D/149 at Lucheux. Bevan adjt. At 149 H.Q. Cold and dull.
16 January –	Round lines. Dull but fine.

23-1-17

17 January 1917

My own darling Con,

Four days gone and only 2 letters written but being on the move has prevented me from writing, Anyhow, am sending this by a man going over so will get to you all the quicker. Just longing for one of your dear letters and hope for one tomorrow.

We have very decent billets here and hope to stop for sometime, excepting for being away for some 3 or 4 days here and there.

As the battery has been split up I am returning the curtains, which they did not want in this battery, so will come in useful at *Lucero*. So far I have seen 2 of the old pal officers and they feel like I do. The one I am in now is not a patch on the other, but hope that one of these days I shall get back to the Captain, but I do not know in the least where he will be pushed off to.

So far I have never finished my letter to Johnnie, and at this place have much less time to write than with the Captain. The work is not nearly as nice or interesting, as it is all done by one man, and the rest get the dirty work.

What has happened to Donald, has he had any more orders for overseas? He seemed so keen on going, but hope that he will not be sent out to Salonika.

I never gave you a cheque on Cox, so I will find how much I am in credit and send you most of it, then you can either get rid of it all or deposit it in the bank.

When I arrived I found dozens of parcels and as they nearly all eatables I gave them away, but not a word. Also there were 2 of your old letters, which I eagerly read. I wonder how your dear self is and also wee Bindy, you will be having great times together and she will become more talkative everyday. That pillowslip is a little too small, 16 inches x 16 inches so will you please make me a couple of ordinary ones and send them along.

Here it has been very cold and bleak and is trying to snow every now and again, but hope that it will keep off.

Well darling, will close with tons and tons of love to both you and Bindy.

Your loving
Harold

22-1-17

17 January 1917

My own darling Con,
Since last writing it has snowed a lot and there are about 3 inches of it, and still going on, luckily it is nice and cold with it all, so no slush about.

Our horse lines are on the road which runs right through a wood and looking down is quite a fine sight, as the trees meet above, and so there is an arch of white and then a long dark row of gees. It is a great thing being on a hard road as there is no mud and easy to keep clean, which saves the men a great deal of work.

My cold is about the same, in fact a little better, the indi has quite gone, it was annoying having it during the leave but better luck next time.

Our Brigade Colonel is a very good sort, and very different to the usual type of army man.

Some ripping person sent me a huge box of chocolates from Fullers, if you know who it was will you let me know, as I have not the faintest idea and should like to write and thank them.

Must close this as post is just off. Heaps and heaps of love to you both.

Your loving
Harold

17 January –   Round sections all day.
                Dull and a few snow showers, cold.

22-1-17

18 January 1917

My own darling Con,

Am afraid that my letters are all very short and no news in them, but there is absolutely none here and as your cartitas have not yet started to come there is nothing to answer.

It has snowed for the last 17 hours and everything is under a huge veil of snow and looks very fine, but what about the day it is going to thaw? Everything will be just like a sea, should like to see about 7 or 8 days of good hard frost.

The Colonel here is a great person, a Livingston-Learmonth and a charming chap. He is a cousin of the Learmonths who are in Guildford. As we are messing at H.Q. we see a lot of him, and over his nightly hot toddy he gives us a very cheery hour or two of it. He has been out in India for a long term, but luckily his liver has not been affected, and so spins us some good old yarns.

We have a great rugby football match coming off on Saturday and I am going to play, what the result of it is going to be I do not know, but can imagine myself a ruined man and stiff for weeks after, but as the doctor is making me play he will have to be responsible for all the results and massage me.

My servant has just gone on leave so until he returns am quite at a loss without him, as he now looks after me quite well. Anyhow I could not let him know, as he has got a wife and family waiting for him and he has not seen them for 14 months and is awfully lucked at getting away.

There is a great spring here, very fine aerated water which we always drink, it is very sparkling and about the best I have tasted.

Well dearest, night night and just tons of love to you both, keep well and let me know all about your dear self.

Your loving
Harold

18 January –   Orderly officer. Gen. White inspected lines. Raid at (no name given) 90 prisoners, 1 officer. Bevan and Hayes left on leave. Snowed all night and day.

☆☆☆☆☆☆☆☆☆☆☆☆☆☆☆

23-1-17

19 January 1917

My own darling Con,

Just a wee line before turning in. Two of the young officers in the battery always go to bed early and after about 5 minutes the house begins to shake, as a result of a wrestling match between the two. One of them is an Irish boy of 20 years, and the other English a few years older, they are both very good natured lads and the former always goes about with a good natured grin which will not come off, not even with a dandy brush.

We have just had news of the German raider being in the Atlantic, wonder how long she will be at liberty, and the damage she will do. It is extraordinary how they get out, and rather throws dust at our fleet, but of course it must be a very tough job from keeping a ship from getting through.

I am going on a few days amusement with the guns in 3 or 4 days, so if you do not hear from me for 5 or 6 days do not worry, as I shall probably get no chance of writing or sending a letter.

It is freezing like anything at night, but hope it will stop before we get on the road as it otherwise will be slippery and our guns will all be on the ground. We have got a very good Sergeant Major in this battery and all the men like him, he treats them as men and not as machines as most of them do, and so he gets the respect which is due to him, and also gets much better work out of them.

I expect by now that Bindy is quite firm on her pins, or does she still wobble a bit? I always picture her strutting about and looking so cheery and bright with her 'boos' and ripping little ways. She will be sound asleep now, or maybe just awake for her 10 p.m. bout, and you darling will be talking to your old Dad, hope you are fit and well and not overfeeding the hens.

Night night my own, God bless you both and keep you fit and well, am just going to turn in.

Your loving
Harold

19 January – Major went to Bellacourt to find gun position. General works in the horse lines.
Lucheux.
Fine day.

☆☆☆☆☆☆☆☆☆☆☆☆☆☆☆☆

25-1-17

20 January 1917

My own darling Con,
It was just ripping to get a budget of 4 letters from you and also enclosing Johnnie's. I am quite with you about our second parting, it was just rotten and only hope that the end will soon come, and then we will do our best to not let it happen again. It makes one just think how lucky Mr. and Mrs. Peters were not to have parted for 57 years, but think that that must constitute a record. Never mind time must now just fly and then we will return to *Lucero*.

It has turned very very cold here and seems to go through everything, and as we have no coal or wood we live in our topcoats. These coal and wood comforts are getting very scarce and hope that they will buck up soon, or the weather get warmer.

I cannot make out why you have received no letter from me unless that clown Bowen forgot to post the one I gave him. I wrote it from Calais so if you do not get it let me know and I will write and talk to him. I wrote last night saying that I would probably not be able to write to you for some days, but now that is off, so will be able to carry on.

About inoculation, it is no good your doing anything on that side, I will talk to the doctor, who is a very good sort and see what he says about it. I do not think there is much need for it, but will find out.

21/1/17

I am very glad your Dad gave you that cutting about church going, and thoroughly agree about it. When our kiddies are old enough to understand we must try and bring them up on a certain line, which we must have a good talk over and decide on. Personally I do not believe in too much religious bringing up. From the first I think we should instill into them what is right and wrong, and gradually bring them up with an open and clear mind. There are many passages in the Bible, which I think are absolutely right, and good and interesting reading for them, I cannot remember what they are, but you will know, and whenever you come across them, I should mark them for future reference. Am afraid that I cannot describe what I mean in writing, but will do so when we next together, and Bindy will also be able to pick up a little of her first lessons. It will be very interesting teaching her and eventually seeing the results of it all. It will be a great life after this war is over and one has to think no more of how to worry and kill the Bosch.

I put in one of my former letters my new address but in case you do not receive it, it is D/149 Brigade R.F.A. B.E.7. I met the old Captain today, he is not looking half the man and has felt the splitting up of his old battery very much, one can quite imagine it, after he has made and trained the whole thing. He is longing to collect it together again and we would jump to it, never mind, we are trying to forget about it all, and must do out best to get used to the ways of this one.

Well dearest, night night, God keep you fit and well and no more feeling sick and rotten, just tons and tons of love to you both.

Your loving
Harold

20 January – Went to Doullens. Rugby match 149 vs. Lancs., beat 14:0. Fine cold day.

21 January – Orderly officer. Went to church 12 p.m. Captain Tytler to tea and went back with him to his billets, nothing arranged. Fine cold day.

26-1-17

22 January 1917

My own darling Con,

Today we have been to a lecture on mange, it was quite interesting, gave me a few tips which might be useful out there. Then we had a full kit inspection of the men, which went off well, and most of the men had their whole kit, which is very unusual, the rest of the day we have been fiddling about, getting our horses ready for the march.

Yesterday I took 50 of our men to church, marched them off in great style and got quite a good sermon, chiefly on what changes we might find in England after this war, and also the good this war has done us. He candidly stated that he misunderstood men before, and that many clergy did the same, and thought that very little religion was in us, but since being out here, he has found his mistake. He more or less stated that men could be so without going to church, as he had seen so many instances out here, especially where men were in action, and under fire, and that he has seen it come out in them in so many different ways. He is quite right, and I am sure it is the time one feels it most, and there are many instances where a little prayer or something or other is done, it is very difficult to express what it is, but it is nearly always there.

Sorry to hear that Helen has German measles, beastly unpatriotic thing to get, and am ashamed of her, you will have to call it something else, she must not assist German trade, anyhow hope she will soon be well.

Fancy I have never finished my letter to Johnnie, which I started before I went on leave. I come down every evening with the intention of finishing it, and each time something comes in the way, if only the officer commanding would go away for the day, I should make a point of it, but there is not much chance of that.

I had a grand hot bath this evening in an old barn, we got a fire going and 3 half tubs put in front of it, and filled with hot water, and soaked in it for ½ hour. There were 3 of us, and in the middle of it and we thought what a picture it would make, 3 officers having a tub behind the lines.

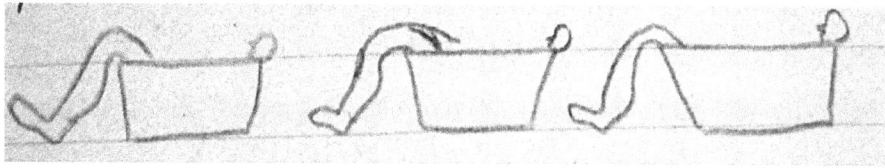

Doesn't it look fine, and the drawings are quite top-hole. Anyhow we thoroughly enjoyed it and everything went off well.

I often wonder if Bindy will know me again but it is too much to expect, as she is still so young, she will be a great person when we meet again and have quite a lot of chatter.

Well darling must close, just heaps and heaps of love.

Your loving
Harold

22 January –   Lecture on horse scabs. Round lines all day.
               Fine, cold day.

☆☆☆☆☆☆☆☆☆☆☆☆☆☆☆

27-1-17

23 January 1917

My own darling Con,

Two of your dear letters have arrived, and it is just ripping to get them. I am very sorry to hear that you have not had any from me, as I especially wrote you from the seaport, all I can think of is that ass Bowen has still got it in his pocket, and will let him know about it. As he is a married man he should know better. By now you will have received some of my others.

Out here it has turned bitterly cold, in fact tonight is one of the coldest I have ever felt, and reminds me very much of the one when we sat up at *Lucero* to see Luenil off to San Raphael.

This evening we went to see the Periots "Blue Bird," which is composed of men picked out of the division. It was very good and consisted of a violin solo, one or two very good songs and top-hole voices, a comic song, recitations and a ventriloquist. It lasted about two hours and we all came away in quite good form, had dinner and now going to turn into bed, that is when I have finished this.

What a pity the photos of Bindy did not come a couple of days earlier, never mind will see them when I get my next leave.

We had some revolver practice today, the shooting is very bad, and glad to say that I was as good as any of them, but this says very little for the others, but think I could pot a Bosch over at 40 yards, anyway he would feel very uncomfortable.

Wonder if I will come across Lucy out here, think it is improbable. Eric will be out here by now, and only hope that Susan will keep in good form and not worry too much. We were both lucky to get extra leave so cannot complain, and hope that the next leave will be for good and all, and everyone at peace again.

The cigs etc. have just arrived and muchas gracias. In another month or so I shall probably be sending some more kit home, as I want as little as possible for the coming spring.

Well dearie I am off to bed, so just crowds of love and huge hug to you both and take great care of yourselves.

Your loving
Harold

23 January – Round lines all day. Went to Blue Birds evening. Div. Periots good.
Lucheux.
Fine cold day.

☆☆☆☆☆☆☆☆☆☆☆☆☆☆

28-1-17

24 January 1917

My own dear Con,

Another day gone and a very freezing one too, in fact we could have skated. Do you remember our skates at Ziweigimmas and Gastade? What great days they were and our great tussles at trying to make the figure 3, also the day the wind ran away from you and you had to carefully sit down to prevent taking a header over the snow bank. Also the day I got so fed up and wanted to take the first train home, I somehow never forget that day, but was always jolly glad we did not.

Con and Harold on ice – date unknown

Fancy that was long before we ever thought of Bindy, and now we are thinking very much of the little fellow, the usual old argument of who he will be like.

Tomorrow we are having an inspection by our General, so will have to get everything very up to date. It is not often he comes and looks at us, and will be glad when it is all over, as I would much rather be in a muddy trench having a few rounds at the Bosch lines or himself.

We seem to be losing a lot of ships now and this raider* being at large is one of our worst troubles, and seems to be worrying the South American liners. It seems

---

*   German armed merchant ships disguised as non-combatant ships, they were used to attack and sink ships of other nations.

extraordinary how they can manage to evade us so much, or else our navy is not keeping such a good look out as it is expected to. Here we hear a new rumour every day about peace, the latest is that Austria have thrown up their hands, but we take no notice of anything until it is confirmed. I often wonder who makes all these things up, must be quite a clever person, but wish someone would drown him.

Dinner is just coming in, so night night and a huge hug to you sweetheart, and a big kiss to Bindy.

Your loving
Harold

24 January – Orderly officer. General work in lines.
Fine frosty day.
25 January – General work in lines.
Lucheux.
Fine frosty day.

30-1-17

26 January 1917

My own darling Con,
The sharp spell of frost is still going on and it is very severe. We try to get our harness and wagons washed and the water gets frozen within 16 seconds, and that is in the middle of the day. The horses get through it very well, and do not appear to suffer but our poor men have a miserable time of it, and are cold morning, noon and especially during the night, and there is nothing that we can do assist them. They live in a huge drafty barn and have wire beds and only their topcoat and 2 blankets, so sleep in their clothes, boots and everything they can, but still remain cold. We cannot light a fire in it, as there is no fuel, and also the roof is a few beams with a haystack on top, so it would catch fire. I am truly sorry for them and think that it is a disgrace that the army have occupied this place for 2 years and have such bad accommodation for the troops that come out for a rest. They are much more comfortable in action. There is fine skating all over the place but not a skate to be had, anyway have no time for it.

Well we were inspected by the General and had a good dressing down for our turn out. I will own that it was not flash, but all the harnesses were clean and well oiled, which is what we want for active service, but this did not suit their idea, and of course every one was freezing including the horses. We had 17 degrees of frost, the men were hurried out at 4.30 a.m. with breakfast at 5.30, then a clean up, harness up and tie in, so you can imagine how their hands felt. Then a 1½ hour wait on top of a bleak hill, I felt just like getting off my horse and having a good row and a knock out with the cretin who had got out of a downy bed and driven up in nothing less than a Daimler. These trying moments often occur, and should like to put them onto a weeks work, just as the men go through it, and then hear what they had to say about it. I think that their idea might change a bit.

Am very sorry to hear that Peter was ill again and only hope that it will only turn out a very slight cold. I have not sent on Johnnie's letter as I have not answered yet, but will do that as soon as possible.

The Major is going to a school of gunnery as an instructor for a few weeks, which he is not at all keen on, so will have a great struggle to get everything in top-hole order before he returns.

I do not at all like this seca (*drought*) they are having out in the camps, and hope we shall soon hear good news, otherwise they will be running into winter without any hay, and if this is the case Johnnie will have to get rid of a big lot of stock before the cold sets in. It makes me very anxious to be out there, it will be a very serious blow if it turns out bad, but must not think of these things too much as it does no good, but our little all is there.

Well darling this is a very uninteresting letter but expect you are getting used to them by now, so will not apologise. Just heaps and heaps of love to you and wee Bindy and take great care of yourselves.

    Your loving
    Harold

26 January – General work.
     Fine frosty day.

31-1-17

27 January 1917

My own darling Con,

Two of yours have just arrived of the 20th and 25th, it is not often one gets a letter in under 2 days, and it is just ripping to get them so quick and makes you feel so much nearer.

No sweetheart, I have not had a headache, do not worry, in fact I have been very fit except for my feet, which have several chilblains and are a bit tender. Also I got a bit of a cold on the top of the other and felt it for a day or two, but has now passed off, but am left with a cough which worries me for about a ½ hour when I go to bed and when I get up, but does not worry me much otherwise.

I was awfully sorry to hear of Esme Penrose's death, what bad luck she had the last year and then to be taken away so suddenly.

I am beginning to settle down a good deal more in this new battery, but cannot quite get used to some of their ways and afraid I never shall. I shall most likely be going into action in 10 or 12 days and onto a quiet part of the line, in fact just as quiet as the last place. But will give you an account of it when I get there.

You will be having a very lively time with the Boswells and hope they will not run you off your legs. I do not envy the schoolmistress and wonder how long she will be able to stand it, and can imagine Sylvia trying to retain the peace.

Am afraid there is very little chance of coming across Eric, as we are so very far apart and unless he moves down will never see him.

This frost is tremendous and in the mornings before we are able to water our gees we have to hack great blocks of ice out of the troughs, and then get the pump going. Luckily there has not been very much wind, which I think one feels more than anything.

I have heaps of warm waistcoats so you can send the one you have to Bindy's prisoner, but hope he is small man.

Glad to hear that Ethel is going to stay with you for a few days and will have a good rest, I will have to come and look after you both. Am struggling hard to finish Johnnie's letter but there seems no end to it.

Well will close, just oceans of love to you and the wee one and take great care of yourselves.

Your loving
Harold

27 January – Orderly Officer. General work.
             Fine cold frosty day.

1-2-17

28 January 1917

My own darling Con,
Two more of your cartitas, I am afraid this will be very short tonight as the post is just off and do not want to miss it.

We have had a great day with our harness, wagons etc., and have got them fairly clean at last, but that has been a hard job, and had to get big fires going to keep the water warm, then it was frozen hard in about 5 minutes. Hope that the General will be satisfied with them.

Bindy does seem to be coming along and will be able to teach me quite a lot when we meet.

I see in papers that there has been skating in England, but think that is has been more severe here and the ice is yards thick. The cold is bringing the wild boar down, and at night one can see them walking about in the horse lines scrimmaging for forage.

Night night and take great care of yourselves.

Your loving
Harold

28 January – General work. Gray returned from leave. Cold frosty day.

6-2-17

29 January 1917

My own darling Con,

The photo of Bindy has just arrived and I like it very much indeed, and will be a ripping one to have in my dugout, but then there will not be much of it left by the time the war is over, as the difficulty is to carry it about when on the move.

We went to the Periots this evening and enjoyed it very much; it was quite a different show to the last one and some very good turns.

Am just off to bed and a hot bath, and have a good night of it to try and get rid of my cold, which has not been so well today. We shall likely be living under canvas for sometime, as where we are going there is nothing bar mother earth.

30/1/17

We now have enough wood and coal for our fires and so are quite comfortable and keep warm.

We are on the move tomorrow and will be a very cold one too, so shall probably walk part of the way. The General inspects us at a march past and hope he freezes.

The footer match was played but I did not play and very glad too as the ground was under inches of snow and frozen hard. The men that played did not enjoy it very much and got rather badly knocked about, all their knees torn, 2 had thumbs badly sprained, 1 slight water on the knee and another sent to hospital, and that was on our side, so do not know what the other lot were like or faired. Anyway, I was well out of it.

What bad luck on your Aunt M. in being left alone, she will feel it terribly but is such a brick, that she will get through it.

I see very little of the Captain or any of the others although we are quite close to one another, but hope to see more of them in the near future, but am afraid that there is no chance of joining together again. Shall probably try to get a transfer and may try to get to Eric's Division.

Glad to hear that you got the curtains safely, they did not take long to get home. The camera was of no use to me and not even allowed to have one, which is quite right.

Ethel will have left you today, unless she prolonged her visit, and hope you had a good time of it together and will have done both of you good.

Yes, I long to see Bindy and can almost see her making huge strides in strength and knowledge, it is awfully interesting to see all her new little ways and sayings and sorry that I am missing it all, as they do get interesting at that age, never mind, I will see the next wee fellow come along with any luck.

Do not worry to send any more papers, as the wrappings are addressed all wrong and we will have very little time for reading. I do not know when I will be able to post this letter as being on the march upsets everything very much, but expect it go the day after tomorrow.

What bad luck that P. Bonnin should have died, and just because the doctor was an ass. I am bothered if I would risk my neck with any flying man that should come along.

Well night night my own and tons of love to you both.

Your loving
Harold

29 January – Went to the Blue Birds. General work cleaning wagons and harness.
Fine cold day, frozen all day.
30 January – Getting wagons etc. ready for the march to Monchiet.
Lucheux.
Fine cold day, frozen all day.

31 January – Marched to Monchiet through Humbercourt, Bavincourt, Gouy-en-Artois. Very bad marching on account of frost, roads very slippery. Monchiet.
Fine frosty day.

☆☆☆☆☆☆☆☆☆☆☆☆☆☆☆

Nelson
New Zealand
2017

Dear Harold,

It must have helped you so much when you arrived in France and at your Battery to find a kindred spirit in Captain Neil Fraser-Tytler, you obviously held him in high esteem and most importantly trusted him. I am delighted to tell you that my curiosity about him led me to some great discoveries about him and his family. I love being able to share my findings with you. I have already told you about his Aunt Molly and her great creative achievements.

You talk of the Captain and his typewriter, the constant clacking of the keys. I imagine that some of his clacking was writing letters to his father, that he later published in a book titled *Field Guns in France*; by the time it was published in 1922 he held the rank of Lieutenant-Colonel. It was thrilling to find that the book was still in print and even more thrilling to find that you were mentioned several times, Neil obviously admired you. I have added these references into your letters, as I have been able to match them with your letters. I do have to repeat one tiny bit here though, as you gave him pause to reflect on the business of war.

> "Musson was top-hole, but being up there with him straight from England, and with some decent feelings left, made one realise what a disgusting business war is."

Neil's grandson Nick sent me some photos of him; the one I have chosen to share with you is the one Neil's daughter Mary hoped I would use. I imagine that this photo is just as you knew him, on horseback in uniform. Here he is on a favourite horse called Woodsman, I wonder if Woodsman was with him in France, there is nothing to tell us that he was, although horses from his home, *Aldourie Castle*, on the banks of Loch Ness did become warhorses.

Neil led an eventful life; he carried on his military career, as you will see in his obituary.

> "After suffering for years from sleepy sickness, contracted, it is believed, in France during the Great War, Colonel Neil Fraser-Tytler, of Aldourie Castle, Inverness-shire, died yesterday morning. He was 48 years of age, and was the eldest son of Lieutenant Colonel E.G. Fraser-Tytler, Lovat Scouts.

Captain Neil Fraser-Tytler on Woodsman, date unknown.

He belonged to a family, which was distinguished in literature during five successive generations.

Colonel Neil Fraser-Tytler, in November 1915, went to France in command of a Royal Field Artillery Battery of the 30th Division, and was mentioned in dispatches four times, receiving the Distinguished Service Order and Bar, and was also awarded the French Croix de Guerre.

On his return to civilian life he published a book, *"Field Guns in France."* In 1923 and 1925 his Inverness Territorial Battery won the King's Cup, competed for by batteries all over Great Britain, and in 1927 the battery were again in the final of the contest. He took an active part in public life, but had to retire several years ago through ill health. He married in 1919, the eldest daughter of Sheriff-substitute J. Campbell Sharp, of Houston, and is survived by this wife and two daughters."

Obituary of Colonel Neil Fraser-Tytler 1938

His wife Christian nursed him for his final years, she went onto play a prominent part in the Second World War, and may even have crossed paths with Bindy, but more of that later.

I have to say that Neil's letters were far more graphic than yours; I wonder if that is because he was writing to his father who may have had more understanding of all that was happening. You wrote to Con in a far gentler way, not really saying too much of the horror unfolding before your eyes. Both of you created a picture of your experiences, and in so doing did a great service for generations to follow, by letting us see through your eyes for a short moment.

I imagine it was a great shock to get back to France after your leave and find that you were no longer with Neil, however, you were able to keep in touch with each other and spend a little time together. I am pleased I have been able to meet Neil and to let you know a little of what became of him. You are all an enigma, this short year of letters from you opened my eyes – at times I wished they had stayed closed and I had never had to know all you went through. Those that survived the war as Neil did carried the scars and burdens for the rest of their days. I imagine that Neil carried on life with the panache you described, finding the treasures in each moment and living a life of daring-do. I wish you too had been offered that opportunity.

With love

Sheila x

February 1917

Con on ice, date unknown

Give your hearts, but not into each other's keeping.
For only the hand of Life can contain your hearts.
And stand together yet not too near together:
For the pillars of the temple stand apart,
And the oak and the cypress grow not in each
other's shadow.

Kahlil Gibran – *The Prophet*

6-2-17

1 February 1917

My own darling Con,

Afraid I have not been able to post my last letter yet, but hope that these will get away today.

We had a big day of it yesterday, started at 9.30 a.m. and arrived here at 7 in the evening. It was only about a 12-mile march, but the roads were like a sheet of ice, and so the gees were continually falling down, and then the difficulty was to get them up, which we eventually did by throwing earth under them. Several of the guns and wagons skidded clean off the road and into the ditch, this often meant unhooking and pulling them out by hand. 2 of the drivers fell with their horse on top of them, and got their ankles badly twisted. Anyhow we arrived here, and slept in big iron huts lined with wood, they were rather cold and draughty, and it has not done my cold much good, but as we shall be in the open altogether, that is under tents, expect it will go. Expect to go up to the line tonight and get settled down for sometime.

The months are gradually slipping along and hope that they will just fly along, as the sooner the push comes the sooner it will be over and out to our wee home.

I get to like the photo more and more of Bindy, it is so like her and her little smile, pity the photo of the two together did not come out well.

Have not had a line from Eric yet, but expect that he has been very busy settling down again.

How are the Boxwell girls getting along at school? They must cause a great deal of amusement to the rest of the school.

Must close now as dinner is just coming on (or lunch). Just heaps of love to you and Bindy.

> Your loving
> Harold

1 February – At Monchiet all day and brought up guns to position at Dainville and Agny. Very hard frost.

10-2-17

2 February 1917

My own darling Con,

Here we are in our new home, it is quite good and much better that I expected, and have good dugouts to live in. The mess is quite a good place, but will have to put a new fireplace in it, as the one we have at present none of the smoke goes the right way, and so we fill the fire up, clear out of the mess for ½ hour to let the smoke get away and then come in and get warm.

All my senior officers have gone away for a few days, and so at present I am temporary Officer in Command, I am glad about it as it gives me a lot to do, and so learn a lot of new points and tips one misses otherwise.

Had a letter from Aunt Janie this evening, she seems very cheery and enjoyed herself at Eastbourne, her letter took 10 days to arrive, so you can imagine what the post is like. She tells me that Uncle Fred has not got the puzzle yet, expect that he will be very fed up with it and cut it off. Also had a letter from Eric, he seems to have got back and settling down again, he is in the same position as I am, and Officer in Command of his lot.

This part is very quiet, almost more that the last and very seldom see a Hun. The cold snap has not broken yet and your hanky freezes in one's pocket, and towel and boots are as hard as nails in the mornings, hope it will not last too long but I think that all this cold is much better than combined rain and mud.

It is about time that Kathleen got home, hope she is very fit and not doing too much hard work.

There seems to have been a German attack somewhere around where Eric was, but it will be a hard job to get through our lines.

Well darling, night night and just heaps of love to you both.

Your loving
Harold

Many thanks for the pork pie, which has not arrived yet, but hope to enjoy it soon.

2 February –   Up at observation post and registered guns, making
2 new gun spots. Gaskell went on leave.
Very cold frosty weather.

10-2-17
3 February 1917

My own darling Con,

Just a wee notita before turning in, I have just shifted my dugout, and am now in an old cellar of a blown-up house. It is a nice and dry and gets plenty of air, and has or will have a stove in it, so will be top-hole.

The last two days we have been very busy getting all ship-shape, and now we can give the Hun a good old straff, he is very quiet in these parts and up to now has not caused us any annoyance.

Glad to hear that Ethel was with you, and also Helen, you will have quite a house full, do not know what you will do when we get back to *Lucero*, and be by our lonesomes.

Today I was with the officers of the battalion that Ronald Drysdale was in, and they knew him very well. The man I met was called Russell, he says that Drysdale is coming out again very soon, but that his foot had never got quite right, at present he is training troops somewhere in England.

By the way dearest will you please get me 1 pair of thick woolly socks to put into my boots, as I cannot get them round here, and send them as soon as possible. Those boots I got at Harrods are rather tight round the instep, but otherwise are very good and thick, they will be top-hole in wet weather. Will you also send me out *The Times*, as we very seldom see a paper and get very out of date.

There is very little news here, in fact none and afraid you will think these letters are very flat, and quite right too.

How is Bindy treating you? I hope that the wee man is very fit, but not too unreasonable, I just long to be with you and will have a very good shot at it soon.

Light is just going out, so night night and sleep well, heaps and heaps of love to you and Bindy.

Your loving
Harold

3 February – 624 rounds of ammo came up. Went round front line during morning. Very cold frosty day.
4 February – General work at guns. Cold and frosty.
5 February – General work. Cold and frosty.

11-2-17

6 February 1917

My own darling Con,
No mail today, and everything trotting along the same as usual, it is still very cold,

it freezes day and night and everything is just like concrete now. There should be plenty of skating in England now.

We just got news today that America* had joined us, wonder how much good it will do. We will get a lot more shipping, and then there is the US navy, which should assist a great deal in patrolling the Atlantic. Let me know what the general feeling in Blighty is, and whether it is satisfactory or not. They will not be able to assist our prisoners in Germany anymore, which is rather a jar.

We are having a very quiet time of it here, but plenty of good work. Have now got our position very comfortable and quite settled down to it again. Everybody has got colds, and I think mine is a slight touch of flu and have had neuralgia for 8 days, so expect it will soon go, but very annoying, especially when I cough.

No news at all, or my head will not think, just heaps of love to you and wee Bindy, keep well and take great care of yourself.

Your loving
Harold

6 February –   *General work.*
           Dainville.
           Cold and frosty.

12-2-17

7 February 1917

My own darling Con,

Thanks, I feel a little better today, and so on the mend and as I have plenty of work to do, time passes fairly quickly.

I got your cartita telling me all about your experience at Frensham, and only wish that I had been there to say what I thought of her. She is just about the limit, and how she makes anything out of it I cannot think, and she deserves to come a cropper. I think she must be fairly independent and runs the place more or less as a hobby, and must say that it could be a good business if it were well run, and a cheery person at the head of it. Anyhow in future we will give it a miss, lucky nothing happened when we were there.

---

*   America severed diplomatic ties with Germany in February 1917, but did not actually join the war until April 6th 1917.

Expect the pond is quite frozen over and skating on it by now. It has been a grand day here and could almost sit out in the sun, would have been great to have had a walk with you. Last night I dreamt that I had just arrived at *Westhanger*, and walked into your room about 6.30 a.m. to your intense surprise, but no luck, woke up to find myself here.

Glad to hear that Ethel is much better and expect that now she is on the mend and will pick up altogether, and so be quite her old self. I must write to her, have not done so far.

There have been lots of planes about today, but they got a very warm reception and had to clear out of it. By the quietness of everything one might think that there is no war on.

Well dearest, must close with heaps and heaps of love to you two dears, and keep very fit and well. Hope you Dad is A1, and will write to him soon, although you must get everyone to excuse me as have very little time for the next 2 weeks.

Your loving
Harold

7 February – General work.
Cold and frosty.
8 February – General work.
Cold and frosty.

13-2-17

9 February 1917

My own darling Con,
Glad to hear that it is getting a bit warmer with you, here it is as cold as ever and does not look like a change.

No, the only thing that the boars did was to scuttle off a short distance, and then wait until one had gone, when they would immediately return and pick up all the tidbits.

It is ripping to hear that Bindy is getting so ripping everyday and intelligent, I can quite imagine her and all her little ways, but expect that she is blooming out in new ones every day.

My feet are quite alright again, and I am feeling much better in myself.

I met the Captain yesterday, and he has hopes of getting a battery, and if so is going to try and get me back to it, it will be just ripping, but sounds too good to be true. Here I am getting on quite alright, but that is because I am on my own, that is senior officer. But then the Major, Captain and Senior Sergeant have to come back, and so will have very little interest or much to do, and that is the chief thing out here, and makes time push along.

I think there is a compass of mine somewhere about; if you find it will you please send it out, also twice a month a plain cake and milk chocolate.

Must close now, just heaps and heaps of love to you and Bindy.
Your own loving
Harold

9 February –   General work.
             Cold and frosty.

16-2-17

10 February 1917

My own darling Con,

Your letters are coming fairly regularly now, and very bucked to get them. I am very sorry mine are getting along so badly, the post must be rotten as I write very regularly. During the move I could not get letters posted, and 2 or 3 went off at the same time, so expect that must have been the delay.

Anyhow, am feeling very much better, and the cough also is going, and I think that the remedy you sent me must have done the trick, as it was from the day I started taking it that it began to improve.

Dearest, you must not worry when you do not hear from me, as I am very fit. If I do by any chance get ill I will wire you, but there is very little chance of that, and if one does one is well looked after behind the lines.

I have heard nothing about America or what she intends to be doing, I hope she will get a move on with that fleet of hers, and should be able to look after the Atlantic.

Tonight I am by my lonesome, but very comfortable and a good old fire going, after finishing this will have a quiet read. I have taken to those mitts Bindy sent, and find them top-hole and much better than any gloves, so give her a great hug and tell her that it is one of the finest presents her Dad has had. Yes please, send some cigarettes and will you send them every 3 weeks. Your pork pie has not arrived, so expect someone has had a good tuck into it, but hope he got tummy ache, unless he was a tommy in the front line, but they do not have such luck as that.

This has been a grand day and the first day I have been able to go without my topcoat since I have been back. I think that a thaw will soon set in as there is more moisture in the air, but there will be an awful mess when it does and yards of mud everywhere.

Donald seems to get plenty of orders and counter orders and must be very fed up with it, but expect that he will soon be moved on and get all the shooting of his guns that he wants. Poor old Susan, she has had bad luck, but hope she will be quite fit again soon.

You seem to be having a lot of trouble getting a stop gap, I expect that is on account of there being so much work and so few to do it, and also they do not care about taking on short jobs. Can quite imagine how useful Bindy is with the duster, and the good sound work she does, I wonder if she will like it as much when she is 17 or 18. It is hard to picture her at this age, we will be quite old then and will be well looked after by her, and can't you just imagine it? Will have to get another Rio Negro for her, even if we are settled in England by then.

I saw the Captain yesterday and he was in great hopes of getting a battery shortly and will try and get us with him, but I think that it will be very hard for me to get a transfer, but will certainly try.

The caramels and such arrived and were fine, some of the best I have tasted.

My batman turned up 4 days ago and was very glad to get him back. He has rather bad luck, as when he got home he found that his sister-in-law had died, and his boy was in hospital with a bad throat and tubercular of the skin, it is bad luck and must have spoilt his holiday.

I was talking to another officer from our old battery yesterday, who had just come back from leave and he found out just the same thing as I did; and that is that his best and happiest days were spent with his wife and kiddie, and were the only ones which shone above all the others. So afraid I will be very selfish on my next, and take you off into some lonely and quiet part next time.

Lucy's address is Scots Guards, 2 Battalion BE7. Have not written to him yet, but must do so soon.

Well darling will close now, God bless you both and keep you very fit and well, and take great care of yourselves.

Your loving
Harold

10 February – General work.
Dainville.
Cold and frosty.

☆☆☆☆☆☆☆☆☆☆☆☆☆☆☆

17-2-17

11 February 1917

My own darling Con,

Yes, time is slipping along and it will be a month tomorrow since I left you at Northgate, so one more month nearer to the day that I shall see your dear self again.

I think Kenneth is a brave man to have hiked 20 miles in the snow, I should strongly object to it, and he had that heat at the other end. It is extraordinary how these people wish to come out again; of course it is much nicer to be with one's own men. Also there is a certain amount of fascination about it all, but mine is to be with the little family, and it will take a good many drag ropes to part me after this is over.

Up to the present I have not been able to finish my letter to Johnnie, but hope to do so before the end of the month, it will have taken quite two months to do, so is not a bad record.

Before I forget will you please send me a good dose of my remedy, you had better send 2 of it, as I hear that parcels are very soon going to be stopped, so better send them while you can.

I had a great walk round today looking at a lot of places, which I cannot mention; it was quite interesting and instructive.

Fancy I have only seen 1 paper in the last fortnight, it makes one feel very out of date, and long for a little outside news, and everything in the line of mail is days before it arrives here. I hear that most people at home are very optimistic, and in great hopes of the war ending this year, only hope that they are right, and it comes to an end sooner than they expect, but it does not look very much like it.

Flurry seems much more cheered than formerly, and so expect that he has got settled down, and to know his men, which makes a great difference and also gives one a great deal more interest in one's work.

Well darling will close, just heaps and heaps of love, sleep well and take great care of your dear selves.

Your loving
Harold

11 February – At observation post. Registered guns, 38 rds.
Fine cold day.

18-2-17

12 February 1917

My own darling Con,

There has been a decided thaw today, and looks as if a general one is going to set in.

Have had a long walk along the trenches with my boss, and this evening I am going to sleep with the infantry. It is very quiet up there and one hardly ever hears a shot fired.

By the way, will you please send me a couple of pairs of medium thick socks, and also some of the ordinary thin ones. I think that I have got a lot of dark blue ones, you might as well send some of those, as they are just as good as the khaki ones, and will wear them out. 4 pairs is quite enough and 2 of the medium thick.

There are a lot of partridges here, and am going to try and invent some kind of a trap and get our dinner off them, they look very nice and plump, and they are the English bird, not the red eyed French bird.

13/2/17

Well I had a great night of it, that is sleep and never woke up till 8.45 a.m., not so bad. All today I have had an easy one, and just shot off a few rounds to pass the time away.

They seem to have had a very rotten time of it in the camp, and only hope that things will now improve and they get plenty of rain and good weather, our cattle must have had a rotten time of it, but luckily do not seem to have lost many.

Post just off so must close. The pork pie arrived safely and jolly good one too, also the Crème de Menthe.

Night night my own, and just tons of love to you both.

Your own loving
Harold

12 February – Went round front lines with Major, and at positions rest of the day. Thawed slightly all day, dull.

13 February – At Battery position all day. Tea at headquarters to see about forward observation post. Quiet day. Fine and cold.

21-2-17

14 February 1917

My own darling Con,

Another scramble to get a letter off, my days are very full at present, and what with one thing and another, they fairly go.

The thaw did not last long and has begun to freeze again, but I hope not as hard as the last spell.

The old Bosch seems to be putting down quite a lot of our shipping, and is about time that we gave him a good lesson, and sunk a number of his submarines. I often wonder how he is getting along and whether he can keep his tummy full, this cold must be making him sit up a bit, and expect that he feels the pinch a bit. In the Somme they appear to have gained a bit more land, and without heavy casualties.

At last we have got a paper, and intend to have a good old read tonight, as I am alone, the other officer has gone down to sleep with the infantry.

I am much better today and well on the mend, and do not feel any the worse for it, and put on flesh or fat.

How are you dearest? You never say, but only hope that you are keeping very fit and taking great care of your dear old self. Time is now getting on, and will only be about 5 weeks before the event comes off. It is hard to realise that it will be so soon and hope to get over for a few days, but can promise nothing.

Night night darling, and heaps of love to you both.

        Your loving
        Harold

14 February –   *Registered battery on new zero line, 42 rds., good registration.*
                      Dainville.
                      Quiet day, fine day.

22-2-17

15 February 1917

My own darling Con,

Well I think that I have read every line in that paper, and have got very little news out of it, anyway nothing of any satisfaction. The only thing that I picked up is that Germany is not starving and expect in the end will just fight it out, and think they will get a pretty good dose of it in the next offensive. I do not at all understand what America is doing or how she stands; it appears to be semi neutral and is, I should think, a very false position, but in the end will lead to open war.

Am very sorry to hear that Susan is still laid up, and hope the asthma will soon leave her. I always thought that it had something to do with the lungs, and that cause of the hard breathing was on account of the passages getting choked up. I only hope that the doctor is right, and wish she and Eric could get out to San Rafael, as I am sure that the climate and rest will fix her up and make a new person of her. Afraid Eric will be very much worried, and is just rotten luck that he cannot get back to her. It is bad enough being away when one's wife is well, what it must be like otherwise I cannot tell.

The guns down in the Somme are plugging away for all they are worth, which means business, they have been quiet for such a long time that one has got quite unused to the huge rumble.

I expect that John Campbell will now be on his way back, and very fed up at having to leave the Argentine, but all the same he must have enjoyed it very much, the trouble is that so much of the time is wasted on the sea.

Yes, I could quite enjoy having had a good hot bath and a good bed with you, but am sure would have got another cold. At present I am on a wire bed, and a very comfortable one too, once I am well under the blanket very little worries me, even if an old rat does dance on my head. There are some beauties about, almost black and very glossy skin, I was making a pal of him, but he did a very low trick on me when I was asleep, and dribbled on my head, so am now after his blood.

Up to the present I have not used the thermal wool, and my indi has been very good, and only had about 2 slight touches of it since I have been out.

The light is just going out so must finish this off tomorrow, so night night and sleep well. Bindy will be fast asleep now, and you and your Dad in the drawing room, having a chat or read, I can see it all so clearly that I might almost be there, and hope it will not be very long. It has been a grand day, no wind and plenty of sun.

Must close up so night night, and sleep well.
Your loving
Harold

15 February – At Battery and went to look around front line for observation post. Difficult to observe Hun front trenches.
Quiet day, fine day.

22-2-17

16 February 1917

My own darling Con,

Just a wee line before post goes. We have had a long trudge this afternoon and feel properly tired, and now I am off to the infantry for the night. On the whole I think that my condition is poor, and will have to do some more manual work before the show comes off.

It has now started to rain, and so everything will be in a fine old state. The Major comes back tonight, and also the other officers, so we will be properly crowded out here and less work to do.

Must close, it is a rotten short notita but no time or news for more. Heaps and heaps of love to you both.

Your loving
Harold

16 February –   At Battery during day and liaison with infantry all day.
Major and Gaskell came back to battery.
Fine day, thaw set in.

24-2-17

17 February 1917

My own darling Con,

No cartita for 4 days, but the parcel with the warm waistcoat, pies and pips arrived safely, many thanks for them, they are top-hole. Ethel sent a huge tin of peppermint balls from Bath, some of the best I have ever tasted, and we are all tucking into them.

I have just heard the Captain is going to get a battery and is off to it in a couple of days. I only hope that he will be able to get a transfer for me, but think that it is very doubtful, as there is very little time to get shifted, veremos (*we shall see*), hope I am wrong and it will come off.

The junior sub in this battery is a very nice boy, Irish, and very much so, only 20, he now sleeps with me, and so have to look after him, or else he gets very uppish. He comes from somewhere round Belfast, and is a very cheery lad. The senior sub has just come back from on leave and managed to get engaged, he is also a very good sort, very hard luck on him having to leave her so soon, but the meeting will be all the better afterwards and there is one thing about it, and that is I would much rather part when engaged than when married.

18/2/17

The thaw has now properly set in, and in a way I am very glad, as it has got very much warmer, but of course there is any amount of mud and slush about, but that is nothing.

Have had a great morning of digging and am going to do a great deal more of it, as it puts me in fine trim, and gets my condition. My cold has almost completely gone and am glad to say am feeling very fit, and if you are as well I will have nothing to grouse about.

Well dearest night night and sleep well, but it is only 3.30 p.m. so will be a few hours before you are off. Just heaps of love to you both.

Your loving
Harold

Would you please send me a stick of William's shaving soap, and a pair of woolen gloves.

17 February – At Battery position all day. Capt. Jones joined battery. Very quiet day. Fired 50 rds. at trench mortar. Fine, thaw set in.

25-2-17

18 February 1917

My own darling Con,

Another night gone and no cartita, that is five nights, but I feel quite content, as am sure that I would have received a letter or wire from your Dad if anything had been wrong, so hope to hear from you tomorrow and that all is quite well.

Those pillowslips are A1 and make my bed look quite nutty, and must say it is nice to have one's head on a thoroughly clean spot. The rat has not worried me any more, so must have given an extra hard tap and broken his friendship.

The Major is going home in a few days on an artillery course for 2 or 3 weeks, lucky beggar, and expect that he will have a thoroughly good time of it, and also get a few days leave after it is over. He only came back from leave after I did, so will have a very nice refresher.

I had a fine hot bath this evening and got into clean clothes for a change which has bucked me up some, and should now like my dressing gown and turn into bed at *Westhanger*.

I meant to have gone and seen the Captain this evening but as there was so much slush about, and felt far too lazy, I did not go, but must see him early tomorrow.

I was in the middle of this when a very sad incident happened and was called out. An orderly rushed in to say that a dugout had fallen in and buried 3 men belonging to us, so rushed out, got what men I could and dug them out. One was very bad, another not so bad and the third alright, but got rather a shock. This happened at 10 p.m., the second man came round in about 5 minutes and was quite well next morning. The first was rubbed and given artificial respiration for 3 hours, but the poor lad passed off. It was bad luck, but these things have to happen in war, and all look upon them as a natural course.

Post just off, so heaps and heaps of love to you both.

Your loving
Harold

18 February – At observation post morning and digging at forward position afternoon, Crinchon River.
Quiet day excepting for a few trench mortar and 50 rds. of 77 and 10.5.
Dainville.
Dull but no rain.

19 February – At Battery morning and observation post afternoon. Mild misty day. Fired 45rds. Heenan returned. Hun heavy trench mortar very active. Walker liaison officer.

26-2-17

20 February 1917

My own darling Con,

This evening I got 3 of your cartitas, and ripping they were.

I expect your are quite right not going to Aunt Janie's, but not from your point of view, as am quite sure that you look very elegant. But you would have been run off your feet, and have done you no good. I am sure you are much better where you are, that is if you are not rushing about too much and taking that siesta, am sure your Dad made you do that, and very glad that he did. Must write and thank him for it, and the cigarettes, which arrived just in time, and am enjoying them very much.

Was very glad to hear that Susan was much better and able to get to Crawley, where I hope she will get a real good rest, and be A1 again.

What about Mrs. R. going to B.A., is that a stunt? I expect the Lockwoods are on their way out there by now, and wish we were with them.

Am going to finish this tomorrow and turn in now, so night night and just heaps of love to you both.

21/2/17

The Times you sent me only arrived yesterday, but the ones from Smiths arrive quite regularly, only one or two days late, so I succeed in getting fairly fresh news, muchas gracias.

There is another thing I should like you to get me, and that is a couple of refills for my torch and a couple of bulbs. The torch is one of the ordinary long ones about 12 inches long, made by Efandem Co Ltd (Bristol.) It is impossible to get them here, and it is the most useful thing one can have out here.

Am just off to have tea with the Adjutant and have a talk with him about a shift.

So night darling and keep very fit and well. Love to you both.

Your loving
Harold

20 February – At observation post for day and in afternoon bad observations.
Dainville.
Misty and showery day.

21 February – At Battery morning and observation post all afternoon, very poor observations. Hun trench mortar very active and broke up wiring on front line. Fired 45 rds.
Fine, misty day.

22 February – At new gun position all day, went to infantry in evening for liaison work. Hun trench mortar very active.
Fine day, misty.

28-2-17

23 February 1917

My own darling Con,

It will be your birthday on the 27th, and hope that this reaches you in time, it should have gone yesterday but I have been away since yesterday morning, and no chance of writing. Just tons and tons of love to you, and hope that you do not feel any older on the occasion, I do not expect you will have a huge party, but hope that Beattie and Helen will be with you, and have a day of it together. I just wish that it were you, Bindy and self, having a nice quiet day at *Lucero*. Anyhow it will have to be next year, and will have a grand time of it, but with the addition of the little fellow.

At present I am in charge of the digging party, and am doing all sorts of things, I have about 150 men at it, and so keeps me going the whole day. Tomorrow the work is going to be inspected by the General, and all he will see is a mud pie with a few in and outs in it, and piles of earth. Hope he will like it, but I think that he is sure to pull a long face and grouse, and will be quite right, as the work that has been done is very bad. I only took it over this morning and find it very hard to improve matters.

A sad thing happened in the trenches yesterday, there were 2 men cleaning rifles, pals and very good men, by accident one of the rifles went off, and shot his pal right through the heart. It is sad, and one can imagine the feelings of the poor fellow that did it, personally I would rather be the dead man than the man who did it. I am afraid he will get a severe punishment for it, but personally I think that he must be going through a severe torture mentally.

Had a long letter from Aunt Bella, she seems very fit and Uncle Fred quite got over his cold and was out skating. He is getting too old for that and should be more careful of himself.

Those boots I got from Harrods are very good, and let no water in, but they are tight on the instep, and give me a lot of work getting into them, in fact too much and are absurdly tight, it is a pity as it spoils a very good boot.

Am surprised to hear that Donald has not yet got away and almost looks as he will stay at home, but a rush might come, and he will be sent out in it, something like I was. Have not heard a word about Lucy, he is a slacker at writing, and think that he really must be in love and no time to think of anything else, wonder if it is Mabel. I must write to him and see if that will have any effect.

I see that the government is trying to get the people to voluntarily economise on food etc., wonder how it will turn out, and if the people will respond to it.

Well dear, just best of love and good luck to you, and take care of yourself. Night night, and a big hug to you both.

Your loving
Harold

23 February – Round new gun position and lunched with Col. Learmouth and arranged about formation of dugouts. Captain Bolton of 19th Kings killed. Misty day.

☆☆☆☆☆☆☆☆☆☆☆☆☆☆☆☆

2-3-17

24 February 1917

My own darling Con,
It is great to hear that Bindy is getting along so well, and making such progress with her talking, but I think that Grandpapa is a very big mouthful, and I should think that Granddad would be easier. I must admit that I prefer it, and probably as she is going to call me Dad, it would be easier for her to catch hold of. What are you teaching her to call you? Now she is getting older she will be treating Alice more as a nurse and really know what her mother is. I should like to wake up tomorrow and find her making her morning visit to us in our room, it must be very cheering.

Have had a great deal of walking today, about 10 miles, and in my present work this will have to be done every day, personally I am glad as it will put in me top-hole condition.

Glad to hear that Donald is doing the course and I am sure he much prefers it to riding. So he is now going out to Egypt, hope he has a good time of it, and will like it. I thought, as it had been so late that he would have been sent out here, but think he will be all the better where he is going.

The Times came and well for 4 days, but have not received one during the last 7 days, and cannot make out what has happened to them, so will you please find out if they are still sending them. I also see that it has gone to 2 pence, so to economise a little I think we might as well go to the morning post, which is just as good and will also save 365 pence.

Do just as you like about investing your £50, I think that it would probably be just as well, and then if we require any more will get it from the Argentine. I have £50 at Cox's and will send you a cheque for it about the 5th of next month. Let me know what you have in the bank. Afraid we cannot invest any more in war loan, as we require every penny we have out there, especially if this seca *(drought)* is going on.

Had a long letter from Aunt Janie, she told me that Edward Musson is a Lieutenant Colonel now, so must have done very well, he is only about 31 but there are a number of the same rank out here who are younger. There is one man close to here who is only 27 and holds the same rank.

The socks have not turned up yet, but do not send any more as I can well manage with what I have until the end of next month, and then hope to be with you. The sponge cake arrived and is top-hole, and not stale. Yes, I like cherry and also currant cake very much, as long as they are plain, also ginger, so you have a huge variety to pick from. Aunt Bella sometimes sends me a kind of chocolate, which I believe she buys from Ballater. I believe it is compressed or something of the sort, would you find out and about March 20th send out 2 dozen cakes of it. It is fine to put in our pocket and munch. The compass arrived safely, muchas gracias.

 Well pet, night night and God bless you and a great hug to you and Bindy.
Your loving
Harold

24 February – At new gun position all day, went round them with General White and Col. Learmouth, good days walk.
Fine, dry and misty, very quiet.

4-3-17

25 February 1917

My own darling Con,
Just a wee notita before the mail goes. Have just come in from a big day of it, and feel gloriously tired, but have heard quite good news, and only hope that it is true. If so you will hear of it before this reaches you, and will show to you the real results of the Somme fighting. Will not say any more until I definitely know what has actually happened, we are quite bucked with the news.

 It has been a grand day, and a spring one at that, it reminded me of our day at, the name of the place has completely gone from my head, but the ripping day we had when we went from Salisbury to New Forest, isn't it Lyndhurst? But of course the scenery is a bit different and the ground very torn and cut up, anyhow the day was like it.

 Poor old Kathleen, she is waiting a long time for her holiday, and hope that she gets it before long.

 That raid you talk about was not in these parts, we are the other way, the raids seem to have been a great success lately, and it bucks our men up very much.

 We are now all getting well over our colds now and should be quite rid of them in a few ways, and then we will talk properly to the Bosch.

 No news at all, so am going to close, my letter of yesterday ran me dry. So night night and keep very fit and well. Heaps of love to you both.
Your loving
Harold

25 February –   At gun positions all day. Fired 50 rds. Fine day, quiet. Enemy evacuated line. Pigs. Dainville.

26 February –   At gun position all day. Enemy retiring, evacuated Gondecourt. Fine day, quiet.

7-3-17

27 February 1917
Con's Birthday

My own darling Con,

Just tons and tons of good luck and best wishes, and hope you have had a happy day of it, what wouldn't I have given to be there, and spent it with you and the wee one. Hope that Beatie or Helen were able to be with you.

    Here we had a quiet day of it, but 3 of our planes were brought down, one in flames, the second nose-dived and the 3rd came down as well, but the observer was shot. To compensate for this one of the Bosch came down in flames, but they have had the better of us for once. Never mind we will do them down next time.

    I got four of your letters last night, and very glad I was too. About going home, am going to do my best to get away on the 21st as it will be my only chance. If I leave it until April, I cannot possibly do it, so better early than late. If anything should happen before do not telegraph as that will be up against everything, but will write to your Dad before. What about the nurse? I hope you have got this all fixed up and that she will arrive in plenty of time and turn out to be top-hole. I do hope that I shall be there for it, bless you.

    I have not heard much more about what I wrote in my last, except that we have gained some ground round Miramont, this is a long way from us; hope that it will mean a lot more. Yes, the submarines seem to be doing some damage, but expect that we shall soon get them in hand, and the bottom of the sea be their grave.

    It must be rather interesting trying to keep under rations, and expect that you will find it quite easy once you get into it, but dotu, do not stint yourself, and take plenty of good nourishment, and Horlicks, I am sure you will be very much better for it. Keep strong and fit for yours and the little fellows sake.

    The thaw has been nice and slow, and on the whole we have had very little mud, and no, the walking is good. My indi has been top-hole and behaved itself very well and I am A1 now, just a slight sniffle, but it is a relief to get away from that intense cold.

Had a short note from Lucy, who is very fit, but no news in it. Funnily enough I had just written to him.

Just finished tea and had a fine old blowout, so will have to sit quiet for a bit, then some exercise.

Night night, take great care of yourself, and a big hug to you both.

Your loving
Harold

27 February – Fired 150 rds. at new gun positions all morning, and haircut during afternoon. 3 of our planes down, 1 on fire, 2 dived and 3 landed safely, pilot killed. Fine day.

28 February – Enemy evacuated Ligny and Le Barque, making satisfactory progress and expect enemy will gradually evacuate a big stretch of country. 77 with infantry. Dull misty day.

☆☆☆☆☆☆☆☆☆☆☆☆☆☆

Nelson
New Zealand
2017

Dear Harold,

Thanks to your diaries we were able to track where you were throughout your year of war. They are the tiniest things, full of information about all sorts of things. The 1916 Charles Lettes diary opens up with a salutation, which assumes that Father Christmas may have dropped it into your stocking: -

> To wish you a happy Christmas
> And a new year more prosperous
> And more contented than any that have
> Gone before.

They really were pocket size, you managed to squeeze a lot of information onto those tiny pages.

Harold's diaries for 1916 and 1917

SKY FULL OF STARS

They were so hard to read but they helped unravel the mysteries for me, and to give me more understanding of what you went through. Jim helped me with grapple with those, we poured over them snuggled in front of the fire, needing a magnifying glass and map of France. Jim was then able to create the maps of your route marches, with places and dates matched. I think you quite enjoyed those marches, and I suspect that you like many men found camaraderie and friendship throughout your time in those foreign fields, you were all there for the same purpose. Ironically your enemies probably found exactly the same thing, and would have gone through all the same angst and emotions.

The 1917 Walker's Diary was the larger of the two, but not as welcoming as it does not have a jolly greeting, only notes the cost of 1 shilling. Still it would be hard to compete with the poem in the 1916 one: -

>Here is a book – its pages yet unsoiled;
>A space is left for record of each day,
>A silent witness of the things to be,
>In the veiled future now upon its way.
>
>The coming months what dreams shall come to pass?
>Shall I note down success or failure here?
>Which times be joyous? Which seem clouded o'er?
>In this – the daily story of a year.
>
>Oh may I write of many happy days!
>Of old friends faithful, and of new ones true,
>Of kindly actions, and of pleasant words,
>Rememb'ring which, brings gladness ever new.
>
>An untrod path, the year before me lies,
>I know not what this book of mine shall tell,
>Yet sure I feel a kindly Providence
>Is over all, and shall make things well.
>
>*Elsie Dickinson*

Your un-trodden path was quite a one, a valiant one that brought you adventures, experiences and friendship as well as loss and sorrow. I have no doubt that you struggled with the duality you found – as a soldier you were required to kill men that on another day you may have raised a glass with. Having made the decision to enter the war you had to fight while still holding the belief of the humanity of your enemy. On another day and in another place they may have been your friends, rather than being in the arena of kill or be killed.

I hold onto the dream that one day there will be no war, and that people really will learn to live without confrontation and in harmony. Maybe if enough of us hold that dream it will eventually come true.

With love

Sheila x

MARCH 1917

Harold with a Straker Squire car, date unknown.

But I, being poor, have only my dreams;
I have spread my dreams under you feet;
Tread softly because you tread on my dreams.
William Butler Yeats - *Aedh Wishes for the Cloths of Heaven*

7-3-17

1 March 1917

My own darling Con,

Another month started and on we go, before it is over we will have quite a large family, and Bindy will have someone to look after, and the act the old mother on. I did not think that at her age she would take so much interest in babies. I was very sorry to hear that she had got another cold, but hope that it was nothing to speak of, and she is quite fit again. She would have enjoyed having a game with that other kiddie.

Here it has been just a grand day, a very fine light and could see miles into the Bosch lines, and could see some of their trains moving about. It is the first day since I have been out this time that we have had any light at all, and hope it means that we will have a good many more days like it.

So you are hard at making clothes again, how well I can picture you at *Lucero* doing the same thing 20 months ago, and how rippingly you did it all. I suppose that most of Bindy's first clothing will come in for the next one, that is if you brought them home, but of course you must have, as when I come to think of it Bindy was very wee when we left, only just over 3 months old. It is hard to realise that she was ever so small, but she was a good wee person. The only night that she ever gave trouble was that night at Hurlingham when nobody could quiet her down, but she slept like a good one after. Hope the next one will be as good, but it is almost too much to expect.

You are quite right, but we are not so far away as you mentioned. Eric is in the same old place I believe, and have not heard from him for sometime. Was glad to hear that Susan was better, but she must be weak after being in bed for so long, but with the spring coming on it will buck her up a lot, and be quite fit again.

The submarines seem to be the giving the Hollanders a bad time of it, and must be a very serious question for them, as they cannot let it go on without causing some serious trouble with Germany. Personally I think that the Kaiser has gone mad, and as he is in a bad hole now he probably thinks that he might as well be at war with the whole world, and so after it is all over he will have an excuse to give his country, that it was impossible for him to be at war with the whole world, and conquer. America still seems to allow them to throw mud in their faces and have their ships sunk. I cannot make out why they do not declare war, and send their navy out to patrol the seas, and assist against the submarine trouble.

You had a good shot at the scones and must have been a fine sight, and hope very tasty, better luck next time.

I do not think you are really feeling very fit, and darling, I hope that you are not feeling too rotten. I do not remember you feeling poorly at this time when Bindy was coming, let me know how you are getting along, and take great care of yourself.

Must close up now with just heaps and heaps of love to you and Bindy.

Your loving
Harold

1 March – Quiet night with infantry, round gun position with Col. Learmouth marking out new position. Daily expect enemy to evacuate front line. Very quiet day. Enemy dump on fire. Fine and good light.

☆☆☆☆☆☆☆☆☆☆☆☆☆☆

8-3-17

2 March 1917

My own darling Con,

Bindy will be a year and a half old in four days, getting quite an old person and expect very wise. She must be most useful at brushing your nighty down in the mornings. Do you remember how Betty Brougham used to brush all the mud off our coats in the hall? I expect that Bindy will follow her example.

I am going to enclose a cheque for £50, which I hope you will get, if not let me know. I will cross it, so that it can only be payable through the bank, which will put us on the safe side. I wrote a few days ago to ask how much we had in the bank, as if it is rather short I will write to B.A. for more, and should like to do so before it runs short.

Dearie, are you quite satisfied with the Doctor? If you are not I would much rather you would say so, as it makes such a huge difference how you feel about it all. I want you to be quite happy about it all, and be so fit and well. I will try my best to be there and look after you, but never mind if I cannot be there, as I will be in spirit.

At last Kut* has fallen, it has cost us a lot of work, and many good lives, but it will upset the old Turk, and give him something to think about. Now we want a real good show here and give the Bosch a good hiding, and do not then think that the war will last very long.

---

* The Second Battle of Kut was fought on 23 February 1917, between British and Ottoman forces at Kut, Mesopotamia, which is present-day Iraq.

It is getting very like spring here, but I hear that this month is usually rather cold and windy, but it has started very well, and we all live in great hopes.

It was great to hear that Aunt Janie and J.S. were down with you and were so well, but poor Bindy, what had she done to be told that she was like me? I call it rotten luck and I expect that she strongly dislikes Jessie for it, but may forgive her. That rest at Eastbourne will do Aunt Janie a lot of good, and she does enjoy herself with the kiddies.

Must close up now, so night night, and take <u>great</u> care of yourself, with just heaps and heaps of love to you both.

Your loving
Harold

2 March –   *Tilloy-lez-Cambrai and Puiseux taken 85 prisoners. Bosch gradually retiring onto Hindenburg line.* On our front very quiet.*
Dainville.
Fine day.

☆☆☆☆☆☆☆☆☆☆☆☆☆☆☆

9-3-17

3 March 1917

My own darling Con,

I was awfully sorry to hear that poor wee Bindy had got bronchitis, and only hope that the doctor is right, and it will not turn into anything serious. It is bad luck and makes me wish more than ever to be home and help you. It is good to hear that she is fairly cheery and takes little notice of things; I hope it will be good news when your letter arrives tonight. She appears to be so quiet and ripping with it all, and must be a dear.

Yes I can imagine how fed up Donald must be, and has he to superintend the digging party? I expect that he will be away by now. I am still looking after the digging here, and have got a good deal done.

The Hun still seems to be falling back, and I rather think that he will go quite a long way, but hope that he does it quickly, it is going far too slowly for my liking, and will have to be pushed along.

---

*   The Hindenburg Line was a German defensive position of The Great War, built during the winter of 1916-1917 on the Western Front, from Arras to Laffaux, near Soissons on the Aisne.

Old England will soon be looking very nice, the spring is just a grand time, and so ripping to see the trees etc. coming along, especially if they are one's own.

We will hardly recognise the trees at *Lucero*, they will have grown a great deal by the time we get out. One thing is that they will give a fine shelter for the house. Hope to get another letter from Johnnie soon with some good news in it.

Phillip is a rotten writer and neither of us ever hears from him, personally I should very much like to hear the news of *Yacuchiri*, and if the fruit is a success, also how is *Monte Palo* getting on. I hope they have had some good rains and good news in general.

Will close with heaps and heaps of love and best of good luck to Bindy, and hope she is quite fit again by now. Night night, and take great care of yourself.

Your loving
Harold

3 March –   Very quiet day on the front. Fired 49 rds. on machine guns and mortars.

9-3-17

4 March 1917

My own darling Con,
Am longing for the post to hear how the wee one is, and only hope that she will be much better, and by now quite her own cheery self.

I can quite imagine 3 Canadian officers round one, as we have heard plenty of it at Hindhead. They can talk, and must say that their twang sounds very unnatural, but I expect that one would soon get used to it, and find them very good sorts, but the twang is hard to get round.

The Turk seems to be in full retreat at Kut, and the whole thing has turned out a fine victory for us. I hope that it will continue, and terminate in a thorough rout. The troops must be very bucked, and can imagine them, but hope they will not overdo it, and that their positions well consolidated.

Fancy the war loan reached £1,000,000, it is tremendous and I believe that we could do it again if required. It is a good investment and a good percentage on one's money, and will be a knock to the Hun.

The Bosch seems to be retiring slowly, but it just shows his weakness and that he is beginning to realise that the Allies are a bit too strong for him. Anyhow he will have a rotten time of it when we get at him.

Have just started a long letter to *L. & Co.*, and wonder when it will be finished, but hope it will not take so long as Johnnie's.

Mail is just off, so sorry that this is so short, but there is no news. So night night, and God bless you both.

Your loving
Harold

4 March –   *Quiet day, general work.*
     Dainville.
5 March –   *Round digging party all day, walked to Bellancourt to look for battery position, walked 15 miles.*
     Fine day.

☆☆☆☆☆☆☆☆☆☆☆☆☆☆☆☆

13-3-17

6 March 1917

My own darling Con,
Just a wee notita to say how do, and hope that this finds you very fit and well.

The news is rotten from Johnnie, in fact it could not be much worse without a catastrophe happening, if it does not rain very soon I am afraid that things will be very serious, and may have a big loss in stock. As it is, it is bad enough to have already lost 40 to 50 head, and by what he says of the aftosa (*foot and mouth disease*)* I can only think that we have lost a big number of calves, which will make a big hole in this year's profits, if the prices of stock do not improve there will be none. It's just rotten luck that this should happen while we are away, and are so helpless to do anything. Poor old Johnnie must be having a devil of a time of it, and there is much too much work for him to do. I would do almost anything to get out and try to get things fixed up, but it is impossible.

You must not even put any hopes on me being able to get away now, as am afraid there is very little chance of it, as the Bosch, by returning, has altered the face of things, and events will probably be big, but I will do my best to get away.

That was a very sad letter from Flurry, but he takes a far too serious outlook on life, and should not let little things like that worry him too much. He has had a rough life of it, and only hope that things will improve from now onwards, I only hope that his wound is not serious and that he will soon be his own self again. I

---
*   A highly contagious viral disease of livestock.

must write to him and tell him not to worry about that little account. You did quite right in opening that letter, but hope that it did not make you feel too sad.

The remedy turned up quite alright, y muchas gracias, I have a good stock on hand now, and should last me at the least 2 months.

I wonder how Bindy is, I hope quite well again.

Since last writing we have had another fall of snow but it practically all thawed out during the day, and luckily there is not very much mud about. I had a great walk yesterday, in the morning about 5 miles and in the afternoon 10 miles, so you see what a pedestrian I am getting, but must say that I am not a bit keen on it. Shall take to the old gee again.

Must close now, hope that Bindy is quite well again, and heaps of love to you both.

Your loving
Harold

6 March – Plane brought down in flames, one of ours brought down, damaged and both men killed. Bosch heavy trench mortar annoying front lines. 3 men killed by trench mortar. Fired 100 rds. Round digging party. Forward observation officer. Major Grant had brought down 26 Bosch planes.
Fine day, good light.

14-3-17

7 March 1917

My own darling Con,

Just a very hurried notita, as am off to see the Captain. It has been a very cold March day, a heavy wind the whole day, but we must expect that during this month.

Had a long letter from Aunt Janie, and was very bucked to get it. She is the only one who has written and let me know how your dear old self is, it was very cheering as she said you were looking much better and fitter, it is just ripping to hear it. Also that Bindy is much better is great, and am sure that she will be very bucked to get out of her camita.

The biscuits etc. came last night, many thanks. Do not worry about making any cakes, as we get any amount to eat, in fact live like fighting cocks.

Will answer your letters tomorrow, so night night, and just heaps of love to you both.

Your loving
Harold

7 March – Spent last night with infantry, expected raid but did not come off. At battery position all day. Went to see Neil Fraser-Tytler and try to get to his battery. Very windy and cold all day.

☆☆☆☆☆☆☆☆☆☆☆☆☆☆☆

13-3-17

8 March 1917

My own darling Con,

Another March day gone and a rare one too, a tremendous wind and several severe short blizzards during the day, luckily I had lots of walking to do and so kept nice and warm. I am now sitting by a good fire, the fireplace is made out of an oil drum, and works very well, and gives out a really good heat.

Glad to hear that you found Mr. Thorny's address, and when you get Flurry's please let me know. I do not expect that he will get home for some time as he will most probably be sent to Malta, or one of those places, but I do hope that it is nothing serious.

Am very bucked to hear that Bindy is much better. Your Dad is far too good to her, you must tell him not to spoil her with all these good things, as when we are in the camp she will not get very much.

Is Helen at home for some time now, or is it just a holiday? I expect the girls will be there during your time.

Yesterday evening I had a long talk with the Captain, who I found in bed with flu, he is going to try and get me a transfer, but do not know if it will come off. I also had a talk to Colonel Learmouth, he wants me to stop on here, but also said that he would not get in my way if I wanted to get back to my friends, so it now remains with headquarters whether I shift or not.

The cigs arrived safely and many thanks, but will you send me a box of Argentines as they last much longer, the other ones burn away quickly and I also smoke a lot more of them, they go about 2 to 1 of the Reina Victoria or Sublimes. Parcels take a long time to come out now, so please get it sent as soon as possible.

Sorry to hear that Harts has been badly wounded, and glad to hear that he is getting on alright. I am very fit now, the cold is quite gone I am glad to say.

Must close up now, just heaps and heaps of love to you and Bindy and take great care of yourself.

Your loving
Harold

8 March –   *At new gun position all day. Very quiet day.*
              Dainville.
              Very cold day and several short blizzards.

☆☆☆☆☆☆☆☆☆☆☆☆☆☆☆

15-3-17

9 March 1917

My own darling Con,

What excitement the Campbell's must have had, a very rotten experience but they must have been very relieved at not having the children on board, it would have made a great difference and saved a great deal of worry. It must have been jolly cold in the open boat and they were jolly lucky not to have got a severe cold. Sorry to hear that you have got one, and hope it as you say only a slight one, you must get over it very quickly and be very fit. Bindy will be very bucked at getting down and out again, and hope that there have been some nice sunny days for her.

Yes, we can have another talk about names when I get back, I like David quite well but whenever I hear it, it reminds me too much of David R., and somehow I do not feel a bit like calling anybody it, but probably that would work off.

I expect you will soon be hearing of the new arrivals at San Rafael, wonder what they will be, and afraid that Brush will be disappointed if another girl. It is about time that some boys came on the scene, as most so far seem to have been of the other sex.

The refills arrived last night, many thanks for them, they are top-hole. We get several illustrated papers; so do not worry about sending any more.

We have had another cold day with short blizzards; the great thing is that it is quite dry and so live in comfort.

D. Guthrie is very lucky to get to the staff and will probably have an easier time of it, and a bit safer. Anyhow he well deserves it, as he has done a lot of hard fighting.

The Times is coming very regularly now I am glad to say, and of course *The Continental Mail* has started to do the same, so get plenty of news.

Well night night my own, just heaps and heaps of love to you both.

Your loving
Harold

9 March –   *Round digging party all day. Very quiet day.*

☆☆☆☆☆☆☆☆☆☆☆☆☆☆☆

Nelson
New Zealand
2017

Dear Harold,

On the plaque in St. Andrews Church in Buenos Aires there is an intriguing name below yours – John Argentine Campbell, another of your chums who has led me on a merry adventure. You mentioned him several times but my curiosity bubbled when I realised that he must have been on a ship that was attacked and sunk. It took a bit of digging around to find it, but I got there in the end.

My investigations unearthed a book called *Seeking John Campbell*, written in 2015 by John Daffurn, it truly was a delightful find. John was investigating the history of a woman, named Isabel Greig who had died interstate. His sleuthing included looking into her ancestry, which revealed that her father was named John Campbell and had Argentine connections. Further research led him to discover there were three men who fitted the bill and that one of them was our John. You can imagine the whoop of excitement that escaped from me.

John was quite a character and a great athlete; he attended Fettes College in Scotland followed by Cambridge University, which he represented in both rugby and cricket. He also played rugby for Scotland and cricket for Argentina. He, like you, also loved polo, and I suspect you had a few games on opposing teams. Of course Horace Laffaye was also of help in his books on polo, noting John's prowess in the game.

In 1914 John decided it was not ethical for him to play polo whilst there was a war in progress, however he was not able to return to England until 1915, travelling with his wife and three children. I imagine you discussed this between yourselves as you made your plans to return to England.

John joined the 6th Iniskilling Dragoons, and like you found himself in France, although you didn't appear to bump into each other there. You tell of John and Myra having been able to travel back to Argentina on extended leave, no doubt you had a little touch of envy, although only for the four day interlude they had in the Argentine between sea voyages. I don't know why they made that trip but I think you and Con may have done especially as Con and Myra met in London on their return, and I'm sure exchanged stories galore. John and Myra returned to England on the *S.S. Drina*, which proved to be rather eventful in the final days of the voyage, as a German U-boat attacked the ship, two torpedoes caused catastrophic damage, and the *Drina* sank, there were some deaths amongst the crew but it seems all the passengers survived.

She lies upside down on the ocean floor, still intact. There was no time to save any belongings and Myra lost all her jewellery, amongst other things, which in your eyes was bad luck. However, it seems John and Myra shopped for a new fur coat and pearls before he went back to France, apparently John saw these as basic necessities, and I am sure Myra did not object in the slightest.

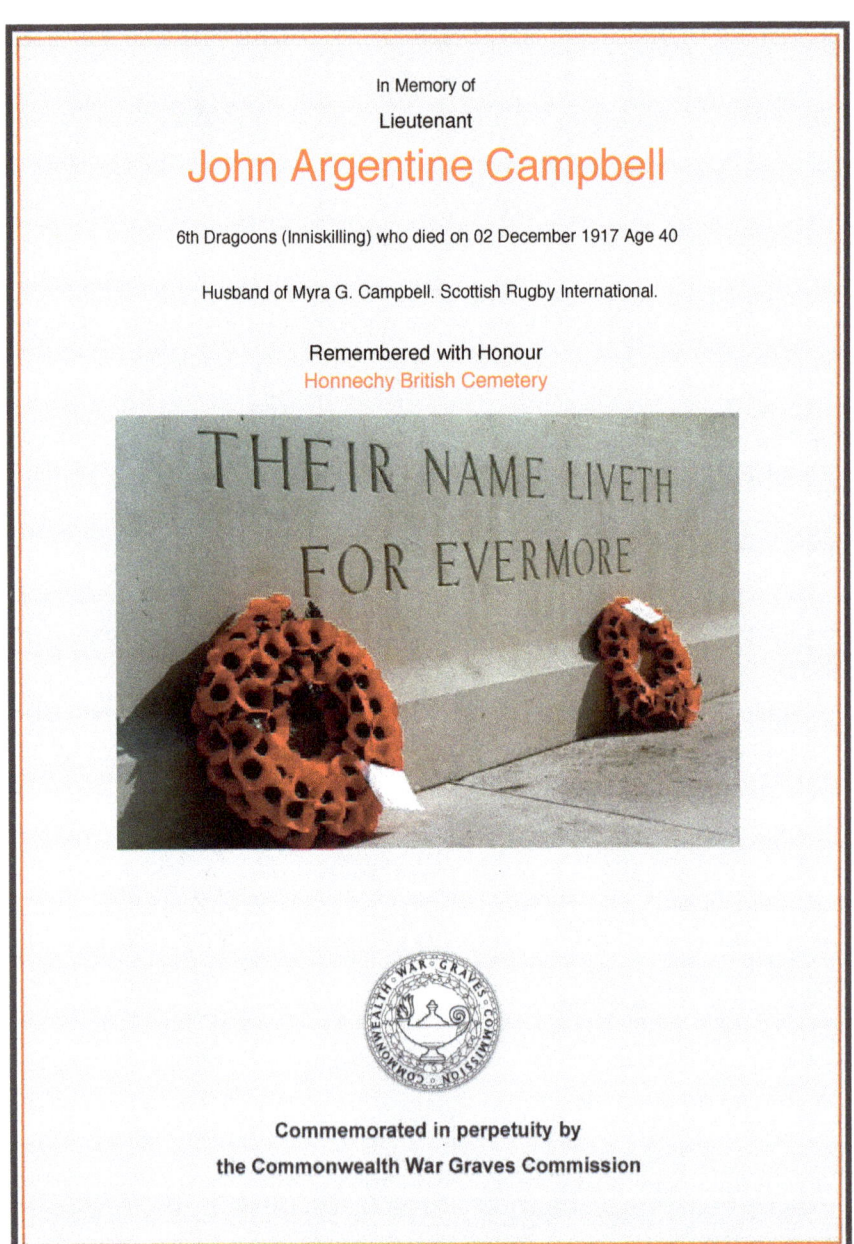

John died a few months after you, in December 1917 from laceration of the intestines; he is buried in Honnechy British Cemetery in France. John was wounded the day before his death; he was taken prisoner by the Germans and treated in a Field Hospital, but to no avail.

Although Myra knew that John was most certainly dead she did not get confirmation until August 1919 when she went to the War Office to collect the few things that had been returned. She was left a knife on a chain, a lanyard, a silver identity disk, a handkerchief and one Franc. Myra returned to Argentina with the children, the boys attended Fettes as their father before them. All three children served in the Second World War.

John and Myra's home was *Estancia El Jabali*, which is now run very successfully by his grandson Jock, who I have been in touch with. Our John was not father to Isabel, but the search led John Daffurn to meet Jock and spend time with him on the estancia. The book was fascinating and a great help to me in unraveling the story of your friend, another of your brothers in arms.

And so you and John are remembered on the same plaque, friends who met the same fate in a land far from their homes. The final words from Rupert Brooke's poem, *The Dead* are written on the plaque, and say it well:

> These laid the world away
> Poured out the red sweet
> 1914–wine of youth–1919

With love
Sheila x

P.S. I thought you might like to see the verse from the poem that the inscription is taken from.

> Blow out, you bugles, over the rich Dead!
> There's none of these so lonely and poor of old,
> But, dying, has made us rarer gifts than gold.
> These laid the world away; poured out the red
> Sweet wine of youth; gave up the years to be
> Of work and joy, and that unhoped serene,
> That men call age; and those who would have been,
> Their sons, they gave, their immortality.
> Rupert Brook – *The Dead*

15-3-17

10 March 1917

My own darling Con,

There is very little news, or else my brain will not work. I have had a big day walking and feel tired, so expect that accounts for it.

The more I see of the army methods and organization the less I think of it, one unit will not combine with another, and do their best to put something in one's way and hinder one. One has to fight like a tiger to get what one wants, and the more unpleasant one makes oneself the more you get.

It is just ripping to hear that Bindy is getting so fit again and will be nice for you to hear her cheery wee voice about the house once more. Aunt Janie has been ripping in writing; I have had several letters giving me the news of you and Bindy after having called you up on the phone. She said that she was most likely going down to Salcombe to stay a few days with Ethel, so hope it will do her good.

Yes, Flurry seems much more cheerful and glad it is only a slight wound, he must have been very depressed when he wrote the other letter, probably it was the first time that he had been in an attack, and looked upon it far too seriously.

Well dearest no more and just heaps and heaps of love to you and Bindy and take great care of yourself. Sorry that this is so short but will try to make up for it tomorrow.

Your loving
Harold

10 March –   Very quiet day, round digging party all day. Fired 18 rds.
*   Dainville.*
*   Much warmer and thaw set in.*

18-3-17

11 March 1917

My own darling Con,

It has been a glorious day, in fact a real spring day and must say that I have quite enjoyed it, especially after all the cold etc. I was surprised to hear the hedges were getting green, here there is no sign of that sort of thing, but if we have a few days like this they will soon come out.

We seem to have done very well at Kut and had a very quick advance towards

Baghdad, I wonder if they will be able to take it and hold onto it, it will be a great thing if we can, and put the wind up the old Turk properly.

John does not seem to have had much time in England, and rather sickening having only 4 days out there. It seems hardly worth it and would not be for us, as the whole time is spent on board and you know my mood there. Hope I shall see him out here, but expect very improbable.

There have been a tremendous lot of planes up today and not a single fight, should very much have liked to have seen a Bosch come down, as have not seen one do so for some time.

It will be Eric's birthday on 18th, so must drop him a line, expect that he is very busy where he is, but maybe not quite so as we are here.

The other night I had a great ride on a bike to see the Captain, a tail wind behind me, so got there fine, but on my return I could not move a lot, so started walking. Suddenly I heard a lorry coming and jumped on my bike and caught hold of a handle on the bus, which got up great speed and whisked me along a very bumpy road, and several times was very nearly over, but succeeded in getting here.

Well dearest, night night, and keep very fit and a huge hug to you both.
Your loving
Harold

*11 March –   Working at forward position. Captured Irles.
         Quiet fine day.*

18-3-17

12 March 1917

My own darling Con,
The weather has now quite changed and has become nice and warm, but has turned to rain, which has made everything very slippy, but if we get a good wind it should clear and dry things up very soon.

Had a letter from Eric last night, he seems fairly cheery but rather fed up with his division. I wrote and asked him if he would try and get me into the artillery of that, but he advises me not to. As I get along well with the people here, am going to remain where I am, especially as it is very late to get a shift now. He did not say a word about Susan, so expect she is quite well again, but a little weak, as it will take some time to get over that attack she had.

Bindy will be very busy again and in great spirits, and often wonder what she will say when she sees the other wee person. It will be amusing to watch her and expect she will immediately go for his eyes, and see what they are made of.

Here everything is very quiet and nothing new to talk about, except that we have one man in our brigade (a new arrival) height 6ft 9½ins., a fine looking fellow and well built, poor gee that has to carry him.

Night night my own and God bless and look after you both.

Your loving
Harold

12 March – With working party at forward position all day, very quiet. Fired 50 rds. Put in for special leave. Dull damp day.

19-3-17

13 March 1917

My own darling Con,

We have just heard that Baghdad is in our hands, and hope we will be able to cling onto it. It has been a very quick advance, and a thorough rout for the Turk, expect it will cut off a lot of his supplies, and from his point of view will shorten the war. I would not be surprised if he will sign a separate peace; that is if they leave him in Europe, otherwise he will fight to the bitter end.

It was bad luck on Myra losing all her jewellery, but on the whole they got off very lucky, do not think that I would care for the experience.

This notita will be arriving about the time, and hope it finds you very fit and well. I am making a good push to try and get home about 23rd and expect to hear in 3 or 4 days what my luck is, and will let you know as soon as possible.

The mail cart is just up, so afraid that this will be a very short one. We hear that there has been another little success down on the Somme and some prisoners taken, all these little things count, and put the wind up the Bosch.

Well dearest will close, just tons and tons of love and good luck and hope to be there in time. A great hug for Bindy.

Your loving
Harold

13 March – With infantry last night, all very quiet. At new position all day, shelled in afternoon, 1 man killed, 2 wounded, infantry sent over about 50 rds. Captured Baghdad. Grevillan – 287 prisoners, 3 officers, 16 mortar guns. Fine day.

☆☆☆☆☆☆☆☆☆☆☆☆☆☆☆

18-3-17

14 March 1917

My own darling Con,

Have nearly finished 2 other letters so have done some quite good work, and must try to get one off to Johnnie after I have done this, but it will be a struggle, as I feel more like a good read. Have just started that book you sent me by Scot, and think I will like it very much.

Have had a very easy day, but a quite interesting one which you will eventually be able to see by my diary, although it is not very fully written up. I am hopeless at writing a good account, and sorry for it afterwards, as it would make it much more interesting and better reading, as now it will take a lot of explaining, and will also have forgotten a good deal of it, if not all.

The other night I was down sleeping with the infantry and I met a chap from Brazil, so had quite a talk in Spanish, but of course his rotten Portuguese was rather hard to understand, but still we struggled on.

There is another officer who has just joined the brigade, he stands 6 ft. 9½ ins., and is well made, feet about 15 inches, he makes us all look like dwarfs in every way. He will have a rotten time in the trenches and have to stoop all the time; otherwise he will get his head knocked about by the bridges etc.

I have a great time with the engineers, when I want them I can never find them, and so start looking round for them, eventually I find they have been doing the same for me, and so we are following one another round, eventually we find one another fed up, and evil words follow, and we depart, nothing doing.

Here everything goes on as usual and no news at all. Post has become very erratic again, and papers arrive about every 2 or 3 days, but this is the fault of the post, not the senders. There must be a great deal of transport now, and so they leave the least important things for the last.

Well dearest night night, and very best of good luck to you and Bindy.
Your loving
Harold

14 March –   Quiet day.
             Dainville.
             Fine.

☆☆☆☆☆☆☆☆☆☆☆☆☆☆☆

18-3-17

15 March 1917

My own darling Con,
You seem to be having a lot of bitter winds at home, many more than we are having here. It would be ripping if you could get some decent weather and get Bindy out, but after this month expect you will get quite a lot of it.

I see by your letter that it is your Dad's birthday on the 18th, so give him my best wishes and good luck, and hope he will have a ripping day of it. I should have remembered it, as it is the same day as Eric's, who I wrote to, but sorry I could not give him good news, as I had to enclose Johnnie's letter, which will not cheer him up very much, but hope to have better news to give him next time.

During the last few days the submarines do not appear to have done so much damage, one does not see much of it in the papers, so hope we have them well in hand now. The Bosch seems to be slowly moving back and giving up a village here and there, and will have to give up a good many more.

Well dearest will close with heaps and heaps of love to you both.
          Your loving
          Harold

15 March –   Quiet day. At observation post half day, fired 120 rds.
             Fine.
16 March –   Round position all day, Bosch slowly retreating between
             Peronne and Monchy. Several explosions and fires.
             Fine day.

☆☆☆☆☆☆☆☆☆☆☆☆☆☆☆

20-3-17

17 March 1917

My own darling Con,
We have now got a piano in our mess, one we poached from another battery, they must have pinched it from some house, by the sound it makes I do not

think that it could have been tuned for the last 50 years. Anyhow, one of the officers knows how to play, so will try and knock a tune out of it tonight, but it makes me long to hear you on it. We must get one when we get out there, and also must teach Bindy to dance to it, that will be your job, I will teach her how to ride and we will have a great time of it. I do not suppose that we will ever get that pony from the Johnsons' and always think that they changed their minds about it, and so never sent it with the troops, which turned out such a clavo (*headache*).

The Major comes back today, he has been on a 2 week course to England, so at spare times I expect that he has had fairly good times of it.

It is turning very like spring now, and grass is trying hard to come out, birds singing and one might almost think there was no war on, excepting for a few guns popping off.

Have just heard that Bapaume is taken, that is the place we were fighting so hard for in October, now they have withdrawn their troops and we have the place, which is always a step further to victory.

Tea is just coming in so must close up. The Major has just come in and is giving us a long account of Blighty and the food question. Also he says that there has been a revolution in Russia and they deposed the Tsar.

No more, with heaps and heaps of love and hope that this finds you very fit and well, and probably will arrive before the new arrival. A great kiss to Bindy.

Your loving
Harold

17 March – Round position all day. Left for Blighty evening, all Bosch country, bit of gunfire. Captured Baparin, Moncy, Transly, Asly le Grand and several other villages. Fired 48 rds. Fine day.

18 March – Arrived London, fine good crossing. Saw Aunt Janie and then left for Godalming, all well. Captured Perronne and about 30 other villages.

19 March – Had a quiet day at Westhanger with Con and Bindy. Nurse Duncan arrived. J.R. to London. Cold windy day.

20 March – Quiet day at Westhanger. About 40 more villages captured, Huns destroying most of them and poisoning all wells etc. Fine cold day.

21 March – **Baby arrived at 6.30, both doing well.**
Captured 40 more villages.
Cold day, several blizzards.

22 March – Captured 10 more villages, enemy giving more stubborn resistance.
Went to London for day, had lunch with Uncle Fred and Aunt Bella.
Asturius torpedoed.*
Cold day, several blizzards.

23 March – At Westhanger all day, quiet day.

24 March – Aunt Janie, Jean, Inesita, J.R, H.& B. lunched at Savoy
and then to High Jinks good. Con going on well.
Fine sunny day.

25 March – Went with Beatie and Bindy to see Susan at Crawley.
Fine day.

26 March – At Westhanger all day.
Advance very slow.
Cold and several snowstorms.

27 March – Had a quiet ripping day at Westhanger. Left at 10.40 for Victoria.

29-3-17

Postcard – 28 March 1917

Just a hurried line, to let you know that I have arrived safely, so far. I got up to town in good time and the tubes were still running and had a fine night at the hotel, and just woke up in time to telephone out to find how you were, and was very bucked to hear you had a good night of it.

It was just rotten leaving you and seems to get worse and worse each time, but never mind, it all brings the war nearer to an end. No time for more, just heaps and heaps of love to you all.

Your loving
Harold

---

* Hospital ship "ASTURIAS."- Torpedoed on 21st March, 1917, at midnight, off Devonshire coast; no patients on board; Temporary Captain G. L. Atkinson, R.A.M.C., Staff Nurse J. J. Phillips, and 12 R.A.M.C. orderlies were drowned; the ship was beached at Salcombe.

31-3-17

British Officers Club
28 March 1917

My own darling Con,

Here I am safely over, and am only going to remain here for a few hours and then on I go. I have just come in from trying to get out to see Kathleen, but now will not have the time; I am very disappointed as was looking forward to seeing her. Anyhow I hope that she will soon have the luck of getting leave, and a good long one too, she has worked really hard for it.

We had a very good crossing, no excitement. It was a bit cold, but that was nothing, and no news on this side to send on.

Well darling, I cannot tell you how much I enjoyed this leave, the whole time seemed perfect excepting just for those few hours when the new arrival came. It all seemed to be so perfect and put the first leave in the shade. Of course it was all over too quick, but still I was very lucky to have got such a good one, and see everything safely over, and both of you getting on so well, I only hope that you will all three keep so, and be a great comfort to one another. As you always used to tell me in your letters about Bindy being such a treasure, I found it out, and there could not be anybody nicer and sweeter, so full of life and such good spirits, and cheers everyone up.

Am afraid that I wasted my last hour or two by being so sleepy, and you must be very fed up about it, but I really could not have been more happy or comfortable than I was then, and can only hope that it will very soon be up, and no more returning to this side.

Your Dad and sisters were so ripping to me, and feel an awful wretch for not having thanked them, but I felt as if I could not, so you will have to do it for me, as I will have no time to write to anybody else but you. I do not know when I shall get to my battery, but hope sometime tomorrow, they are not in the same place as I left them, but not very far off.

I left an indelible pencil on the hall table, so hope that you got it. Well darling until tomorrow, God bless and keep you and the 2 little ones very fit and well. I will try and drop a hurried tomorrow, but do not be surprised if you do not hear for a few days.

Your loving
Harold

28 March –   Left for France, arrived at Boulogne 1.30, left for the front at 10.40 p.m. Fine day but rained during the night.

29 March –   *Arrived Doullens 9.30 a.m. and left for Beaumetz at 11.30, arrived at battery 7 p.m. It has moved forward to Le Chat Maigre west of Mercatel. Cold rainy weather.*

☆☆☆☆☆☆☆☆☆☆☆☆☆☆☆

6-4-17

30 March 1917

My own darling Con,
Here I am with the battery once more, I got to it yesterday afternoon after a good journey. Got into a very comfortable train, but did not have much sleep as there were about 20 V.A.Ds. on the train and all just come out to France for the first time. The lot that were in our coach, 3 of them, were a very cheery lot and very nice, so kept us going most of the time with millions of questions, what was this like and what was that like, so the time fled very quickly. The latter part of the journey I did by motor lorry, and then finished it up in an old cart and on my gee, so had quite a number of different transportations. I found my battery a long way from where I had left it, all very fit and having a quiet time of it.

It was very interesting to see the old Bosch country behind their lines with their noticeboards etc. up. But the country they have made a mess of, not a lot that is not blown to pieces, all the bridges, roads, crossings and railways blown up, not a decent tree, both small and large wiped out. The Bosch had some very fine dugouts and gun positions, and they have been so well blown up that the pieces cover a radius of about 200 yds. We are now in one of his dugouts, which he tried to blow up and set fire to, but he did not succeed, most of the charges we took out and threw them away. We have got about 30ft of earth above us, and 2 good passages out; it is all well lined with wood and makes a very comfortable place. All the main roads were lined with fine trees, but these are all on the ground, there is one thing about it, and that is that we will have plenty of firewood. We have got plenty of work to do now, and it keeps us going the whole day, which I must say that I much prefer to otherwise. On the whole the Bosch has left very little material about, but quite a lot of bombs. We are still following him up gradually. I cannot put any more news, and this that I have put is of no importance, but will give you a slight idea of the country, it is very much after the style of Salisbury Plain, but not so many woods.

Well Beatie, like a dear, gave me some food, but as luck would have it I did not require it as I was always in a place where I could get it. When I arrived here I had a big tea, and had the eggs for it.

There is another officer posted to this battery who was at St John's Wood with me, in the class before me, but just as he got his commission he broke his wrist and has been home ever since.

When I came away, I said a very rotten goodbye to the girls, but I felt as if I could say nothing or burst, so did the former, but now feel such a rotter about it, as they were so ripping to me the whole time, and gave me all your time, so dearie will you please do it for me, and I will try to write one of these days. Afraid I have left you all the work, but will try to do better next time.

Well dearest, night night, and sleep well. This has missed tonight's mail. Just tons of love to you and the 2 girlies.

Your loving
Harold

30 March – Went to forward position with digging party. Quiet day.

5-4-17

31 March 1917

My own darling Con,
In a way this new life is quite like the Somme, except that there is next to no shelling. But now I live in a small dugout and have sent half my kit behind the lines, so travel quite light.

The more one sees of the country the more bare and desolate it appears to become, the Bosch is quite an expert in laying the country to waste, and up to all the dirtiest tricks that one could imagine, but our men are now up to most of them, and so get very few casualties. Now I hope that we will give him a rotten time of it, and repay him for all he has done, but it just makes one's blood boil to think that men like these should live, and it is all on the shoulders of the Kaiser and general staff.

Am in great hopes of getting a cartita from you tonight, and am just longing for the post to come. You will be getting up in a day or two and hope you will not be too weak on your pins, and soon be as fit as ever on them, just wish I were there to see you all again.

Expect that Nancy is changing quite a lot and getting quite the look of a baby, and a good colour too. We never talked about christening her, expect that this should be done quite soon, that is in 4 or 5 weeks, anyhow you get it done whenever you like and think best. Hope that you have not had any qualms on the names; I like them just as much as ever and am sure she will be a regular little Nancy, and be a fine couple with Bindy.

Bindy is such a fascinating little lassie and will be very hard to beat, I picture her so well going into your room and saying "baba" and "hush" and running about and playing the payaso (*clown*).

The weather has not been anything to brag about, the last two days have been cold, windy and showery, but hope it will soon change for the better.

I have clean forgotten Flurry's address again, so will you send it along. When I arrived from the boat on this side I met a chap called Musson, but no relation, he is the first of this name I have ever met here. He came from London, very cheery and had just arrived out for the first time.

Well dearest will close, with heaps of love to you both and the weeny one.
Your loving
Harold

3| March –   At observation post morning and then battery all day, fired 30 rds.

Nelson
New Zealand
2017

Dear Harold,

I know you loved your girls deeply, found them fascinating and had plans and dreams for their futures. I will have a chat with you later about Bindy, but it is funny to think that the little girl you adored grew up to be my mother-in-law.

Wee Nancy Katherine was only 6 months old when you shuffled off this mortal coil, and I think you only met her in her first few days of life. She looked a bonny lass, I know you had hoped for a boy, but I suspect you were not disappointed for too long after she was born. Nowadays with modern technology many parents find out whether they will have a little boy or girl, I rather liked the element of surprise when I had my babies. I have to tell you I did chuckle at Con obviously being in bed for so many days after the birth, but that was a luxury you were able to offer her.

Here is your wee scamp up on her hands and knees starting to explore the world.

Nancy Katherine Musson, date unknown

Your girls had a good and privileged childhood, based in England in a home Con built, and travelling at times to Argentina. They had lots of love and support from Con's father, who they called Dandan, and from aunts and uncles. They both attended Hayes Court School in Kent as boarders, and later went to a Swiss Finishing School.

Both girls were war babies, and sadly both of them had to live through another war, known as the Second World War. This was an equally vicious war with more sophisticated weapons, including the atomic bomb that was used against Japan. This war lasted for 6 years, and included the most dreadful genocide of Jews, Gypsies, and those with disabilities carried out in German concentration camps.

Both of your daughters served in the armed forces during the war, Nancy joined the Women's Royal Naval Service, as a Probationary Wren on 01 July 1942, thirteen days later was working as a Motor Transport Driver in *HMS Victory*. I feel she may have struggled with her health; she was given sick leave twice in 1943 and was eventually discharged on 18th May 1944, after a spell in the Nervous Diseases Hospital. It is noted on her records that her character was very good and her efficiency was average. She was awarded the War Medal 1939-45, the criteria for receiving this was to have served for 28 days. We were initially unable to find Nancy's war history as there was no death certificate for her, but thanks to John Daffurn, who undertook some research about Nancy, on our behalf, we now have her records. Nancy did not claim her medal, Jim and I claimed it on her behalf, and are now proud to share with you.

Nancy's war medal

Sadly I don't know anything more about your wee girl until her untimely death on 7th September 1946 in a dreadful air crash on her way to Argentina. I have thought of this so often and how terrible it must have been, there is no official grave for Nancy, and even writing this brings tears to my eyes. I imagine this must have been a dreadful time for Con and Bindy, saying goodbye to a beloved daughter and sister. I do have first-hand experience of losing a sister, and I watched my mother's decline when my elder sister Valerie died, the pain for her was unbearable and she eventually lost her mind. I still crave the company of my sister. I hope you were there to meet your girl as she made her journey to the other side.

I have the official accident report from the Flight Safety Foundation for you. Nancy was on board an Arvo 685 York 1 aeroplane belonging to British South American Airways.

> An Arvo plane, named *"Star Leader"*, was destroyed when it crashed shortly after takeoff from Bathurst (now named Banjul), Gambia. All 24 on board were killed.
>
> The aircraft was on a flight from London to Buenos Aires via Lisbon, Bathurst, Natal, Rio de Janeiro and Montevideo. It had arrived at 02.43 hr. at Bathurst where a new crew took over. At approximately 04.08 hr. the York took off again for Natal. The weather was fair, with visibility 10 miles and cloud base 1500ft 3/10 strato-cumulus. The wind was WSW at two knots. Shortly after takeoff the aircraft had crashed in the bush nearly two miles south of the airfield. The port wing first struck trees 40 to 50 feet high and then crashed through more trees as it rolled over to the left. The airplane burst into flames.
>
> The accident flight was the captain's first York flight on a scheduled service, and it was also the first take-off he make in a York loaded to more than 69,000 lb.
>
> PROBABLE CAUSE: "The captain losing control of the aircraft very shortly after it had left the ground. The cause of the loss of control cannot be determined, but that it was due to a mishandling of the controls by the captain is the most likely explanation."
>
> *Aviation Safety Network*

It must have been so awful for all of those on board the plane, even though I imagine it all happened very quickly. Also on board was John and Myra

Campbell's daughter, Joan, no doubt the girls knew each other and maybe were able to offer each other some kind of comfort in their last moments.

Air travel is so common now, thousands of planes are in the sky at any time carrying people across the world and it is thought to be one of the safest forms of travel. Huge planes can carry around 500 people, probably not something you can really imagine.

In the probate records it is noted that Nancy left £4334 19s 5p to her mother. I imagine that on the whole Nancy lived an enjoyable life and had many adventures. She was brave enough to answer her call to duty just as you had, life for women in the services would have been hard, but they played a vital role in the war effort.

Here she is, a young woman, and I think has very much the look of you, as I said before, your genes have travelled well through your bloodline.

Nancy Katherine Musson, 21st March 1917 – 7th September 1946

I find this picture to be rather haunting as she gazes out at us; I wonder what were her hopes, dreams and ambitions that were cut short by pilot error. We will never know.

In sadness and love
Sheila x

April 1917

Cenotaph, Wakefield New Zealand – Anzac Day 2015

They went with songs to battle, they were young,
Straight of limb, true of eye, steady and aglow.
They were staunch to the end against odds uncounted,
They fell with their faces to the foe.

Laurence Binyon – *For the Fallen*

6-4-17

2 April 1917

My own darling Con,

No mail at all tonight, paciencia (*patience*) until tomorrow.

Things have been very quiet today and nothing of interest has cropped up. One of the officers is most likely going to another battery as Captain; I am rather sorry, as he is a very good sort and will quite miss him. Our small mess is very crowded, so it will relieve it a bit; one of us have usually to retire early, so as to make room for the others but this we do not mind, as there is usually one or the other of us a bit tired.

I have now started to take the Iron Jelloids, so you will see me blooming when next we meet.

Afraid that this is going to be a very short notita as have no time for more, must close, just heaps and heaps of love to you all and take great care of yourself.
      Your loving
      Harold

P.S. Another village just taken.

1 April –	Bosch shelled battery, no harm done.
	Quiet day, cold wet day.
2 April –	At observation post all day, very quiet.
	Cold and heavy snow showers.

8-4-17

3 April 1917

My own darling Con,

It was just ripping getting in this evening and finding one of your dear letters, and also one from Beatie waiting for me, it was just glorious getting them and nothing I wanted more. I am sorry that you did not have a very good night of it, but expect that you will get fitter and fitter every day, and so have much better nights. Yes, Bindy seems very full of baby and will get thoroughly interested and make great pals with her.

I remembered Kathleen's address alright, but could not get out as time was short.

Yesterday we had a wretched day of it, cold all morning and in the afternoon had a very heavy fall of snow, which has now turned to a fine old slush and stopped all work. We are all very sick about it, as it hinders us quite a lot, anyhow I hope it will soon improve.

Dotu, am very sorry about the photo and was an awful ass to forget it, especially as you told me once or twice about it. It can't be helped and will have to get it done next time.

Thank goodness today has been a fine one and had quite a lot of sun. Last night was quite an eventful one, I went to bed and suddenly heard a slight rumble, so looked round and found that a bit of the wall had fallen out. I went to sleep again and was suddenly woken up, and found that the whole face of the wall had fallen out, some of it fell on my pillow and I had to dig it out, and then went off to sleep again. When I woke up in the morning all the floor was flooded and door blocked up, so got the servant to dig it out, such is life in the army.

Well dearest must close with just tons of love and good luck to you and the little ones.

Your loving
Harold

P.S. It comes very strange including little <u>ones</u>, and cannot yet realise that our family has increased.

3 April – 2 of our balloons brought down by shellfire. Shot 360 rounds. Cold wretched day.

4 April – Brought 4 guns up last night to east of Boisleux-Au-Mont, registered them on zero line and shot 420 rds., first day of <u>the</u> bombardment. Took Croisilles and Henin-Beaumont yesterday, took 40 prisoners, our casualties 160. 1 plane down – ours. Cold and sleet all day.

10-4-17

5 April 1917

My own darling Con,

It is just ripping to get one of your letters every day, but you must not write when you are not feeling up to it.

Yes, Lucy is a lucky beggar, although he does not think so. What a pity he did not write sooner, I should have very much liked to have seen him and had a good chat, never mind we will meet one of these days.

At last we have got a grand day, no wind and fine hot sun, which makes all the difference to one's life here. Since I last wrote we have moved forward once more and are quite well off for shelter etc.

So Nancy was out for the first time I hope she enjoyed it and did her a lot of good. The news is quite encouraging about her becoming pretty, and I expect she will beat the crowd and be very brainy. So Susan will be one of your first visitors, you must let me know how she is looking, and only hope that she is getting rid of her asthma.

Yes, when I got back I found all the kit that I wanted, also the choc and cigarettes. The former is very good and very much appreciated by all. You might send me some more whenever you can, also some peppermint balls; I have quite a hankering after them, and afraid will have to deal with them as Nurse Cruikshank did. I often wonder what she is doing now, and also Nurse Bacon.

Is Bindy making pals with Nancy now, and taking much interest in her? They will both revel in a day like this and be out most of it. All the hedges and trees will soon be sprouting and looking so ripping shortly, I wish I were there to enjoy the spring with you, such as that day at Beaulieu, which to me always seems to stand out so much.

By the way you can send me a parcel occasionally and I will write to Aunt Bella to carry on, as they seem to reach here at times.

Must close up, with just heaps and heaps of love to you and the two girlies and keep very fit. Love to Bindy and Nancy.

Your loving
Harold

10-4-17

6 April 1917

My own darling Con,
Just a wee notita as I am orderly officer, and means one has a good deal to do nowadays.

You say that you did not know whether we had moved or not, we have, and are in quite a good place. I think that it mentioned in one of the papers the names of the places taken, so will not be any harm in telling you, xxxxxxxx,* quite close to the town or villages as it may be Morcatille. They have left all of them in ruins and generally damaged everything they could come across. The whole thing has been

---

* I imagine censors crossed out the place Harold mentioned.

very interesting to see, and now I will be very glad when all is over and at peace once more, the good old Argentine sun burning down on us, and so realise that there is one, as the one they have here is a very poor fellow, and shows itself very little.

We had a lovely day yesterday and nice morning of it today but it is beginning to change once more and rain, but hope it will not be much as we want the ground to get dry as soon as possible. It makes such a difference to the men, on dull wet days they go about with absolutely a fed up look about them, and on sunny days they are just the opposite.

Must close up as on a job. Just heaps and heaps of love to you and the wee lassies.
Your loving
Harold

12-4-17

7 April 1917

My own darling Con,
Afraid that this will be a very hurried notita again, but one's time is very full and afraid that letters might be rather scarce for some time, but will always try and get a field postcard off.

You will be up for a few hours a day by the time this reaches you, or maybe up altogether and feeling very fit. Am longing to see you all three together, you must send out a photo of yourselves as soon as you can.

I was up all last night, and could not have struck a worse one, rain, sleet and wind, when I came in at 11 a.m. this morning I turned straight into bed and had a good sleep until 5 p.m.

Must close, with just heaps and heaps of love to you 3.
Your loving
Harold

7 April –   *Quiet day – fired 4200.*

13-4-17

8 April 1917

My own darling Con,
Am at the present moment at the observation post, and as there is no light at all, am going to aprovechar (*take advantage of*) the moment to write a notita. Am glad

to say that the weather at last seems to be on the mend, and only hope that we will get a real good spell of it, and once more get the ground decently dry and fit for moving about.

Your notita of the second arrived last night, and see by it that you were hoping to get up the next day, you will be very bucked about it, but expect that after 2 hours you will be quite willing to turn in again. Your description of Nancy and her improvements make me very keen to see her again. Does anyone think or form an idea of who she is like? I personally believe that she is going to follow her mother's good looks.

I had a long letter from Eric, in which he enclosed one from Phillip with absolutely no news in it, all he says is that he has to send about a 1000 kilo of fruit to Buenos Aires and nothing more, he is very hopeless and not at all satisfactory. He also says that his brother Frank has just arrived out with 3 months leave, on what excuse I do not know, as he was only managing a place. If he can do it, I and Eric will have a good shot at it next winter, as our work is far more important, in fact urgent, as we only left the place for a year, and must try and get out and fix them up again, especially after the bad times they have been through. Expect that we shall soon be getting a letter from Johnnie, and hope that there will be much better news in it.

I also got a letter from Patsy, he is somewhere in the push and dislikes it as much as ever. He says that their estancia has had a very bad time of it, and have had big mortality in their stock, he is longing as much as we are to get out again.

Sorry to hear that Beatie has had tooth trouble, it is rotten and there is nothing much more painful. I should go and have the wretched tooth out.

It is hard to imagine Donald among all that sun and glory, it makes one just long for it all, and feel the sun burn through one's shirt, and also be fairly certain that they do not get too much rain and also that it very soon dries up.

Old Bosch land in front is being badly pounded about, he must be getting a rotten time of it. I think that you would enjoy sitting here on a fine day and watching it for an hour or two.

No more news so just heaps and heaps of love to you all, and keep fit and well, tomorrow is <u>the</u> day and only hope all goes well.

Your own loving
Harold

8 April –   Z day,* Canadians took 2000 prisoners, remainder took 1000 prisoners very fine days work. Fired 3000 rds. Horton wounded, died 3 days after.

---

*   Marks the start of the Battle of Arras, which was actually April 9th 1917 and seems Harold noted it a day early.

☆☆☆☆☆☆☆☆☆☆☆☆☆☆

16-4-17

9 April 1917

My own darling Con,

Another very hurried note, as we are all upside down and on the move. We have given the Bosch a nasty knock, he has had to move, and only hope we will able to keep him on the run, it will finish the war much sooner, and it makes it far more interesting. Wagon is just off.

Sorry you have been so long without letters but I have not missed more than one day at a time, but am sure it must be that there is a tremendous lot of traffic.

It is great to hear that Nancy has put on ½lb and that you are all very fit. Just tons and tons of love to you all.

Your loving
Harold

9 April – Good progress on the right. Rotten weather.

10 April – At forward observation post at St Martin all day. Troops made very fine progress and Cavalry went through, many casualties. Blizzards.

☆☆☆☆☆☆☆☆☆☆☆☆☆☆

16-4-17

11 April 1917

My own darling Con,

The push up to the present has been very satisfactory, I think we have got something like 14 thousand prisoners, a large number of guns and quite a lot of country, and we will have to keep them on the move. The only worry is the weather, which is as bad as it could be, all yesterday we had blizzards and snow, about 3 inches of it and bitterly cold. I should not think that we have had an April like this for years. Luckily we have not had to sleep out, but a lot of other troops have and suffered quite a lot for it, but it is tremendous how well they stand it and just shows that they are in fine condition.

Before I forget will you send me 2 refills for the Tommies' cooker, and some plain and milk chocolate, as thick as possible. We eat a lot of it now, during the day practically live on it, and hard biscuits, but really get any amount to eat, as when we get in we have a really good hot dinner, and then sleep like pigs.

Another few knocks like this to the Bosch and he will have to chuck the sponge up.

Sorry to hear that Beatie had to have the tooth out, but it is much better with it out and no pain.

I really believe that this is a worse country for rumours than old England and one cannot believe any of them, in fact if you did we would soon be in Berlin.

Must close up, you will be thinking that you have rather a rotten mate in life, but time is really very scarce. Well dearest just heaps and heaps of love to you and the 2 kiddies.

Your loving
Harold

11 April – At gun from 5 a.m. – 6.30, firing. At 6.30 went to observation post. Tanks went into action at 7.30, did good work and cleared trenches of Huns. Took their front line at Heninel, no prisoners. 6 corps moving forward and captured Monchy-le-Preux. Blizzards all day, cold and raw.

16-4-17

12 April 1917

My own darling Con,

We have had from up to 3 inches of snow since last night, and the country is in an awful state, the worst of it is that it still looks like going on, but never mind it must change for the better sometime.

We have made quite good progress since last night and will probably move forward together again, which means making a new position and digging in once more. Our horses are having a hard time of it through exposure, 7 died last night and the others look very rotten, it is hard luck on them and only wish that conditions would improve.

I got a short notita from your Dad telling me what he thought of you, and told me not to answer it, so will you tell him that I will take him at his word. He seems to think that you are both going on well, but says that he does not like small babies nearly as much as big ones.

Am enclosing a letter for Lucy, so will you please send it on to him, you can read it if you like.

Yesterday I had a very interesting day of it, I saw 4 tanks in action, they are very interesting things and go very slowly and can get over anything, the Bosch do not like them at all, and fairly fled before them. They did very good work and I think that they are a very good thing, but want to be a bit faster and would then be a very fine thing. One of them was knocked out and burnt up. Bosch is getting a very bad time of it, and does not like our heavy artillery at all.

There is no news here, so will close with just heaps and heaps of love to you and the little ones.

Your loving
Harold

12 April – Captured Heninel last night and second line of Bosch Hindenburg line. Casualties light. Blizzards and rain all day.

☆☆☆☆☆☆☆☆☆☆☆☆☆☆☆

18-4-17

13 April 1917

My own darling Con,
We are still making very good progress, at present we are not in action, and out of range of Bosch.

I was up in the famed Hindenburg line today, which we have broken, it must be a great knock to him, as I am sure that he meant to hold it. It is in a very bad state through our bombardment, and the only places that remain intact are his concrete machine gun emplacements, but even these we have taken pieces out of. He picked his ground very well, and had a grand view out onto us, but it has not served his purpose as we did not let him stop long enough there, now he is out in the open and so easier to get at, and teach him a good lesson.

Am hoping to get a letter from you tonight, but as everything is more upside down than ever it is not likely, although I must own that they bring everything up very well, considering the difficulties that get in their way and have to contend with.

I have been down to the wagon lines for the first time since I came back, and must say that it is very nice to see the horses once more, although they are in rather poor condition. Today has been quite a sunny one and has warmed them up a bit. We had them all loose in a paddock, which they thoroughly enjoyed, some careered about, others grazed, and a few lay down and had a good bask. The men are also thoroughly enjoying a good rest, and love a lie in the sun.

Well I wonder how you are all getting on, and expect glad to see a little sun, especially Bindy who seems to revel in it. No more news so will close, with just heaps and heaps of love to you all and keep very fit.

Your loving
Harold

13 April – No attack, quiet. Went into Hindenburg line on hill 105, many of our dead about. Line badly smashed to pieces by our fire. Found wounded officer. Cold day.

14 April – Took about 200 yds. Hindenburg line. Moved up to new position north of Croisilles. Quiet day, fine and sunny.

15 April – No attack but straffed the Bosch heavily in evening. Croisilles. Rotten day, rained all day.

☆☆☆☆☆☆☆☆☆☆☆☆☆☆

24-4-17

16 April 1917

My own darling Con,

I got 3 of your cartitas last night, I was very bucked to get them, and hear that you were all fit and well, and having decent enough weather to let the kiddies out. Here there has been none to speak of, and are all beginning to believe that the European climate is nothing but rotten.

Sorry I missed 2 days, but one of them I sent out a field postcard, there may be a good many days like this, until we go out of action, but do not think that this will be for some time, but one never knows one's luck.

Things are going well here and have given the Bosch a real good knock, which will take him some time to recover from, and hope to give him a worse one very soon.

It is great Kathleen getting her leave, you must all have been very bucked to see her, and am very sorry to have missed her, I bet that she will thoroughly enjoy herself. Personally I did not think that she would get it as it was very late, and there are a large number of casualties going through now, and they must all be very busy at the base.

I have not said anything about myself, as am very fit, and I will always tell you when anything is wrong, but after what we have been through during the last 3 weeks, it makes one almost proof against anything, as living is rather abnormal at present. Everyone is very cheery and takes everything jolly well; it is nothing when one is doing well and winning, and this I hope we are.

Another good tooth of mine is rapidly disappearing, the right hand lower eyetooth, but up to the present have had no pain from it.

I got all your enclosures from *L. & Co.*, and hope to get some more favourable news from Johnnie soon, and hear that he had been able to sell some of the stock off at a decent price.

We have all been on iron rations for the last 3 days, they are very good and give one plenty to eat, but nothing is left over.

Must close with just heaps and heaps of love to you all and bless you all.

                  Your loving
                  Harold

16 April –	Quiet day, fired 350 rds. Total number of prisoners to date, 16,000, 194 guns. Rotten day.
17 April –	Quiet day, but good news from French front. Fired 350 rds. French captured 12,000 prisoners. Rotten day.

24-4-17

18 April 1917

My own darling Con,

I got one of yours yesterday and was very sorry to hear that Vaughn was missing. It is indeed hard luck on the mother and father, but can only hope that he is a prisoner and safe.

Have not seen much air fighting lately but 2 came down in flames the other day, that is about a week ago. Yes, I knew we were going to make a big attack before it came off, and am glad to say that it has been a great success, and hope that it will go on being so. Last night we got the news that the French had captured 12,000 prisoners, and also wiped out a counter attack, all this news is most excellent, and may have very big results. The Bosch must be having a terrible time with our artillery, and am quite sure he does not love us. Our infantry have done very well, they have gone through a lot and done their work in a very fine way, and shown themselves to be much finer at their work than I expected. I have every admiration and respect for them all, and they deserve every credit that can be bestowed upon them.

The weather continues as rotten as can be, and one can get nothing dry, and are all very dirty. I have not had a bath or a change since I left you, and am almost beginning to like it. It is impossible to do in these circumstances, but if we can only get a hot sunny clear day I think everybody will indulge in a bath etc.

Will you please send out:

2 tins black boot polish	2 cakes coal tar soap
2 tins brown boot polish	1 tube Colgate
1 tin boot oil	1 tin Braggs

Also you might send every 8 or 10 days some biscuits, pork pie or anything you might think best, and always chocolate, they seem to arrive well and now want them, especially choc and biscuits, either Bath Olivers, oat meal or any dry biscuit.

Well, Nancy seems to be doing well and getting quite a little corner of your heart. I wonder how old she will be when I see her, expect quite talkative and taking a great interest in everything.

There was not much news in the *L. & Co.* letter, but hope that Johnnie will write soon.

Fancy all of the prisoners we have taken, I have not seen one, except the dead ones, but hope to see a good haul soon.

Give my love to all, and just tons and tons to your dear old self and the 2 bairns.

Your loving
Harold

18 April – At observation post all afternoon, fired 350 rds. Bosch straffed Croisilles. Croisilles.
Slight improvement in weather.

24-4-17

19 April 1917

My own darling Con,

We have been very quiet here for the last 2 to 3 days, but do not expect that it will last very long, as we cannot let the Hun sit down for very long, and must be up and at him and keep him on the move, give him no rest, so wear him down.

He is a very stubborn beast and makes use out of every little bit of vantage he can, but still I think that his number and time is up, and he will call out for peace in 2 or 3 months. Anyway we all hope so, and so make an end to this so called war.

I am a little south of where you think but well in the fun, and am only hoping for better weather, which does not seem to be improving and get no sun at all.

I met another of the men that was at St John's Wood with me, he has got the M.C. but for what act I do not know. At the school he was about the worst man at his work, so it just shows how little you can judge a man.

By the way I left my gold safety pin at the Grosvenor Hotel on the night of the 27th in room 314, so will you please write and try to get it for me.

Yes dear, about nurse's pay, just pay her and be done with it, after all everything has been very satisfactory, and I am jolly pleased with everything. Expect that she will probably have gone by the time that this reaches you, but you must not get rid of her until you feel thoroughly fit, and that you and Alice are able to look after her with ease.

I got a notita from Helen and will try and answer it soon, but will not promise, you can let her know what I think of the war.

Well dearest will close with just tons and tons of love to you and the 2 bairns.
Your loving
Harold

19 April –   Quiet day but preparing for a big attack on 22nd unit. Fired 340 rds. Dull day with occasional drizzle.

25-4-17

20 April 1917

My own darling Con,
Yesterday and today have been without rain, at least had a little yesterday, the ground has begun to dry up very quickly and hope it will go on doing so.

The pies, biscuits and choc arrived this morning, and many thanks for them, they have just come at the right time, and the choc is a great thing. The pies were great but rather churned up, but all enjoyed them thoroughly. I do not remember if I asked you to send me a couple of refills for the Tommies' cooker, if not will you please send them along, and also 3 of my ordinary white hankies. Afraid I am always asking for odds and ends, and never seem to get properly fixed up. About the weekly parcel, it will be better to send it once a fortnight, as food will be a little more plentiful now. We have not had anything fresh since I last wrote, but something will be coming off before this reaches you, and will let you know all about it then, that is if the weather is good to us.

Do you know if John Campbell has been up with the Cavalry? I have been on the lookout for him, but so far without success, he must be further south as P. Inglis saw him.

It is getting much more like spring and the butterflies and beetles are coming out and grass beginning to grow, which is a good sign of summer coming along.

Well no more and hasta mañana, with heaps and heaps of love to you three.
              Your loving
              Harold

20 April – Quiet day, fired 360 rds.
              Fine but cold and windy.

☆☆☆☆☆☆☆☆☆☆☆☆☆☆☆

30-4-17

                                        21 April 1917

My own darling Con,

Something very funny must have happened to the weather, 3 days without rain and quite a lot of sunshine, but it has not been very warm, in fact today is rather cold and feels like a good frost tonight.

We moved to a new position yesterday and have had a great dig in, and the whole battery is very comfortable and almost rain proof, if not quite.

I had a nice packet of sweets from Susan from Stewarts, so must write and thank her for them, or if I have no time will you please do so. Our food rations have increased once more, and are very good, it is extraordinary how regularly they come up, especially when we are on the move.

Old Bosch has visited us quite a lot with his planes the last 2 or 3 days, but we do not care a bit about this, and merely laugh at him, as he probably sees such a lot that he cannot distinguish one thing from another.

Am very sorry you are not getting my letters very regularly, as I only miss a very exceptional day, and hope to miss none, in fact I have only so far sent one field postcard off.

Glad to hear that Aunt Janie and Bella went out to see you, the former wrote and told me all about you, but did not say who she thought that the wee one was like, she is very enthused with Bindy, but she is with all kids and loves them all.

This time I am sharing a dugout with one of the other officers, but do not like it nearly as much as being alone, so in the future will strike off on my own.

Well dearest of all, night night, and take great care of yourselves, and just heaps and heaps of love to you all.

Your loving
Harold

21 April – Quiet day, fired 360 rds.
Fine day, cold.

23 April – 1 of our planes brought down. Big attack at 4.30 a.m. with 2000 prisoners and 1 field battery, counter attack drove us back, regained all lost ground by fresh attack at 6 p.m. Fired 2400 rds. equals 35 tons. Bosch put up a heavy barrage. Windsor killed, B. Bat. – many killed and wounded on both sides. Grand day.

☆☆☆☆☆☆☆☆☆☆☆☆☆☆☆

30-4-17

24 April 1917

My own darling Con,

I had just started a letter to you yesterday when orders came through that we had to fight and had a very heavy one too. Our first one we started at 4.30 a.m. and had a big do and took 2000 prisoners, then we had to retire into where we started as there was a hold up in one spot, anyhow that part was disappointing, but could not be helped, and as we made such a firm bag of prisoners we were all very cheered. This fight finished at about 3 p.m. and the Bosch seems to have been very annoyed and plastered the whole place with his rotten shells. Then at 6 p.m. we had orders to restart the fight, and all worked like niggers, and gave Bosch a bad doing and gained all our objectives in about one hour. We captured a battery of field guns, so on the whole had a very successful day, and once more did the Hun down, and will go on doing so. He did not plaster his shells round us, but on the country I was observing on, one could not see anything but bursting shells and <u>dust</u>, both his and ours, it really was a fine sight and to cap all the weather is just grand, could not want for better and all the men are very contented and bucked.

At present I am sitting behind a bank having a good bask and write in the sun, after having got up at 12.15 p.m. I was up from 4 a.m. yesterday to 4 a.m. this morning, and now feel quite comfortable, except there is no sign of a bath.

I am very sorry to hear about Vaughn, it is bad luck and especially on him, he was so keen and young and everything to look forward to in life. Yes, one just longs for the end of this, and the awful slaughter that is going on.

We alone yesterday sent over 30 tons of steel to the Bosch, and there were dozens of others doing just the same work. The tanks are taking a great part in this war, and are doing very good work; it is very interesting to see them ploughing their way along.

The parcel of shoes and refills arrived and muchas gracias, also a parcel of chocs from Jum, so am full up and enough to last me a month.

Must close as am just off out. Just heaps and heaps of love to you all.

Your loving
Harold

P.S. Am enclosing a letter for Susan, please forward.

24 April –   Number of prisoners increased to 3000, our losses
were heavy. Fired about 400 rounds.
East of St. Martin.
Grand weather.

29-4-17

25 April 1917

My own darling Con,

Just a wee notita before the mail goes. There has been nothing new since I last wrote and everything has been fairly quiet and have done no more fighting, but in a way hope it will not be long before we are, as it means the end all the sooner.

It is rotten to think that the Bosch is doing his best to sink all the hospital ships, and that puts the finishing touch onto it all, and I can only think that here is nothing bad enough for him to do. Yesterday I could have knocked 100 of his Red Cross men out and several Red Cross wagons, but not one us fired on them, I cannot help thinking that is was a ruse on his part, but one never knows.

It was a sore blow to Bosch in losing Monchy, as it commanded a very fine view of all our country, and now he will never get it back.

I dreamt last night that I was back with you, and found Nancy very intelligent, what struck me most was that she knew so well how to wipe her mouth, but of course she appeared to me to be about 1½ years old at least.

No news so will close, just tons and tons of love to you and the 2 wee bairns.
Your loving
Harold

P.S. Please send me plenty of my remedio as soon as possible.

25 April –   Fairly quiet day, fired 350 rds.

☆ ☆ ☆ ☆ ☆ ☆ ☆ ☆ ☆ ☆ ☆ ☆ ☆ ☆ ☆

New Zealand
2017

Dear Harold,

As I have mentioned before, Anzac Day is an important day here, of course it does not only remember and honour your war, but also the wars and conflicts that have come after. Even as I write this letter to you the world is in a tricky state, there are power hungry leaders who create a lot of discontent. However, there is little point living in fear of what may or may not happen, it is far better to fill the days with love and awareness of all the goodness in humanity.

Perhaps Ben, our youngest grandchild has the right idea. Anzac Day is hard to grasp when you a small, last year Ben who is a Kea – the branch of Boy Scouts for its smallest members, was part of the service. He sat at the front of the hall in his uniform, it is hard to be solemn when you are small, but he did well. He also gave us a note, which happily states: -

> Dear Grandma and Granddad,
> Happy Anzac Day. I love you.
> Lots of love
> Ben

Two of Angela's children, Alanda and James are serving officers in the British Army, both hold the rank of Major and both have served in Afghanistan in the theatre of war. Their younger sister Grace is married to a retired Army officer. Angela's husband, Terence is also a retired army officer. I am sure between all of them Angela has had more than a few nerve-wracking moments.

There has been so much happening to acknowledge all that happened a hundred years ago. I was also delighted to have your name read out at the Tower Of London, where a moat of ceramic poppies was created around the Tower to commemorate the start of the war in 1914, there was one made for each of you who died. I also had the names of Wilfred and Raymond read out. A ceremony was held at 7.25 p.m. each evening, when 180 names were read out, ending with a bugler playing the Last Post, this was recorded to enable people all over the world to view it. I am the proud owner of one of the poppies; it is rather delicate and sits for safety in a wine bottle.

I think you can tell from these letters to you that you have left your footprint on my heart.
With love
Sheila x

☆☆☆☆☆☆☆☆☆☆☆☆☆☆☆

30-4-17

26 April 1917

My own darling Con,
So Bindy is getting particular about her dress already, she seems to be beginning early, and I expect has quite good taste. It must be awfully interesting watching her pick up all these little ways and fads, only wish that I could join you in them and try and give you a hand, but would be an awful chambon *(klutz)* at it, and probably better where I am, or putting an old cow out at *Lucero*.

Here there is nothing fresh, but expect to give you some news in 2-3 days, and hope that it will all be good, and a great success.

If it was not for the submarine trouble I think that we would have the Bosch tight; but I do not think that they will ever starve England out. I also think that they should get the food issued out on a firm basis, and nothing issued without a ration ticket, and in this way could get a good reserve in hand, but these sort of things are never done in England until too late.

I hear that the Americans are going to send over an army of 10,000 men fully equipped in 3 months time, I wonder if this is so and what they will be like, anyhow hope that the war will be over by then. They seem to be going the whole hog and doing all possible, and so hope that their fleet will be able to assist against the submarines. I really do believe that we are once more going to have supremacy in the air, our new plane is good and think that it puts the wind up the Bosch, it will be a great thing and I must say am much more hopeful with regards to the air service than I was 10 days ago.

　　Must close, with heaps and heaps of love to you all.

Your loving
Harold

P.S. Please send some cigarettes and bicarb.

26 April –　　*Quiet day excepting for a few bursts of artillery, went to look for new observation post but could not see zone from any point. Fine day.*

1-5-17

27 April 1917

My own darling Con,

Just a wee line to let you know that I am on my way out with a party of 10 men, for 10 days rest. We go behind the lines for this time and hope to have a nice easy time of it, then we come back and 10 more go out.

　　Nothing new has happened since I last wrote and so very little news. I see the account of our last fight is in the papers of 25th and 26th, there are several little points I could add, but on the whole it is fairly correct, although they do not make one realise the rotten part of it, and the number of infantry laddies that will never see their homes again. It is truly sad to see them and think that there is such a lot of fine life sacrificed, and men maimed just because there is such a person as a mad Kaiser and politicians.

　　The weather still keeps good and is a great blessing to all. I wish I knew Mabel's address, as I shall be somewhere close to where she said that she might be, and should like to look them up. I met Mr. Bryant of V. Valleria yesterday, he is still just as cheery and fat as ever. He will be at this rest camp with me, says that they have had a rotten time of it with the seca and lost about 900 head.

　　Must close and will write a good long one from rest. Heaps and heaps of love to you, and the 2 little lassies.

Your loving
Harold

27 April – Quiet day. Came down to wagon lines and remained there the night.
Borleux, St. Martin.
Grand day.

☆☆☆☆☆☆☆☆☆☆☆☆☆☆☆

4-5-17

28 April 1917

My own darling Con,
Here I am out at rest, we are all enjoying it very much and hope to enjoy it still more. There is quite a good chance of getting to Amiens for a few days, and even Paris is talked about, but if the latter comes off I do not expect that I shall go, as the preference will be given to the men who have been longest without leave, but it would be quite good fun if we could even get a couple of days.

The weather is just grand, and today has been the best of the whole lot, and only wish that I could have had you over, and spent even these few days with you.

The submarines seem to be doing a great deal of damage and increasing every week, it is the hardest question of the war to tackle, but hope that they will get some good solutions to the problem and wipe them out.

The Bosch is sustaining a great many casualties here and do not know how they can keep it up. All the men that are out at rest here are very cheery; it is extraordinary what a difference the fine weather makes to them, and a change of food.

29/4/17

This is just grand, and had a great slack in bed until 9.30 a.m., a good breakfast and then a read, now I am writing this in a garden in the sun. It is a grand day and very much like spring, hedges, gooseberry bushes etc. all coming out, the birds coming back to life, singing and whistling about, and making life thoroughly agreeable. With a few days of this weather we will have plenty of grass for the horses, they do revel in getting loose and roving about the paddocks. Back here it is hard to believe there is a war going on, and a very fierce one too. This village 6 weeks ago was under shellfire, but luckily not much worried, and now well out of range, the name of the village is La Cauchie, there is no harm in telling you this. It is a very 'Sunday' day; one can hear the bands etc. at church, and church parade.

We can get any amount of fresh eggs, butter and milk and lucky about all kinds of groceries, so we are doing ourselves proud. The old French folk are very busy in their gardens digging and planting seeds etc. in the line of vegetables, but no flowers. All this makes me picture the spring out there, and just long to be in our own wee garden, pottering about and see Bindy plodding about on our wee lawn. I wonder what things are like out there, and hope there is a big improvement from the last news.

About Nancy's Godfather, I most certainly will not be it, and do not see the right of it. Most certainly if Gilbert cares to be him, I can think of nobody better as I reckon that he is just about the right age, but maybe a couple of years too young, which does not matter. The Scotch never have anything of that sort, and as far as I can see they are of no use, the only thing is that it pleases a great many people to be <u>it.</u>

Today I am going to have my hair cut and a good bath, and am sure will be all the better for it.

Just finished my bath and feel quite a different person, the first I have had since I left *Westhanger*. Must close up as post is off, and must also aprovechar (*make the most of*) this rest and get a lot of letters off. Tons of love to you and the 2 kiddies.

Your loving
Harold

28 April –	Went to La Cauchie with 10 men for 10 days rest, arrived at 12 p.m. and all turned in. La Cauchie. Grand day.
29 April –	Spent very quiet day, wrote, read, slept. Took German front line at Oppy and 950 prisoners. La Cauchie. Very fine day.
30 April –	Went to Ameins by motor bus and spent a great day there, returned at 3 a.m. all thoroughly satisfied, sent blouse to Con and chocs to Kathleen. Very fine day.

May 1917

Isla Beth Kennard –
Anzac Day 2015

They shall grow not old, as we that are left grow old:
Age shall not weary them, nor the years condemn.
At the going down of the sun and in the morning
We will remember them.

Laurence Binyon - *For the Fallen*

8-5-17

1 May 1917

My own darling Con,

Another month has gone by, and so nearer the end of the war.

Well I did not write yesterday as we all went to Amiens and had a great day of it, a big bus was allotted to us and 13 of us went. We arrived there about 11.30 a.m., did a little shopping and then had a great lunch, which we all thoroughly enjoyed, and must say that the cooking was most excellent. There seems to be no restriction to the amount of food one can eat, and one can buy anything including new potatoes, the wee small ones too, which I was very surprised at, and do not think it right, as they should be left to grow to full size.

From after lunch onwards I shopped and bought several little things for us. I saw a very nice shop, a place you would love to be in, and as I was walking about with Bryant, we rolled in much to the amusement of all the girls. We had a great time picking and choosing, we had half the shop down and eventually I chose a blouse, which I hope will arrive safely, and that you will like it. It looked so beautifully cool and summery, I liked it very much, so hope it will fit, but I think it slightly on the large scale, but expect you can get it fixed up. You may not like the black prints on it but somehow I thought that they looked very nice. I pictured you in it, with that hat we bought in Buenos Aires at Eric's wedding, although I expect it is out of fashion by now, and am very sorry I did not see more of you in it. There is also a little pinafore for Bindy and a hat for Nancy, the latter is a very curious looking thing and doubt it will fit, or if the shape is any good, but looked like summer. I also sent Kathleen a box of chocs, so hope they will arrive safely.

The weather here is just grand, I am out in the sun most of the time and just love it. We hear the guns going hard in the distance, which means that someone is going through a rough time of it.

I had a long talk with Bryant, and of course it all led to the Argentine. Mr. Booth and Roscollar have had a very bad time of it, lost 900 head and a great deal of their alfalfa. It must just have been awful up there, and one can just imagine what the sand clouds were like, dunes and a medaro *(block)* forming at one's door after every bit of wind. I can only hope that things have improved, and will go through a better winter than last. Byrant himself seemed very cheery, and as most of us do, he wants the war to end quickly.

Amiens is quite a fine town, and one can get almost anything one wants there, lots of people about, but that are no gayeties on now, the dancing hall is turned into a restaurant and well run too. We finished dinner about 9.30 p.m. and left there at 11.30, arrived here at 2.30 a.m., and turned in after a very satisfactory day, and then lazed in bed until 11 a.m. with a grand sun shining in at the window.

Beatie seems to have had a rotten time with her teeth, but hope that she has quite got over all that by now, and is very fit and bushy.

What about Helen, is she coming out here as a V.A.D.? Expect she would thoroughly like to, and if she does must let me know her address in case I go anywhere near her. They seem to be going to bring a great many more doctors out here, which means opening a lot of big hospitals out here, which seems to be the only thing to do, considering the dirty tricks the Hun is up to.

Must close now, with just tons of love, keep very fit and God bless you all, my own.

Your loving
Harold

1 May –   Had quiet day at La Cauchie writing letters and slept. Very fine day.

8-5-17

2 May 1917

My own darling Con,
Just a short notita, as I am off out for the afternoon.

I cannot make out why you should go for 5 days without a letter; there must be something very wrong about the management and transport, as you should get a letter practically every day, as I only miss a day here and there. So if you go without a letter for several days you must not take any notice of it, as everything is all right, and no Bosch is going to worry me.

We are having most gorgeous weather; everything is coming out fast, and got quite a tinge of green. Pansies and several other flowers are out, that is in the line of primroses of various descriptions, but no good old-fashioned primrose.

The flying men are very active today and have a grand day for it, hope they will be very successful and knock spots off the Bosch.

Have just written a very long letter to Johnnie, and hope that it will reach him, am afraid some of them must have gone astray as he has never answered them and always complains of not having received any.

Am sending that parcel off for Bindy and Nancy, but now I look at the bonnet I do not like it at all, so you can give it to Mrs. Chandler or someone who has a kid, and will make a better shot next time.

Must close up, just heaps of love to you and the 2 bairns.
Your loving
Harold

2 May –   *Went to Doullens, shopped and had tea.*
                 La Cauchie.
                 Very fine day.

9-5-17

3 May 1917

My own darling Con,
Another gorgeous day, a huge battle raging in the distance, and are all anxiously waiting for news, and only hope that will be very good. In a way I am very sorry not to be there and see all that is going on, and know that things are going well.

Yesterday I went to Doullens for the afternoon merely to put in time and for something to do. We are all getting into our summer clothes, it is nice after having been trussed up the whole winter with all one could put on. This life we are leading at the present moment is too easy, and one is rather apt to get bored with it. The weather reminds me more and more of the day we spent at Beaulieu and only wish that you were here to complete the reality of it.

My two gees came over yesterday, and so I am contemplating a ride this evening, and try and get a jump or two.

I had a long dream the other night about *Lucero,* and dreamt that the trees had grown to a fine size, but that a lot of them had died and the remainder had grown so thick that we could not walk between them, afraid that it has made me long more than ever to be out there and look after them etc.

You must all be enjoying the weather and expect that it has put Bindy in great form, and she will be strutting about the garden as if the whole place belonged to her, and looking as fit as a fiddle.

A huge box of apples arrived for me from Aunt Bella, I think that they were on the road for at least 2 months, but arrived in very good condition and the men thoroughly enjoyed them. They are all very bucked with this rest and is making quite different men out of them, and look quite smart again.

Have not heard for sometime from Eric, hope Susan has got good news of him.

Must close now, oceans of love to you and the 2 wee bairns.
Your loving
Harold

3 May –   *Big battle going on. Had quiet slack day. La Cauchie. Went for a canter evening. Very fine day.*

10-5-17

4 May 1917

My own darling Con,

Am not getting any letters from you at present, so expect that the Battery is keeping them until I return, and will then get a budget of them. Expect to go back about next Tuesday or Wednesday.

    The shipping news seems to be very serious and the number of boats that go down is very great, and looks very much as if the Bosch has got the upper hand in that respect and hope we will soon devise some means of upsetting them.

    The weather continues gorgeous and seems to have properly settled down. The little garden I am sitting in is coming away fine, it is extraordinary the amount of work the 2 old folk get on with. The old man must be over 70 and the old girl not much younger, one sees them digging, hoeing and also loading manure, which is a very heavy job even for a young man, they pitch into it like anything and get it done. They run a small farm, 1 horse, 2 cows and a few hens, of course we get crowds of fresh eggs, butter and milk and almost live in the lap of luxury, it would be top-hole if the gooseberries and currants were on the go, we would be putting on kilos and kilos.

    Am having another very slack day, whenever I do this I have a fine old siesta in the sun and am getting a very vivid colour. We will have a great time of it when we get out fixing the garden up, and expect that there will be very little left when we do get back, and so start all afresh, excepting for the trees, hedges and shrubs which should be plentiful.

    Yes, Mrs. Cory Smith must be very bucked and will give her a great interest in life, but it is extraordinary what a number of girls have arrived, and rather bad luck especially as England will want the boys later on. Anyhow we are too jolly lucky to get anything and in another 2 or 3 years they will be grand, just to even think of them playing about on the grass under the willows, ash and paraísos, it will be a sight to do one good and be proud of.

    Three of the other stable mates went off to Amiens again but the more staid and married ones remained here, and I think are much the wisest.

    Let me know if this notepaper arrives alright, but am afraid that it might have the ends torn off it.

By the way, will you please send the small camera including some refills as soon as possible; that is what you sent sometime ago to Mr. Wilson to bring out. Hope to get a few good opportunities to use it.

Must close with just heaps and heaps of love, take great care of yourself and the little ones.

Your loving
Harold

4 May –   Battle not going well, no ground gained and a large number of casualties on both sides. Chersy taken by us and then retaken by Hun. Heavy cannonade all day. Grand day, very hot.

5 May –   Went to Doullens, hot dusty journey, brought provisions for mess. No news. La Cauchie. Fine day, very hot, small shower and got much cooler in evening.

13-5-17

6 May 1917

My own darling Con,

Yesterday we went to Doullens for the day and am afraid that I did not write. We had a very dusty journey there and arrived quite white with it. Anyhow we had a good wash and then lunched, did a lot of shopping for the mess, had tea and came back amidst another dust bath, so had another wash and felt very fit after it. After dinner we had a gamble at 21 and managed to win about 30cts. after 2 hours of it, so the betting is not ruinous.

It is much colder today and very refreshing as the last 2 days were very hot and steamy. Everything is beginning to look very nice and all the early trees have come out and look just grand, and the others are beginning to turn green, so in another 2 weeks everything should look just grand.

There has been another terrific battle, swaying one way and then the other, and should think that the honours have been divided, probably slightly in our favour, but one thing is that the fighting has been of a terrific struggle, and will continue so for sometime. We have now been out at rest for 9 days, and so expect to return at any moment now. On the whole we have had a great time of it and had our full share of sleep and rest and should be fit for another good struggle, and hope a successful one.

If you have not got that letter of mine asking you to send out that parcel you sent to Mr. Wilson to bring out sometime ago, and was returned, will you please send it as soon as possible, am very sorry I had not got it with me now.

Am going back to the battery loaded up with provisions and fresh vegetables, so they should enjoy them when I get back as they have not had anything of that description for some time. Am hoping to get some of your letters today as have not received any for 8 days, that is the penalty we have to pay for coming out to rest, and a rotten one too.

The Major we have with us is a very quiet harmless sort of a person, no go in him at all which is rather a pity, as it makes such a difference to all, so give him a miss in bulk and go out on our own.

What about this new rationing scheme? They seem to be getting a move on, and hope it is not going to be too severe, and also that all baby foods will be plentiful as it would be rotten to think that they would also suffer, but personally I do not think that it will ever come to that.

I see that Chile has broken off diplomatic relations with Germany and wonder if Argentina will do the same thing. If all these countries do it, it will be a big financial loss to the Hun and take him a long time to recover from it, in fact many years to gain his former forte.

Well how are the 2 kiddies treating you? You will have a great job looking after them but expect it will ease off after a short time and become less and less, until they are 4 and 5½ years when we will have to make a proper corral for them.

Well darling must close now, with just tons of love to you and the wee ones.

Your loving
Harold

6 May –	Took Chersy last night, number of prisoners taken 950. Day very quiet on front. Grand day.
7 May –	Quiet day at La Cauchie, evening ride to Belleville. Fine hot day.

☆☆☆☆☆☆☆☆☆☆☆☆☆☆☆

13-5-17

8 May 1917

My own darling Con,
A grand budget of your letters arrived yesterday, and was very bucked at getting them. Glad to hear that Bindy's cold was much better, and hope it has quite gone

by now. I cannot quite make out what you mean by saying that there is something wrong with Nancy's insides, is it that she cannot digest her food properly, or is there some wrong formation? I hope to goodness it is not the latter, and that it is only some baby complaint, and it does not worry her too much. Whenever the doc finds out what it is let me know.

Glad to hear that Susan was intending to stop a night with you, and hope you have been able to get her to stop more, it will be nice to have a good chat.

The spring cleaning must be an awful nuisance and you will be jolly glad to get it all over, those wretched drains must be an awful nuisance, and would most certainly put me against ever thinking of carrying on renting the place. It is very nice of the Turners offering to put the whole family up, and will be a great load for them, they must be very good sorts. I wonder where the R.G.A. (Royal Garrison Artillery) husband is, you might let me know his battery and will try to look him up, as there are a lot of heavies round us. At the present moment I can hear them rumbling away, and expect to be up there tonight or not later than tomorrow midday. This rest has been a great thing and the weather has treated us top-hole, and are all very fit except for one officer who has got a slight touch of cold or flu, and so will now be ready for a couple of months in the line.

I see by the papers that they say we are having very dry weather, so we are, but it is all to our good and the only thing we want rain for is the crops, which could do with a real good gentle rain, but are at present not suffering at all.

The 2 parcels arrived safely, which included pork pie, polishes, refill for the Tommy cooker, hankies, choc and cigarettes, y muchas gracias *(thank you)*. I do not think that it will be advisable to send any more pork pies during this warm weather, as they are quite liable to get a bit messy, although this one appears to be top-hole. Also I do not think it necessary to send any eatables excepting an occasional bought plain cake or a little chocolate, and that thick bar choc I like better than any, including the Aberdeen choc.

By the way how does our banking account stand, let me know when it is down to £60 and will write for another supply. I should not like to get it lower than this, as one never knows what might turn up and must be prepared.

Glad the bayonets turned up and hope that they have made a good job of them; they will quite a nice recuerdo *(souvenir)* to ornament our hall with.

Yes it will be great for Ethel having Eleanor down there and expect that Jack and her boy will have a great time of it together, it must be grand down there now, and should like to go and have a couple of weeks with them.

Nancy looks a curious wee person, but cannot see very much of her to say whether she is really handsome or not. But the nurse looks as if she had a night out and rather the worse for it.

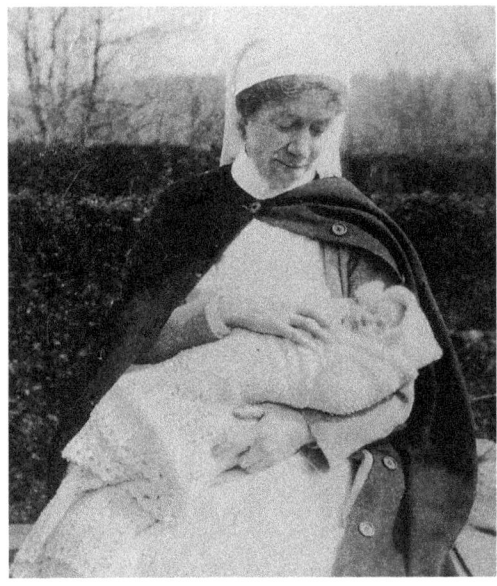

Nancy and nurse - 1917

Must close up now with oceans of love to you and the wee ones. Keep very fit.
Your loving
Harold

13-5-17

8 May 1917

My own darling Con,
Just a very hurried note before we go, the lorries are waiting for us and expect to be off in about an hour's time, and be back with the guns tonight. It is raining hard, ever since early morning and must say it is very refreshing, and no dust flying about, but all the same hope that it will soon stop and get the sun again.

We had our last gamble last night and I came off with about 30cts., which was rather good as I was left without a red cent.

Must close up with just tons and tons of love to you and the kiddies.
Your loving
Harold

8 May –   *Returned to guns, arrived about 7.30 p.m., very quiet.*
              Rained heavy in night until 12 p.m.
9 May –   *At observation post this morning, shifted gun position to ridge.*
              Fine day.
10 May –   *Came out of action to wagon line, reformed wagon lines and made dugouts.*
              Had football match in evening, gunners vs. drivers. Drivers 2 to 0.
              Grand day, very hot.

15-5-17

11 May 1917

My own darling Con,

Just a wee notita to let you know that we have come out of action for a week, I have been jolly lucky as I was the first to get out on the 10 days rest, then the secon lot went and now it has been stopped, and this new idea come in of sending the whole battery to the rest, so here we are.

We came out yesterday and started the rest by a football match, in which I played and quite enjoyed it although I did get rather done, but enjoyed it very much, and had a good cold sponge down in the open, which was grand and felt very bucked after it.

I see that the Germans predict a very hot and dry summer, and by the way things are here it looks like it in every sense of the word, but hope we will get a certain amount of rain to keep the crops going.

By now you will have got back to *Westhanger* and thoroughly settled down again. Yes, I expect the Turner girls are a very stout and sound lot, and no rot about them, but I do wish that they would dress decently; as I must own that it does make a very great difference to one.

Glad that you like the blouse and should think that it will go quite well with navy blue and expect you will look a great nut when I next come home. Yes it would be ripping to see the kiddies, and they look top-hole in the photos, but Bindy is trying to nurse someone nearly as big as herself and looks very serious about it all. Nancy looks fine in the one where you are holding her and very fit, and changed from the time that I saw her.

The cigs arrived safely and please thank your Dad very much for them. The only thing about them is that the tobacco is very dry, and with carrying them about I lose about half, as all the tobacco crumbles out. Please send me some in about 10 days time.

I got your cartita last night with poor old Flurry missing in it, it is just rotten to see one's pals gradually taken away, but can only hope that he is a prisoner and well looked after, let me know whenever you get more news. I wonder if anybody knows his mother's address, as I should like to write to her.

Must close, with tons of love to you and the 2 lassies.

Your loving
Harold

11 May –   *At wagon lines E. of Boiry-Becquerelle. Quiet day. Fine and hot.*

☆☆☆☆☆☆☆☆☆☆☆☆☆☆☆☆☆

18-5-17

12 May 1917

My own darling Con,

I am orderly officer today, which means getting up at 6 a.m. but as it is such grand weather I feel just the same as when out there, and that is when one is up. It is grand but the getting up is poor fun, but should revel in a great gallop over the country with you, one could go for miles without coming to a fence or a hedge, and all over grass so you can just imagine what it is like.

I have lost Thompsons, my tailor's address, so will you please write to him and ask what he would charge for a drill tunic, I want thin material, I thought that if he sent you several different patterns you might choose one for me, I want a real light summer drill and stars on shoulder straps, plain sleeves. If he does not charge an exorbitant price will you order one and have it sent out.

13/5/17

Also a pair of trousers, the khaki pair you have of mine, I would go to some other tailor but none of them have my size or measurement.

We have been shifting camp again, so had to finish this yesterday, that is the 3rd time we have been moved in 4 days, and am getting fed up with having to make a dugout each time, so am going to invent some sort of small tent which will not take up any room, and one that I can rig up in about 5 minutes.

The weather continues top-hole and we are all getting very tanned and fit. At present we are supposed to be at rest but our officer commanding is very hard on the men and works them too much and gives them no encouragement, which I call rotten as they have been fighting hard and deserve all one can do for them. I am so fed up about it that I cannot take any interest in anything and will be glad when we get into action once more as the men have a much better rest there and not booted about so much.

The pinny and cap went in a separate parcel about 7 or 8 days later, so expect that you will get it about now. This is a very uninteresting notita but will try and do better tomorrow, the war has calmed down for the present.

Well night night darling and crowds of love to you and the little ones.

Your loving
Harold

12 May –   Orderly officer. Quiet day.
                 Fine day.
13 May –   At wagon lines all day, quiet day.
                 Fine day.

☆☆☆☆☆☆☆☆☆☆☆☆☆☆☆

19-5-17

14 May 1917

My own darling Con,
We had a nice little rain last night, which has bucked everything up a lot. I went over to see Major Tytler, he was in great form and in the midst of having sports for his men, which they all seemed to be enjoying very much. They had wrestling on horse back, marking the pigs tail, a potato race with potatoes being lumps of chalk, an obstacle race, 100 yards sprint and 2 or 3 other similar events, and wound up with 2 casks of beer. The officers had champagne for dinner, which I think they rightly enjoyed and so far does not seem to have done any harm. What a difference between batteries, and one can see it the minute one sees the men. Here are our poor lot, not even given a half-holiday and are supposed to be in rest.

I should think it very doubtful whether you could join me anywhere and lately have not heard of anybody's wife coming over, but it may be possible next winter, that is if I cannot get leave to go out to B.A., which I shall long for.

I had a letter from Eric yesterday, he has been having a good time, and training behind the lines with the artillery, so conclude that he must be attached to them for carrying ammunition. Aunt Janie writes and says that Susan is quite her old self again, and picking up a lot, it is great to hear this and will buck Eric tremendously.

I suppose that you have had no news of Flurry, I have not seen his name in the papers as missing, and can only hope that there is some mistake and that he will turn up fit and well.

It has started to pour and blow and looks like a wet evening, but as we are all snug and well dug in it does not matter, and will do a lot of good to crops and grass, and will soon have tons of it for our gees, and will be grand for them to get in good condition and a decent coat on. I wrote to Johnnie and asked about your mares and whether they had any foals.

Must close with heaps and oceans of love to you and the kiddies.

Your loving
Harold

14 May – At wagon lines all day. Very quiet day, driving drill etc. Received notice of Military Cross. Boiry-Becquerelle.

Henin Hill

Battery sports, mounted and dismounted, were held, a well-run show, stage managed by two of the wagon line officers and a battery Sergeant-Major. Owing to the canteen having done so well, we were able to spend 1,100 francs on prizes, free drinks and so on. One of the comic events was an obstacle race in P.H. gas helmets.

Lt-Col Neil Fraser-Tytler, *Field Guns in France* – Pg. 169

"A" Form. Rec. 19-5-17. Army Form C.2121
MESSAGES AND SIGNALS.

TO 2 Lieut H M Murson

Sender's Number: AC 174   Day of Month: 14

I wish to congratulate you on your well earned award of MILITARY CROSS

From: Genl WILLIAMS

Lieut & Adjt.
149 Bde R.F.a

Enclose this, rather nice but do not know why I should have the chuck by it

---

SKY FULL OF STARS

21-5-17

15 May 1917

My own darling Con,

I do feel sad at the news of old Flurry, the more I think of him, and what I know of his life the sadder I feel about it. He did have a hard one, and mostly kicks and no sugar and now this on top of it all, it is truly hard and one cannot understand why a man like he was, full of common sense, practical and well read should not have got on in life. One seems to have most of the luck and another none and probably the latter deserve it very much more. I expect that one day we will find out the reason for it. I still somehow hope for the best and that he will turn up one of these days, and be able to catch hold of his honest paw, and give it a good old shake. There must have been very heavy fighting round there, much more than we ever hear of, and can only hope that things will break through, just think of the joy it would give the Serbians to get their old country back. I bet they will fight for it like devils.

Captain Bingham was wounded the day before yesterday, but do not think seriously, unfortunately it was through a premature from one of the 60 pounder guns. At present things are quite quiet here, but never know when they will wake up, in a way the sooner the better, as we must get this war over this year.

I cannot think why I had the luck to get the Military Cross, and can hardly realise that I have, and feel as if it was only a dream, as I have done nothing out of the ordinary, and never even knew I had been recommended for it.

Must close now as am off to camita, and will finish this tomorrow, so night night and take great care of yourselves.

16/5/17

I am going to return Flurry's letter to you, as I am sure to lose it. Have just read it over again and he seemed very cheerful and must have had a good rest, and enjoyed the spring and hot weather and can only hope that he was happy in his last moment.

By the way when my new tunic is ready will you get the ribbon on it, it goes over the left hand pocket in centre, and about $\frac{1}{3}$ of an inch over the seam. I had my old tunic finished, so have to wear the good one, which is rather rotten.

Must close, heaps and heaps of love.

Your loving
Harold

15 May – Orderly officer at wagon lines. Boiry-Becquerelle.

	Fine day, cooler.
16 May –	Driving drill morning, at new gun for afternoon.
4 men wounded –	Bombardier Young, Greaves, Simpson and another.
	Boiry-Becquerelle.
	Quiet day, dull and showery.

☆☆☆☆☆☆☆☆☆☆☆☆☆☆☆

Nelson
New Zealand
2017

Dear Harold,

I can see from your letters how much you cherished friendship, and probably none more so than with Flurry. I too have become so fond of him, he somehow completed my journey with you, the man from the place I now call home.

Once again I found Flurry through Horace Laffaye's work, and once again curiosity took over. It was a truly pivotal moment in the creation of this book when I discovered that Flurry was from New Zealand, it meant that there was a place for our story here, as well as England and Argentina, my triangle of countries. There have been moments in this creation where I have cried, and this was one of them. Like you, Flurry found a place in my heart. I have to tell you that at times he is called Fluffy as Isla got his name wrong; I doubt he would have minded.

He was born in New Zealand in 1886 in a tiny place called Te Karaka, near Gisborne. He was one of three children. His given name was Florence, a name more normally given to girls, although used more commonly in Ireland. His parents, John and Deborah were both from the Emerald Isle, John from County Cork and Deborah from County Kerry. They married in 1881 and I believe were farmers. I don't know when Flurry left New Zealand for a new life in Argentina, or how and when you met each other. You were both part of The Borderers polo team and shared a love of horses. I searched for his family and initially thought there was no one left, but have been thrilled to find he does have family through his sister Margaret, and I am now in touch with them.

Flurry is noted as a mayodomo, or manager, of *Estancia San Juan* in Las Moscas, he is remembered on the *Holt Memorial Cairn*, which was rededicated to the fallen from the province of Entre Rios in 2014. It was quite a ceremony with dignitaries present and all the names read out. The cross is known locally as Cruz de los Ingleses, the Prince of Wales inaugurated it in 1925, no doubt he was on another tour representing his father. So much can be shared through the magic of the computer that I have been able to watch the ceremony and hear Flurry's name read out.* It was quite an occasion, I am sure if the Prince of Wales had been able to leapfrog through time he would have been impressed with the service.

---

*   There are several clips on You Tube of the ceremony; the following one is the reading of names. https://www.youtube.com/watch?v=hMhI3ADpvCc

Holt Memorial Cairn, Ibicuy - Provincia de Entre Rios, Argentina 2014

Flurry is also remembered on the cenotaph in his birthplace, Te Karaka, a rather magnificent memorial topped by a lion. Mr. and Mrs. Hutchison who lost their son gifted it to the community.

The Cenotaph, Te Karaka, New Zealand

Flurry is recognised in New Zealand for his part in the war, even though he chose to serve in the British Army rather than with the many troops who enlisted in New Zealand. He travelled to England before you and was commissioned into the North Devon Hussars; he was posted to Salonika with the 10th Battalion of the Devon Regiment and was initially listed as missing on the 24th April 1917, in the first Battle of Dorian. You kept in touch with him throughout and I know it was devastating when you found out that he had been killed. His body was never found. I am so glad that I found him and can tell what little of his story that I know.

LIEUTENANT F. CRIMMIN,
of Te Karaka (Gisborne),
Missing, believed killed.

You mentioned that Flurry had not had the easiest of lives; I assume you lent him some money that he was bothered about and wanted to repay it. You encouraged Con to send him gifts and parcels; I bet he was thrilled to get his Christmas hamper. I hope were able to write to his mother when he died as you planned to, and offer her a modicum of comfort.

I imagine that one of the things that you felt contributed to his difficult times was the death of his father John, as reported here:

The inquest on the body of John Crimmin, which as found hanging in the wool shed at Rangatira station, Karaka, was held at Rangatira yesterday before Mr. J.A. Ceaser, J.P. and a jury comprising Messrs. Jas, Orr (foreman), J. White, J.E.C. Price, C. Neenan, D. McDonald, and W.J. Brown. Detective Nixon represented the police. Evidence was given by the deceased's wife, Mrs. Debra Crimmin, who stated she saw her husband last at four that morning. He told her he did not feel well, and said he had a pain in his chest, but seemed quite cheerful. He went to see Mr. Patullo with the object of proceeding to Kanaekanae, and stated he would return for breakfast. As deceased did not return, Mrs. Crimmin went to the station, and saw his horse tied up at the shed. Witness was unable to proceed with her evidence and fainted. – Frank Patullo, station manager said he found Mrs. Crimmin at 5.30 a.m. in the shed and she was in a great state. Crimmin was there apparently dead. She said she found her husband hanging by a rope in a sheep pen, and immediately cut him down with a pair of shears. Witness knew no reason why deceased should commit suicide, except temporary derangement of the mind. Crimmin had held his position for the past 15 or 16 years. He was about 42 years of age, and came from Ireland 23 years ago. He was a fairly healthy man, and steady. – The jury found that the deceased hung himself while in a despondent state of mind, owing to ill-health, which caused temporary insanity.

Poverty Bay Herald 2 December 1902

It must have been devastating for a young man of 16 to have to deal with the death of his father by suicide, something that would take a long time to come to terms with.

It was such an irony that you heard of a Flurry's death on the very same day you were awarded the Military Cross for you bravery. I cried for you both. Flurry has his own verse in the *Ode to the Borderers*, written at *Estancia Marabu* in 1913: -

> The first to be mentioned is "Flurry"
> Who is always ahead in a scurry
> On any old screw
> He will back up his crew
> And gets many a goal in a hurry.

No doubt you saw your future with Flurry as part of it, playing polo and sharing your victories and defeats together, but it was not to be.

In Memory of
Lieutenant

F Crimmin

Royal North Devon Hussars who died on 24 April 1917

Remembered with Honour
Doiran Memorial

**Commemorated in perpetuity by
the Commonwealth War Graves Commission**

Flurry also has his certificate from the War Graves Commission showing the Doiran Memorial in Northern Greece, where he is remembered. There are two inscriptions carved into the stone, written in both English and Greek, as well as the names of the fallen.

"In glorious memory of 418 officers and 10,282 other ranks of the British Salonika Force who died in Macedonia and Serbia 1915–1918 and to commemorate 1,979 of all ranks who have no known grave but whose names are on the panels. They did their duty."

"The land on which this memorial stands, is the free gift of the Greek people for the perpetual commemoration of those of the British Salonika Force who fell in the war 1915–1918 and are honoured here."

The Doiran Memorial also has a lion on it, a great match for the cenotaph in Te Karaka. Lions on memorials act as guardians for the fallen, and signify courage and strength. Two lions guard Flurry, one in the place of his birth and the other in the place of his death.

I hope that his end was not too horrid, that it was quick yet also that he had found time to make his peace. There is so much that we will never know, only little cameos of your lives, but a little insight is better than none at all.

Congratulations on receiving the Military Cross, Harold, I am delighted your bravery was recognised.
With love
Sheila x

22-5-17

17 May 1917

My own darling Con,

My batman is just sewing the ribbon on, so shall be a great nut strolling about this afternoon, but somehow I feel very much I should like you to do it, any how you can do it on my new one.

I did not enclose Flurry's letter in last, as it was only one of those folding envelopes, so am putting it in this; and hope it will arrive safely.

The weather has quite changed and has rained a lot, and continues damp and dull, but after all those fine days we can put up with a bit of this sort, and will do the country a lot of good. By the papers they seem to be complaining a lot about the drought in England, that it has done damage to the crop and corn. I do not think they really know what it is to have a dry spell, although the ground and soils of England do not retain the moisture like the Argentine soil.

You must have a great gathering of cousins for Sylvia's birthday, and hope you all had a great time of it, and that the two bairns did not get too mauled about, they must have had a rare old dose of it, that is if Sylvia is at all like Maudie. But when we get out there Bindy will be able to look after herself, and be very particular of the way she is handled.

That husband is a lucky fellow (Turner) and I bet will have a nice easy time of it and jolly glad to get back, even if it is only for 6 weeks.

I see by the papers that Russia is very unsettled, but hope she will behave like a man and stick it out to the end, but it looks as if it might easily be the other way, which will rather upset our plans and may prolong the war, but anyhow think that it will be over this year. As everything is run by politicians one never knows where one is standing, or what will suddenly turn up.

What about Nancy's christening, isn't it about time that it should be done? 7 weeks old and getting such a huge girl, and will know what cold water is like and probably kick up a fuss. Glad to hear she does not howl so much, but expect they all do at the beginning and some keep it up and others don't, so hope that ours are the don'ts.

All the gees are just going to be groomed so must push off and see them, so hasta mañana. Heaps of love to you and the wee bairns.

Your loving
Harold

17 May –   At new position 1/2 day and at wagon lines rest, easy day. Put Military Cross on first time.

Boiry-Becquerelle.
Rained during night and day, cool.

23-5-17

18 May 1917

My own darling Con,
This battery have done very well, Captain Jones, Lt. Gray and B.S. Major all mentioned in dispatches, we are all very bucked about it, as we have done as well as anybody.

Our seven days rest is now up and we go back tonight, but I think only for 3 or 4 days, but one never knows, so we always expect anything.

It is very bucking to hear that Nancy is getting along so well, and also to hear that her inside is quite alright and hope it will always be very fit and well. It is funny to hear that one so young as Bindy should take such a liking for a baby, and must be ripping to see them together, and when I do, will thoroughly enjoy it and have a great time of it, and hope that it will be very soon.

The last rain has freshened the weather up a lot and made things very nice and cool, and as you say the spring is just grand and I revel in it, and do not think that I will ever get tired of the sun.

So Donald has gone near Gaza, he will have pretty warm weather there, and get as brown as a berry and properly acclimatized for the Argentine.

Am enclosing a wee bit of ribbon, as I know that you more than all helped me to get it, and sorry that you cannot wear it, but the King will not allow it.

Well dearest, must close as am off to the guns in a short while. Best of love and take great care of yourself, and heaps of love to the kiddies.

Your loving
Harold

18 May –   At wagon lines, moved up to new position evening,
6 guns. One of our planes brought down.
Boiry-Becquerelle.
Fine day, windy.

19 May –   At guns morning and observation post noon. One of our planes brought
down and one Bosch plane brought down on our lines. Guns fairly busy.
Grand day.

☆☆☆☆☆☆☆☆☆☆☆☆☆☆☆

25-5-17

20 May 1917

My own darling Con,

We are having another stiff day of it, and had a fight this morning and is still going on, so do not know what will be the issue of it, but I think successful, it has gone fairly alright so far, just one or two little stickys here and there.

It has been a hot day but must say I thoroughly enjoy it, and does one a lot of good, but is rather like a mild north-wind day in the Argentine, just north of the Torro.

So you went to Guildford for an outing and expect must have enjoyed it after your long stay at Godalming, and only wish I had been there and taken you up to London, and if I were you, I should most certainly have done so and must say that you well deserve it. Anyhow we will have a great time of it when we do get there.

There is no news so will close, am feeling very tired. Yesterday we had great excitement with a Bosch plane, it came very low over our heads and anti-aircraft guns and our planes and we were all sniping at it, and down she came and we captured both the men.

So hasta mañana, and hope to have good news for you shortly. Heaps of love to all.

Your loving
Harold

20 May –	Attacked Hindenburg line 5.30 a.m., took front lines and failed in support lines, attacked 7.30 p.m. Took 170 prisoners, fired 1000 rds. At observation post 9.30 till 2.45, at guns rest of day. Fine day, hot and muggy.
21 May –	Fired 200 rds. Came out of action in evening. West of St Leger. Fine day, hot.

☆☆☆☆☆☆☆☆☆☆☆☆☆☆☆

27-5-17

22 May 1917

My own darling Con,

Here I am, out again and had a good fight the day before which turned out successful. We got all we went for, and took about 170 prisoners, and also gave the Bosch a bad time of it in his counter attacks, in fact the men he brought up to counter attack had such a bad time, that he had to give up. We could see them coming at a run over the ridge, and gave them a rotten time of it, they must have got a great number of casualties. It is one of the finest pieces of work I have seen done, and a good lesson to the Hun. I expect to be out for 10 to 12 days and probably to a long way from here. I am very bucked at this, as if the weather holds up, will enjoy the march thoroughly and be grand going through country that has not suffered through this war.

I got your letter last night with the letter from *L. & Co.* enclosed. It is bad luck and do not know what to do about it, in fact I cannot do anything and is a great relief to me that Johnnie is in charge and doing much better than I could, although it is much more satisfactory doing it oneself, and to be on the spot. The great thing is that they seem to have a good rain and with another about now, hope to pass through a good winter, and am sure the grasses will come up better than Johnnie expected. I must say that I like doing alfalfa at this time of year, and hope it will make good grazing on cutting next year, when I hope we shall all be out there and settled down once more. We will have to try and get some new agreement with Rodriguez or give the camp up next January, I have written to Johnnie about this and so he can do as he thinks best. The furniture is the nuisance, and if we give up the place must try and get it stored at Blancos, Charlone, and that means getting our house built as soon as we get out there.

We had a big rain last night and all this morning, it has done a lot of good but everything is all slush and mud, but these long days soon dry things up.

Had a letter from Ethel last night, she seems very cheery and all the kiddies are very fit. She intends stopping there for the winter, as this bad time out in the Argentine is affecting her, as the sugar factory is not paying any dividends, very glad we sold our shares when we did.

Must close now, will write to you when on the march. Heaps of love and take great care of your dear selves.

Your loving
Harold

22 May –	At wagon lines all day, getting ready for march.
	Boiry-Becquerelle.
	Rained hard during night.
23 May –	Marched to Habarcq via Boisleux-au Mont, Ficheux, Wailly and Dainville

24 May –   Marched to Maisnil St. Pol via Izel-les-Hameau,
                    Ambrines and Maizieres-Fermes – 14 miles.
                    Habarcq.
                    Grand day.

30-5-17

25 May 1917

My own darling Con,

Have missed two days and have only a few minutes to write this, so will be very short.

About the tunic, you can choose what colour you like, but should like a drill, but if the thin cloth is nicer will take that. I want the stars and collar badge, the belt you can miss out.

We have been on the march the whole time and are all tired, but is doing us a lot of good, and nice to get away from the line for a few days, but will not be long out. They have taken us out from a hot place, and are putting us into another one, the famous salient of Ypres, so will have a gay time of it. I think that Eric must be somewhere round there and hope I shall come across him.

We are having grand weather and getting more sunburnt each day, and I am so fit that have given up my remedio for the last week or two. I got your Dad's letter, he asked for particulars re M.C. It has not so far been in *The Times* and will tell you in my next what it was for, which is not very much.

A huge parcel arrived from you, but so far I have not opened it, muchas gracias. At present we are camped by a little stream in a very nice spot amidst trees, but are only here for one night. The country we go through is just grand, lilac and everything out and looking top-hole.

Will write a long one tomorrow, so night night dearest, and heaps of love to you all.

                        Your loving
                        Harold

25 May –   Marched to Amettes about 15 miles via St. Pol –Valhuon, Pernes and Aumerval.
                    Amettes.

1-6-17

26 May 1917

My own darling Con,

Here we are after another day's march, and this time had quite a short one, and a grand day for it. It is just ripping going through the country and seeing all the trees, hedges and flowers about, tulips, lilacs and rhododendron in full swing. As we get more north the people are much more friendly and have better houses, cleaner and take much more pride in themselves and what belongs to them than the southerner does. We are now in the flat country and can notice a large difference in the quality of the soil and crops, and look well excepting for some of the early sown wheat, which is rather scraggy.

Am glad to say that some of our men are going on leave now, but do not expect it will be for long, most of them have been out here for 20 months, so will hardly recognise their wives or children, and must thoroughly enjoy themselves.

Had a ripping letter from Susan, and glad to hear that she is much better, and only hope that the specialist she was going to confirms Dr. Hurley's ideas. She says that Peter is a huge fellow and is bullying Janet's girls now, afraid he will be a terror. It is rather funny Nancy getting Eric's smile, must be in the family and hard to get rid of, the extraordinary part is that Susan says it is a very nice one.

Well dear you seem very anxious to know what I did to earn the M.C., it was nothing, and what thousands of others have done and not nearly so much, in fact I was jolly lucky to get it, and do not deserve it in the least. I have not been told what it was actually for, but one of the two following things or both. The day after the famous Easter Monday battle I was sent out to find out where our infantry were, and also to send in good information of how the battle was going on, and the advance we were making, so up I went and found out the former exactly, and also saw how the battle was going and sent in my reports. It was one of the most interesting days I have had and saw a lot, there was one funny spot in it. I was with the infantry forward and we got word that the village in front of us had been taken, so the Colonel asked if I would go over with them, on which I said yes if my officer commanding would agree, so I rang up and was sometime getting over, in which time the infantry went over and got quite a shock, as soon as they got over the bridge the machine guns started and down they had to flop, losing a few men, so the rest retired.

The second thing is that I went up after another fight into the front line to try and find an observation post, this I could not find as there was no place of vantage to observe from. I joined 2 more officers, and then we heard a shout about 20 yards over the parapet to the rear, where there was a wounded officer, so up we got and found him shot through the thigh, we got a stretcher and had him back, the dirty Bosch were sniping hard but with rotten shots, so we got back and then sent the fellow off to the dressing station. This is only for your information and must on no account tell anyone. Personally I believe the M.C. was given on account of the former, and also for my work on all the new gun positions I was making before I went home. Anyhow I shall probably hear one of these days.

At present am sitting on the bank of a canal, a grand evening and gorgeous sun, which is very bucking. Well dearest, must close with just heaps and heaps of love to you and the kiddies.

Your loving
Harold

26 May –   Left Amettes for Wittes via Amis Lieres, St Hilaire, Mazinghem, and Lambre-Aire. 11 miles
Grand day, hot.

☆☆☆☆☆☆☆☆☆☆☆☆☆☆☆

Nelson
New Zealand
2017

Dear Harold,

Your granddaughter Angela is the guardian of your medals; she keeps them on your old wooden chest, with a photo of you and flowers in a shell case – just as Con did.

Your medals are in a frame with the cap badge of the Royal Field Artillery on the top.

Harold's medals

On the reverse is the acknowledgement from King George VI that you gave up your life; there are some letters that you simply wish had never come your way.

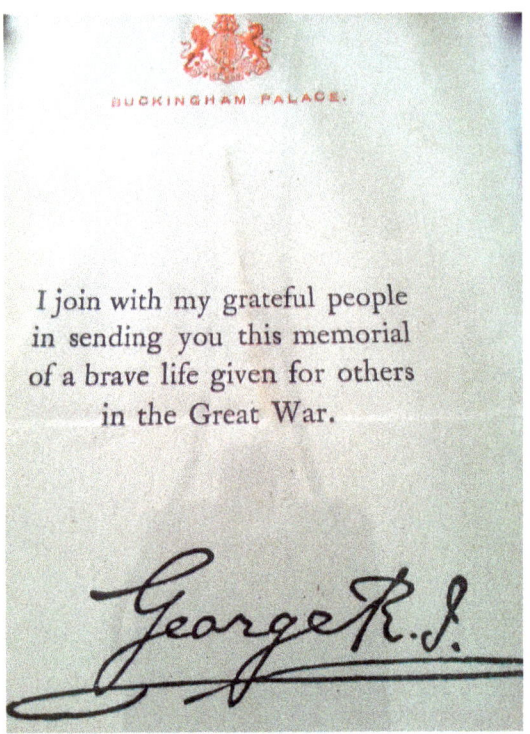

The round plaque on the top was given to those who died and is known as the Dead Man's Penny. It is engraved with Britannia holding a trident and a lion, dolphins signify Britain's sea power and a second lion is tearing up the German eagle. The words engraved around the edge are "He died for freedom and honour". Britannia holds an olive wreath above your name; however there is no mention of rank to show there was any difference between all who gave their lives.

Your three medals hang underneath. You wondered why you got the Military Cross and had a couple of thoughts, this is the official version as noted in the Edinburgh Gazette on the 20th July 1917: -

2nd Lt. Harold Methven Musson, R.F.A.: Spec. Res.

For conspicuous gallantry and devotion to duty. He was acting as F.O.O., and established himself close to the objective. When the advance was held up he went forward under heavy fire and joined the infantry, and returned with information of their position. Throughout he sent in most valuable information.

In an earlier letter I mentioned briefly that Isla had read her poem at the Anzac Day service in Wakefield, New Zealand. What I didn't mention was that she was wearing the miniature of your Military Cross, which had made the journey especially for that day, bundled up and flown from England to New Zealand. Isla wore it on the right side of her chest as etiquette dictates. She read the poem beautifully, standing on the stage talking into a microphone so we all could hear, including those who had not been able to fit into the hall and were listening outside.

And so we have shiny medals to admire, ones for bravery, ones for simply being there and ones for the ghosts that will never know they got a medal and a letter from the King. The heavens must be extra busy in times of war and conflict as the queues form from all sides for their entry into the hereafter, friends in death rather than foes in life.

With love
Sheila x

1-6-17

27 May 1917

My own darling Con,

Here we are very comfortably billeted, but only until tomorrow when we will be on the move once more. This place is a fine old farm, by a long way the best I have been to, very clean and comfortable. Of course the chief attraction are 2 girls here and we have a great time with them, they are most cheery and keep one on the go the whole time. Yesterday they took some photos of us and themselves, which I will enclose in my next of reads. I can quite understand why Eric had such a fine time in one of his billets, they are the first really nice lot I have struck, and will be a great shame to get away tomorrow. Never mind old girl, expect I will get over it one of these days.

Have just woken up from a fine siesta under a cherry tree, one of the oldest I have seen and just full of fruit. The blossom has been very fine this year and with any luck should be a great deal of all kinds of fruit. The men are all enjoying a bath in the canal and have had an easier time of it today, and so are more cheery and just revel in this weather, and are very fit.

I see that the Italians have started their offensive, and done fairly well, and would be a great thing if they would only capture Trieste, it would be a fine blow to Austria, who will put up a great fight to retain the place.

About my getting leave as Madge mentioned, it is quite out of the question, and I have never heard of it being done, and at the present time am certain that it is not done, so you must not place any hope on it. Will you thank B and H for their letters, afraid that I will have no time to answer them, as must write out to B.A. as soon as possible.

My trousers also arrived, y muchas gracias. Do not trouble to send any more chocolate out, as I eat very little now the weather has got warmer and give some of it away.

No news so will close up, just oceans of love to you and the bairns.

Your loving
Harold

27 May –   At Wittes all day, had a fine old slack. Gorgeous day.
28 May –   Battery marched to Borre via Boeseghem, Steenbecque, Hazebrouck and L'Acffe. Captain Jones and self came forward to reconcile battery position and returned to Borre.

☆☆☆☆☆☆☆☆☆☆☆☆☆☆

4-6-17

29 May 1917

My own darling Con,

We are still on the move, and am afraid have missed a couple of days, have hardly had a minute to ourselves, and when we do finish our day's work I am quite tired and too slack to do anything. The incoming post has been very good, and had a letter from your dear self every day. In your last you say that I did not answer a question of yours, but I did and expect that you have got it by now.

Now I have to learn a fresh language, and it sounds very funny to hear it spoken all round one, but will soon get used to it, but am sure never learn a word of it.

This has been a fine cool day, and thoroughly enjoyed it. Am afraid that this will be a very short one as post is just about to go, and must not let it go empty on my account.

It must be just grand to spend these days in the garden with the kiddies, and quite imagine the fun one could get out of it, and can quite see that little girl of ours flying about.

Well night night, and very sad that this is such a short one, but better a little one than none at all.

Your loving
Harold

29 May –   Marched to Watou, Belgium. Quiet day. Fine.

4-6-17

30 May 1917

My own darling Con,

Here I am on the last days march and it has been top-hole all the way through, and so quite ready to have another go at Bosch.

The Italians seem to be doing really well, 23,000 prisoners is quite a good haul. Altogether we must have taken about 30,000 and hope it will soon be over 100,000.

The part of the country we are now in is much more fertile than the one we left, everything seems to grow so strong and well, and the flowers top-hole. I am sure we appreciate them much more coming out of action, as all these lovely flowers show up so well after the torn up and mutilated country we have left. Also it is great to see the cattle grazing in grass up to their knees, and all the calves about, reminds me very much of the lecheras (milk cows) at *Lucero*. One thing we must get out there is a hawthorne hedge, they look just grand, not clip it, just let it grow wild. In a few years time, with any luck we will have a top-hole place, and never want to leave it.

Glad to hear that Beatie is much better and her old self, how does she like being at home? I had a letter from Kathleen the other day; she seems to have thoroughly enjoyed her stay at home and saw a great change in Bindy and liked her very much. She was away for a long time and expect it will be a good while before any of us get away, as there is plenty of work to be done, and the sooner it is done and over the better, and all get home for good.

The cigarettes arrived quite safely, and are quite alright, it is no good trying to get the Argentines as they do not import them now.

The last raid on England seems to have been rather unpleasant, I cannot make out why so many people are up against us making severe reprisals and do double the damage that he does to us. If we persisted in it am sure it would do a lot of good, as it is we sit down and twirl our thumbs, it makes everybody here fed up and long for something to be done.

There is no news so will close. Just heaps and heaps of love to you three.

> Your loving
> Harold

30 May – Marched to east of Poperinge and came into Ypres, brought 2 guns in and took 4 guns over. Came in by Dixmude gate. Quiet day. Fine.

31 May – At observation post during night, quiet. Quiet day, shelled town as usual. Fired about 100 rounds. Fine day.

☆☆☆☆☆☆☆☆☆☆☆☆☆☆

Spring / Summer 1917

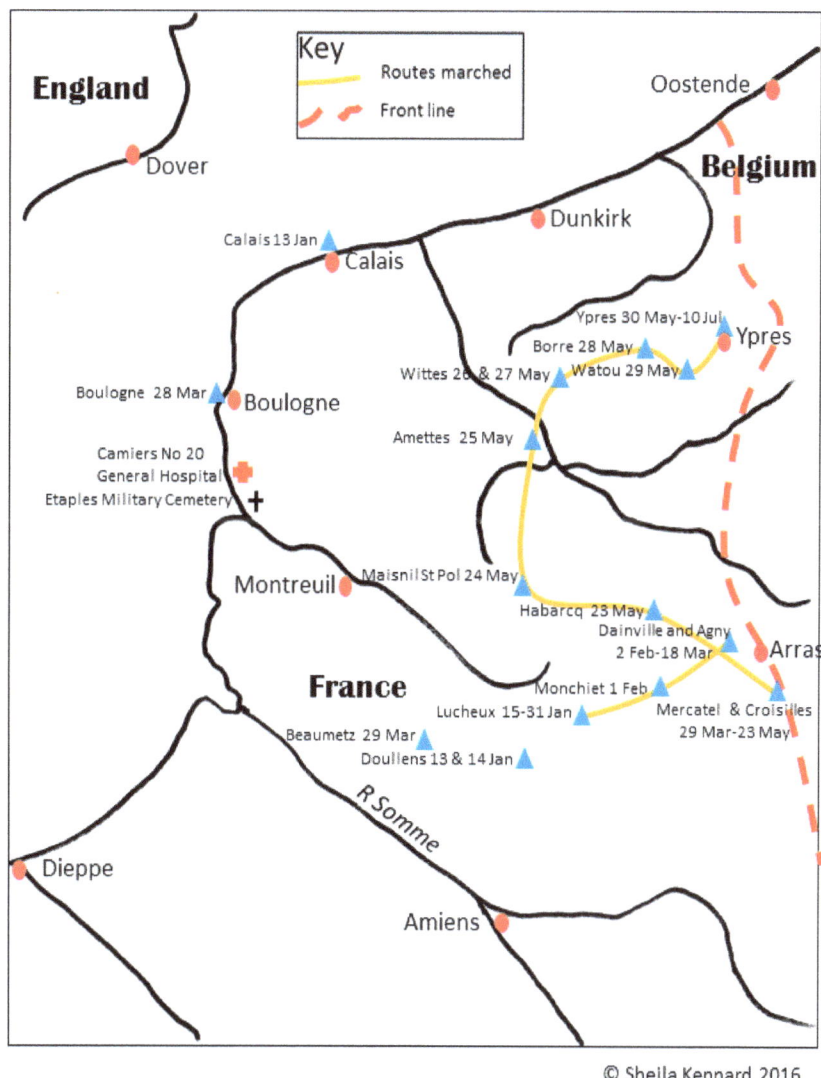

Places and dates mentioned in Harold's diary of 1917 – including the route marches.

June 1917

Bindy, Nancy and Nurse, 1917

You may give them your love but not your thoughts,
for they have their own thoughts.
You may house their bodies but not their souls,
for their souls dwell in the house of tomorrow,
which you cannot visit, not even in your dreams.
You may strive to be like them, but seek not to
make them like you.
For life goes not backward nor tarries with yesterday.
Kahlil Gibran *The Prophet*

6-6-17

2 June 1917

My own darling Con,

You will be getting very fed up at getting these rotten short notitas, but one's time seems to be filled up every day.

I had a short notita from Eric last night, he is quite close to here and wants me to meet him at a place close to here, and will try to do so next week, that is in about 7 days, as I will not be able to get away before.

Where I am now it is very hard to get used to all the different sounds, and everything appears to be much closer than it really is, if a shell bursts it sounds right over one's head, but in reality it is 100s of yards away.

I have got my dugout decorated with your photo and several snaps of the kiddies, which make it look top-hole, I share it with the Captain, and so can keep him in order.

Lucero will once more be going through the winter months and all the leaves etc. will be off, but hope that it will not be such a bad one as the last, and that the stock will be well fed, and not forced to use the hay that they bought from San Rafael, as that is rather too expensive, although hay will be dear all over the country.

Last night we did not have dinner till 11 p.m., nice hour, but were too busy with the Bosch to have it before, but better late than never, anyhow we had a good one, and then turned in and had a fine old sleep.

It is extraordinary how the weather keeps up, fine everyday, and not much wind which is great, of course one does not feel it so much out here, as in the camps, on account of the ground being uneven, and more trees about.

Mail just off, so tons and tons of love.

Your loving
Harold

1 June –	Shelled battery heavily, Sgt. Croft killed, Gn. Wilson and Coleman wounded. Fired 150 rounds, town shelled. Ypres.
2 June –	At observation post afternoon, quiet day except for the other batteries being heavily shelled. Town shelled. Fine day.

7-6-17

3 June 1917

My own darling Con,

I got three of your cartitas last night and very bucked to hear that you are all so fit, but afraid that you must have felt that hot day very much. Here we have had some very hot ones, but have thoroughly enjoyed them, and feel very fit on them, and very glad that we have left all that old weather behind, and hope that the war will be over before any more comes.

Fancy a year ago being that grand day at Beaulieu, on the whole it has gone quite fast and I never thought for a minute then that one would have gone through such a lot, and that the war would not have come to an end, and that I should have been away from you for so long, and also lost one of my greatest pals.

I got *L. & Co.'s* letter, with copies of Johnnie's, and must say that the news is much better, but wish that he would get rid of the cattle and not risk too much. Also he does not give any detail of the cattle we have and where they are, also the number of deaths we have had, so cannot piece things together and have them all pictured in my mind. Also he has never acknowledged any of my letters, so do not know if he has ever got them, my next one I will send on to you and you can forward them, as I think that it is the safer way.

Glad to hear that you are going to have Nancy christened, and that the 2 godmothers will be present. Expect you will have got a proxy godfather. Had a nice long letter from Gilbert and appears to be very bucked at becoming godfather, so am afraid that he has not arrived at years of discretion, or he would know better. He takes it rather seriously, but of course it is nothing except an honour to be Nancy's godfather. I will try and drop a note to him if time permits, as I must first of all write to Kathleen.

Yes, I should most certainly like to have time with you and the wee kiddies once more, but am afraid that it will not be for a long time, but one never knows, and may be sooner than I expect. Bindy must be getting a great walker and very bucked with herself.

The cake arrived safely, but very crushed, they either have to come in tins or wooden boxes, but do not worry to send any more, as we get any amount to eat and can well do without them. Also it is too hot for chocolate, and have still got some of the Kincardine and Cadburys left, so shows how little I eat it.

So you have Nancy in shorts, it is much better now that it is getting so hot; personally I have no use for those very long baby skirts, and cannot make out why they should be so long.

Well dearest night night, and heaps of love to you all.
Your loving
Harold

3 June – Put up a practice barrage, fired 150 rounds, otherwise a quiet day. Town shelled. Fine.

8-6-17

4 June 1917

My own darling Con,
Another grand day practically gone, and have had a nice slack one, but had a very strenuous one last night, will tell you about it when I get home and go over my little notebook.

Just had a very hurried note from Eric saying that he would meet me on the 8th, so hope that nothing will crop up to prevent it.

The cigs arrived safely from Van Raalts, and will thoroughly enjoy them. Last night we got the electric light going, but about 11 p.m. it suddenly went out, so think that Bosch must have taken a dislike to it, and had to light the candles once more, which is rather a come down.

No news at all, so I am going to have a short sleep before dinner.

Just heaps and heaps of love and take great care of yourselves.
Your loving
Harold

4 June – Last night heavily shelled by gas shell from 10 p.m. to 3 a.m., put over about 7000 rounds, no damage to battery. Several casualties in other batteries. Ypres.
Fine day.

5 June – At observation post afternoon. Bosch knocking blazes out of 18 pounder batteries, otherwise a quiet day, fired 600 rounds.
Fine day.

10-6-17

6 June 1917

My own darling Con,

You seem to be going to have a big haul of visitors and should think that will be glad when it is all over, although it is very nice to see all your friends and relations, but I think that a steady stream of anybody gets rather tiring. A pity that you could not get along to Aunt Janie's, as she would have just loved to have you and the kiddies for a few days, but all the same I think that you were quite right in not going, and you could not leave your old Dad alone. Aunt Janie wrote me a very disappointing letter and felt very down hearted about it all. She said they were most likely going up to Ballalie either at the end of this month, or first week in next. How perfectly ripping it would be to go with them for a month or so, the weather must be just grand in those parts, and to feel a good salmon on the end of one's line, one can almost feel his vicious tugs to break away for freedom and life, and I do not blame him.

So the pram has at last arrived and looks good, and can quite see Bindy not wanting to get into that cramped little one of hers.

Very bucked to hear that Nancy is going to be christened on the 16th, and if I have the chance will drink her health on that day. She will be nearly 3 months old, nearly as old as Bindy when we left Argentina to come home, so will picture her as such. Do you remember what a chuckle Bindy had on her, used to go into fits and thoroughly enjoy a good joke. Does Nancy still continue to have Eric's smile? If so she will never have such an open laugh as Bindy has. She looks ripping in her photo, and would love to catch hold of her, even if only for a few minutes.

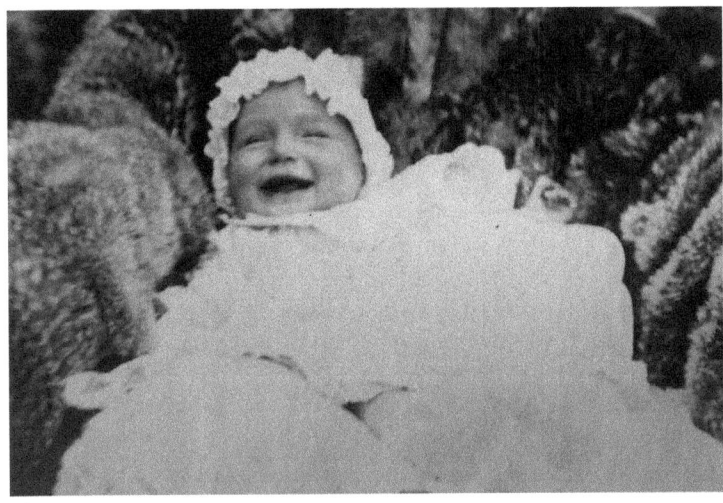

Nancy, 1917

Yes, the roses make one long to be out there, but I think that everything does, and makes one want to at get them and look after them a bit. Afraid that the monte *(woodland)* must have had a bad mauling by the locust, which will put everything back a good deal, and the fruit trees will have done badly, but with careful pruning should come away alright. The ligustrum hedge (privet) we put in round the tennis court and kitchen garden has had a very poor time of it, what with frost, seca and locust, will be jolly lucky if it ever comes away. The gooseberry plants have no hope for, and will have to start all those things afresh, but never mind it will be good for us.

At present am sitting in a snug little O.P. and a grand breeze blowing through a slit with all the smell of fresh green leaves and flowers blowing in with it. There is a fine old moat close to here which has been very battered and torn by shell, in fact everything is ragged and torn, and in this there is a white swan that has been there the ever since the war started, the only thing not hit by shell. It swims about proudly as if nothing in the world was wrong, it is rather extraordinary to see it sailing about.

Chaplain Thomas Tiplady, Army Chaplains' Dept.

For three years the storm centre of the British Battle front has been at Ypres. Every day and night it has been a standing target of thousands of guns. Yet, amid all the havoc and thunder of the artillery, the graceful white form of a swan has been seen gliding over the water of the moat. It never lacked food, and was always welcome to a share of Tommy's rations. (Then) a shell burst near the swan, and it was mortally wounded.

Somehow the swan seemed a mystical being, and invulnerable. It was a relic of the days of peace, and a sign of the survival of purity and grace amid horrors and cruelties of war. It spoke of the sacred things that yet remain – the beautiful things of the soul upon which war can lay no defiling finger. Now it had gone from the water and Ypres seems more charred than ever, and the war more terrible.

Richard van Emden: *Tommy's Ark: Soldiers and their Animals in the Great War.*

---

6 June – At observation post morning, very quiet day. Bosch put a few gas shells over, fired 600 rounds. Fine day.

7 June –   Big attack at 3.10 a.m. from Messines to Wytschaete, very successful, gained all objectives and took 4000 prisoners. Finest opening of attack have ever seen, saw 4 mines go up and thousands of rockets. At observation post all night. Grand day.

8 June –   Heavy fighting still going on, total of prisoners 6000 all going well. Had dinner with Eric in Poperinge.
Ypres.
Fine day.

☆☆☆☆☆☆☆☆☆☆☆☆☆☆☆

Nelson
New Zealand
2017

Dear Harold,

Today is Anzac Day in New Zealand, I didn't go to a service, instead I baked Anzac biscuits as a different way of remembering. Such a shame I can't send those back through time for you to munch on. I do wonder what happened to all the tins that cakes were sent in; it must have been so nice to get those food parcels, however I did think sending pork pies was an interesting idea, and imagine they may have arrived in quite a state.

I did ask Ben if he would like to wear Nancy's medal when he was part of his local service as a Kea, but he declined, he was concerned that a pin may make a hole in his shirt. He has the most delightful way of thinking laterally about things.

This is also the last letter I will be writing to you, although you will be reading a couple more before the end of our book. I wanted to end on a day that had also marked the beginning of our journey of creation.

I also wanted to draw your attention back to the swan on the moat at Ypres. The swan looks so serene as it glides over the water as battles rage nearby, a living demonstration of beauty and grace. So symbolic of all of you who no doubt tried to be as serene as possible, whilst paddling like mad inside to simply stay afloat and alive. I loved that the swan lived for so long; I guess it was inevitable that it would meet a horrid end, as did so many young men on the battlefields they did not choose.

I do also want to share with you words from my daughter Laura, as she remembered Anzac day and her beloved grandparents, who all took part in the Second World War.

> Today in particular I remember my 4 grandparents who each went out and fought for our freedom in WWII. Noel Kennard, the Captain, an eternal shy nomad and storyteller, a man who fascinated me, the man that gave me my love of words and the English language. Bindy Kennard, the Colonel, who growing up one of my closest allies, she always made me feel 10 feet tall, Kathleen Kitchen, the Nurse, with her gentle warm, but feisty spirit whose smile was always such a warm safe place and Hedley Kitchen, the Soldier Musician, who I will still always remember as my toughest goodbye when I left the UK to embark on what would be a new life, I have carried that hug and those tears with me everyday since. Today I thank them for all they did for us and the world we live in, but most of all I thank them for making me who I am today. I carry a bit of each of their fighting spirit and who they were in my DNA, and to be a part of these four greats is nothing but a privilege.

Noel and Bindy Kennard
Kathleen and Hedley Kitchen

I have mentioned before how proud you would be of your great grandchildren, which of course is the point where you and I meet, and combine forces with the blessings of our genes.

I wonder how much Jim is like you, one aspect that makes me chuckle is around your obsession with socks and shoes. For you it was a case of having enough pairs to keep your feet warm and dry, for Jim it is getting ones that fit, and keeping them away from the dog, who likes to carry them around and so puts an accidental hole in them. You both have big feet, although Jim's are more enormous than yours were.

I have loved writing to you, sharing things that I think you would have liked to know. None of us know when death will come to call on us, your invisibility cloak slipped on the day you were wounded. For so many who did return life was never the same again, the wounds were often the invisible ones that gnaw away at the soul. Those returning from your war and the Second World War didn't talk much of things they went through, although for some it was their finest hour. Jim and I grew up knowing little of what our parents went through, I only learned of my father's experiences when he was ill and he started to speak of things when very poorly. He didn't remember telling me, but was delighted when I gave him a written copy, which he then expanded on.

I hope that by exposing us both in this book that we can make a little bit of difference to the state of the world. Peace and understanding has to be the best way forward for us all.

With love

Sheila x

13-6-17

9 June 1917

My own darling Con,

Well I had a great 5 hours with Eric, who is very fit and well, and has great hopes of getting home on leave in 2 or 3 days, which will be just ripping for them. No, it is no good in me trying to get leave at present as I was the last to get it, and must now wait patiently until my turn comes round.

Eric is going to try to see you, and also have a good talk about getting leave to go out to Argentina this winter, and try to get away about the beginning of October. It is urgent after the bad year we have had, and also the rent for Rodriguez camp will be up, and so must try to get a new lease, or a bit of Salsis camp. The great trouble is that we could not take the girlies out; and so should like to have your ideas on the subject, and whether you would care to come out or not. Eric is going to put in for it too, and so would be just great if we could all four go, and leave the kiddies behind, as I should not like to risk taking them along, and would not be worth it for the short time we are out there, as most of our time would be spent on the sea and rushing about on the other side. Anyway you think it well over, and have a talk to Eric, and let me know what you think about it. If you did not come over I would go out and return as quick as possible, and spend the remainder of my time with you.

I left my hat and coat in the hall, so hope that nobody has pinched them, but expect you will find that one of the girls has put them away.

Well dearest, since last writing there has been a great fight, and have done very well, have not heard the details completely yet, but think we have taken about 6000 prisoners and some guns, and got all we went out to get and a little more. I have seen several big attacks, but never saw such a fine sight as this one, and that is from a spectacular point of view, 3 or 4 huge mines went up of ours, and the display of signal rockets on the part of the Bosch was a grand sight, and then the guns and bursting shell was a finishing touch. I wish I could write well, but have not got the gift to do so. We were not actually in the fight, but very near it and so could see most of it. Hope to hear today the definite results, but expect that you will see them in the papers long before we know. I am at the wagon line for a few days and help to take ammunition etc. up to the guns, which on the whole is not a bad job.

Am going over to see Eric in an hour's time so must close this, and will write a long one tomorrow. The mail is coming very well, and get your cartitas 2 days after your write them.

Just heaps and heaps of love to you and the little ones, and keep very fit.

Your loving
Harold

P.S. Please send me a couple of thin khaki shirts, there should be some at *Westhanger*.

9 June –   Prisoners 7000. Went over to Proven in afternoon to
            see Eric and saw the Red Cross sports.
            Fine day.

☆☆☆☆☆☆☆☆☆☆☆☆☆☆☆

14-6-17

10 June 1917

My own darling Con,
I went over and spent the afternoon with Eric, and had a nice quiet time of it. There were some Red Cross sports on, so went over to see them, they were quite good and the men seemed to thoroughly enjoy them. It was very hot, but that made it all the better, they had one very cool competition that was tilting the bucket. If you missed putting the stick through the hole a bucket full of water came down on your head. I think that the men enjoyed this more than anything. I am expecting Eric over this afternoon for tea.

"Tilting the Bucket" - Picture courtesy of the Lurdy Blog (www.lurdy.wordpress.com)

I think that our old battery hold quite a record, there was Captain Tytler and 4 officers in it. The Captain got the D.S.O. and Croix de Guerre, and 3 of the officers the M.C. He is very bucked about it, the officer who has not got it was recommended for it, and by some bad luck did not get it as I am quite positive that he deserved it as much as any of us.

I started this about 2 hours ago lying down, and I must have fallen asleep as have just woken up and find it is 4.30 p.m. already and nearly tea time, no sign of Eric so conclude he has been held up somewhere.

Glad to hear that you have taken some snaps of Bindy and hope that they turn out good. Eric showed me a lot taken of Peter, he has got a huge fellow, and looks very cheery, some of them were very good but a lot made him look far too old and not at all like himself. Eric is very keen on seeing him again. He is taking you home a cartridge case from a Bosch 5.9 howitzer. I thought of having it made into a flower bowl and mount it on a black oval stand. If you think of something better let me know. I am also going to try and raise a gong, as I told you about when I was home, but afraid that there will not be much chance of getting all the pieces unless I once more go down south.

We are in very good quarters, but for the time of the year they are too shut in and deep down, and one feels very mouldy in the mornings. The mess is a very swank place, fine white tile table, plush sofa and several small tables and chairs about, and the place crammed with flowers, so you are not the only one who can have flowers on your dinner table.

I expect that picture in the Academy of guns going into action is very exaggerated and showy, as in today's warfare we go in at a slow walk, plump them down and away go the gees at a slow walk once more, it is very tame and nothing thrilling about it, except when Bosch livens one up with a whizz bang or pip squeak, and then we make for the strongest dugout and nobody is to be seen. That old style of dash and run is a wash out.

No, it is not worth sending the book out, but thanks very much for thinking of it. Afraid I entirely disagree with you Dad and PW's idea of reprisals and if they were out here for long they would quickly change their minds, they would not worry our prisoners any more than they are doing and if they did we could return the compliment, and as we have more prisoners than them, could give them the llapa *(bit more.)*

Must close now, heaps and heaps of love to you all.

          Your loving

           Harold

10 June –   Took ammunition up. Total prisoners 7350 and total guns 47. Quiet day. No. 1 gun knocked out, 500 rounds of ammunition blown up. Fine hot day.
11 June –   Quiet.
            Fine hot day.

☆☆☆☆☆☆☆☆☆☆☆☆☆☆☆

17-6-17

12 June 1917

My own darling Con,

Last night I met Eric and we went to a divisional performance, which is the best I have ever seen. It was really top-hole, and there were some turns every bit as good as you would get at the Palace or any of those places, and we thoroughly enjoyed it all. Of course the scenery was not so luxurious, but was plain and good. When one is there it is hard to believe that they are so near the line, and so much pleasure in one place is missing in the other. It does all the troops a lot of good to see these shows, and bucks them up tremendously.

The country round here is very dry, and could do with a real good rain, but rather looks as if we are in for a real seca, the crops are still looking well, but will soon want a real good refresher. Luckily the roads are very good here, and all the main ones paved with these square blocks of granite, so not much dust flying about.

This last battle we have had has been a great success, and got all we wanted to, and glad to say that the casualties have been fairly light, and the Bosch very heavy. I think that the Kaiser must be beginning to scratch his head, and wonder what he can do next, but will have still more cause to scratch it sooner.

Last night I met Leonard Lacy, who has managed to get the Military Cross. He has grown into a fine lad, and is very like Monty. Very nice boy and gets on jolly well with everyone. Taking that family all round, one could not find a better one, there is something very fascinating in them, and could not have better manners. He is in the Army Service Corp and Lewis is in the King's Horse. Both of them have applied for the R.F.A. and if they get in means 4 weeks in Blighty, and then a very exciting career after.

The Bosch has not got his own way now, and we are always on the top of him, on the ground and up above.

This evening am going over to dine with Eric, and he is most likely to come over here tomorrow, so will have had a good innings with him. Must close, as the post will be soon away.

Heaps and heaps of love.

Your loving
Harold

12 June –   *Quiet.*
            Fine.
13 June –   *Quiet.*
            Fine.

☆☆☆☆☆☆☆☆☆☆☆☆☆☆☆☆

20-6-17

14 June 1917

My own darling Con,

Here I am just had my bath, 1 p.m. and I have got a notita from you. Only got to bed at 6 a.m. after a very big night of it, and now ready for tonight once more and for the next 2 or 3 nights, nearly all my work is done during those hours, then I hope things will become normal once more. Have been living in a tent for the last week, they are very nice and one makes oneself very comfortable. At the moment I am having my lunch, which consists of bully and very choice lettuce and radishes, and inevitable bad half-cold tea. We are having very hot weather here, but must say that I like it, top-hole, and the rain seems to be keeping off, but nearly every day it looks as if we are going to get a thunderstorm, and each time it disappears.

Have not seen Eric for 2 days so hope he has got home. Susan will be most frightfully bucked, especially getting him home at this time of year as you can spend nearly all your time in the open and probably have one or two little outings on the rivers, it is about 7 years since I spent a summer in England.

When I got your letter this morning I had more or less half woken up, and when I was reading about the roses and flowers I quite thought that you were writing from *Lucero* and describing them, what wouldn't I give for it. You will have got my letter by now telling you about my idea of trying to get out this winter, and am most certainly going to have a very good try for it, as the more I think of it, the more I see the necessity of it, see what your Dad thinks about you coming. If we both decided to go out I think that we could probably hire a cottage by Ethel's, or somebody like her, and then she could keep an eye on the kiddies, or at Eastbourne. About leaving them at *Westhanger*, it would be too much for them, and also in the end harder to break away, as your old Dad would feel it much more. It is a very knotty question, and will have to be gone into very carefully, one thing is that we have got plenty of time, about 2½ months, as should like to get away about the middle of September. It would be top-hole to be landing there in October, would get in for all the roses and the best part of the spring, we could go and stop with Johnnie.

By the way when I first came home I wrote to the Daimler Company asking the price etc. for spare parts of cylinders for the car. I think their answer is in my dispatch case, if so will you please quote the number of their letter, and ask them to send the prices as soon as possible, and will send them straight out to B.A., and have it ready by the time we get there. I get keener on it every day, and looking very much forward to it. I think that the Colonel will work it out for me.

You are having a rare lot of visitors, and glad to hear that Bindy is assisting you to entertain them. She must be becoming very attractive and long to see her.

Must close up and get ready for tonight. Just heaps and heaps of love.

Your loving
Harold

14 June – At wagon line all day and moved lines to Ouderdom.
Hot day.

15 June – Gray took 2 guns up to new position at Zillebeke. Took ammunition up.
Farrier wounded and Moaks died.
Fine hot day.

21-6-17

16 June 1917

My own darling Con,
Yes, Thompson's have been a very long time over my tunic and if you have not received it by the time this reaches you, I should tell them to keep it. It is a pity as it would be very much appreciated during this hot spell, on second thoughts do not cancel it, as they may worry you, and it is not worth it, I will stir them up when I get home.

I believe that Eric may have gone home, as have not heard or seen him for the last 3 days, hope so.

That last air raid seems to have been serious, and we do not appear to have brought any of them down. This still convinces me more that we should visit them as often as possible, and in and by every conceivable way and means. Personally it makes my blood boil to think of the feebleness we show in not retaliating in the same way, and so bring it home to the German public that there is a war on, and we can return them in their own coin. Hope that they did not come anywhere near you and that they will keep away.

It has been very hot here, and the crops are beginning to suffer a bit, and the trouble is that it does not look a bit like rain.

At present I am not up at the guns, but with the gees, that is why I get the night work, as we cannot take the ammunition up by day. It is not a nice job, and Bosch makes himself unpleasant at times, but the great thing is when we get back we are not under fire, and can have a decent rest.

Also it is rather nice country and the people round here are very clean, and have quite a different appearance to the French, on the whole they are much fairer, thicker set and look much more like Dutch and most of the girls can now speak a fair smattering of English, and some well. The only trouble about them is that everything they have got is for Tommy, and we have a great job to get anything from the farms, and have to send a Tommy to get it.

Glad to hear that the spuds are doing so well, and after the hard work put into the place your Dad well deserves a good result, round here there are lots of spuds. You mention in your letter that Beatie and Guyen have gone to a 'pension' but do not say where or what for; so afraid am rather vague on the subject.

Must close with heaps of love to you three, and take great care of yourselves.

Your loving
Harold

16 June –   Went up with ammunition, quiet night. Ouderdom.
17 June –   Gray went up with gun from Ypres and Zillebeke, quiet night. At wagon lines all day. Very hot.

☆☆☆☆☆☆☆☆☆☆☆☆☆☆☆☆

22-6-17

18 June 1917

My own darling Con,

The tunic arrived this morning and is quite a good fit, excepting that it catches badly under one arm when I want to lift it up, but this I can soon get fixed up, as we have a tailor in the battery who is quite useful.

No, it has not rained at all here, and everything is just shouting for it. It looks rather like it now, and hope we will get a good thunderstorm tonight or early tomorrow morning. The heat was bad yesterday and hardly any breeze to buck things up, today there is and it is quite nice.

It is just ripping to think that you will come out with me, as I thought that you might not want to leave the kiddies, and it has just got to come off. Of course there is always the risk of a submarine, but think that we will just have to chance that. Will have to make full arrangement about the kiddies, and then get back as soon as possible, and be with them for 2 or 3 weeks.

When you write to Jum give her my love and all congrats on the new arrival. Yes, your Dad was fairly close to the bombs, that is the second time and hope his last, as it is not a very pleasant experience, and a thing one never gets used to and never takes a liking to.

The reason everything sounds much louder is that we were in a town and so the echo and walls make a very big difference, thank goodness we are now out of it, and well in the country, some of the trees have even got a few leaves on them. Yes we had roses on the table, but nothing half as good as the *Lucero* lot.

Will close as there is no news. Just tons of love to you and the wee ones.

Your loving
Harold

18 June –	Went up with ammunition last night, shelled, took gas and 190 rds., no casualties. Bombardier Booth killed, 2 guns knocked out. Sgt. Mason badly wounded. Very hot, started to rain.
19 June –	Major Kirkland wounded. Moved to new gun position. Eric came over to tea and dined in Poperinge. Fine rain.

23-6-17

20 June 1917

Darling Con,

Just a very hurried notita and enclose a letter to Johnnie. Also as Eric is here have not much time.

We had a fine old rain here, and it has done a lot of good, still looks like more and expect it will, it is still quite warm.

Have not had a notita for 2 days but as they have been coming so well I cannot grouse.

Heaps and heaps of love to you and the 2 kiddies.

Your loving
Harold

20 June – Quiet day. Went up to Shrapnel corner and fixed up wagon that had got turned upside down.
Rained during night, fine day.

25-6-17

21 June 1917

My own darling Con,

Well I had a nice quiet evening with Eric, and very much enjoyed a good long talk. He had no further news of his leave, but was expecting it any moment; so hope it will come soon, and that he will have a jolly good time of it.

Fancy J. Fair getting the Military Cross for that job, I do call it a rotten shame and it is making it all very cheap. Our Major went away the day before yesterday wounded, but glad to say not seriously, and will probably get a couple of months rest, which he will be jolly bucked about, and also give us a bit of a rest.

Well Nancy's christening seems to have gone off very well, and as you say she is a very lucky girl, and her godmothers have been far too good to her.

Yes this hot weather is rather too hot, but now it has turned very cool, and is very refreshing although I did not feel the heat much. I am quite fit excepting for my teeth which are rotten, and am going to try to get back to have them fixed up. Also I have a boil or two coming out which upset one a little, but those will soon go, and it is a long time since I have had them, whenever I see the doctor will have a good talk to him.

Have just received 2 huge parcels of anti-fly outfit from Sir A. Yarrow, so must try it as soon as the flies come out, and if it is really good will take some to the Argentine, although I think that nothing will beat that little flapper Aunt Bella sent.

Some of the crops are looking very pretty here, as they have a lot of red poppies in them, and they are such a ripping red, it would be worth collecting the seed of them, but quien sabe *(who knows)* where I will be by then.

Fancy it is nearly a year since I came out, and it also feels it, and seems a very long time since the Somme battles. We have moved and done so much since then that it appears as if we could not have done it all within a year.

Lucy has been very lucky, and hope he will go on being so, and not be in such a hurry to come out here. I was only wondering the other day what could have happened to him, he is a slacker re writing. Expect he will get another couple of months at the barracks, and then wind his way out.

Sorry to hear that Bindy was not well, what about too much christening cake? Anyhow hope she is much better.

Heaps of love to all, and a huge kiss.

Your loving
Harold

21 June – At wagon lines all day. Suspect Bosch to be retiring. Ouderdom. Showery.

22 June – Went up to guns evening. Bosch planes brought down and 2 of our balloons. Bombardier Morris and Waring killed. Gunner Yates seriously wounded. Showery.

27-6-17

23 June 1917

My own darling Con,
Nancy's bit of cake arrived safely yesterday, and looks very good and will have it for tea, hope she enjoyed it, am sure it would do her a lot of good. Was Bindy allowed any of it? But expect Aunt Janie spoilt her with tea, sugar and all the tidbits. Got a fine box of chocs from Susan, so in case I have not time to write will you thank her for me.

I know where you got the rumour of me getting my Captaincy, but at present there is nothing doing and you will be the first to know when I do, so will you put an end to the rumour. I do hate these things going round, afraid that Eric was the culprit as I told him that it might come along.

Before I forget, will you please send along some more of my remedio, Colgate toothpaste and Wrights coal tar soap.

It is fine and fresh after the last rains and has bucked everything and everybody up very much, trees etc. look so fine and green and seem to freshen one up.

My tunic is rather tight under the arms, so when we go back to rest will have to get a tailor to fix it up. The material is just the right thing, and so you appear to be a very good judge of what is wanted.

Am afraid that there is very little we can find out about Flurry, the only thing is that if he has got any old keepsake I would like it sent out to his old mother, so will you write and find out, or if you like I will.

Am very keen on getting those snaps of Bindy, and hope that they are good, as I have none of her grown-up self.

Am glad to hear that Aunt Janie has rented the flat, as I am sure she was getting very fed up with it, and as she is getting on she feels the burden and worry of running it. Also it will be great for Susan to have a place to go of her own.

Yours with the snaps has just arrived and I like one of them very much. About the Daimler, among all my papers you will find a letter from Daimler saying that they can supply the prices I require, so will you fish it out, quote the prices and correspondence and tell them to dispatch them to *L. & Co.* as soon as possible and I will write to *L. & Co.* about it. Let me know what Daimler say.

Heaps and heaps of love to you and the wee ones.

                      Your loving
                      Harold

23 June –   At wagon lines all day, went up to guns at 10 p.m. with ammunition, arrived back 4 a.m. Gas shelled us badly. Bosch brought down 2 of our balloons. Fine.

28-6-17

24 June 1917

My own darling Con,

I got yours about leaving the kiddies with your Dad. I do not think that it would do the slightest harm to them; my only meaning was that your Dad might get so attached to them that later on it would be a very hard knock for him to lose them. But most certainly if you think it would upset him to take them away we will most certainly not do so. The great point now is to cheer him up as much as possible, and not give him any worry at all.

Re passport for you, I do not see why there should be any trouble, and will have a good fight to get one, as far as I can see there is no reason why they should not give you one. Anyhow we can find all this out soon and if Eric has not got the time I will get someone else to do so, anyhow there is not much need to worry about it at present and lots of things may turn up before then. Anyway I hope all the submarines are all knocked out by then.

Just tons of love to you and the two girlies.
Your loving
Harold

24 June – 2 guns knocked out, blew up 500 rounds. Bosch brought down one of our balloons. Captain Jones evacuated with nail run through his foot. Went up to guns, Bosch shelling back areas and batteries hard, put up several dumps.

☆☆☆☆☆☆☆☆☆☆☆☆☆☆☆

30-6-17

25 June 1917

My own darling Con,
Just another very hurried notita, as am just off up to the guns to remain there. The weather is just grand here, nice and cool and thoroughly enjoy it, so hope you are having the same. No, we have not had any very fierce winds, which we can well do without.

The subs seem to be at it hard again, I often wonder how many we do capture or sink, expect a good few, but if we are, they must be making them at a great pace. Of course they think that it is their last chance of winning the war, and probably it is, so must do our best to keep them under.

Yesterday we brought down two Bosch planes, and they had the cheek to bring one of our observation balloons down in flames, but the two men parachuted down in fine style.* Personally I should not like the sensation of having to jump and trust to the parachute, don't know how to spell it; anyhow you will know what I mean.

The kiddies must be enjoying this weather and expect out the whole day long, even for their siesta, or won't Bindy sleep outside?

Must close now, heaps and heaps of love and more to yourself than anybody.
Your loving
Harold

25 June – At guns and observation post. Went to see Col. re gun position and will remain in same. Fairly quiet. Fine and warm.

---

* Balloon shot down by Heinrich Gontermann, a German fighter ace.

3-7-17

26 June 1917

My own darling Con,

Afraid I am too late to catch the post tonight, but it will go tomorrow, so here goes. Am again at the guns and very busy, as I told you in my last the Major was wounded and the Captain ran a nail through his foot and gone, so at present I am in charge of the guns and a rare old mess there is, will tell you all about it when I see you, so do not forget to ask, as it will be rather interesting.

Will you please get a copy of what Eric is sending you and send them to Lt. F.W. Walker, Bushmills, County Antrim, Ireland. Am enclosing a fine picture, which is not so bad and I hope you like it.

Am just off to camita, so night night and heaps of love.

27/6/17

I sent you a field postcard thinking that I would not have time to finish this, but will have a whack at it now, although there is no news to give.

Have heard from the Major and he is at one of the general hospitals, and getting along quite well, and ought to be home very shortly. I see by the papers that the Americans have sent a lot of doctors and nurses over, and have taken some of the hospitals over; I bet they will turn out good and thoroughly up to date, and do their work well.

I met a fellow called Watson from Esperanza, quite nice to get a whiff of the place. I do not expect that you know him, as he was more of Batteria way, he has just been awarded the Military Cross and is very bucked about it. He is in the trench mortars and at present having a fairly easy time of it.

Am living in a wretched cellar once more and do not like it at all, and be glad when we get out into the open. We are having grand weather once more and feel fit, but do not like the job of running the battery, and be glad when the Major is back to take it over, as the responsibility is a little too much, especially where we are.

Yes it must be great to see our little lassie amusing herself on the lawn and in the garden and expect that she finds any amount to do, and will turn out a great gardener. Have all your visitors come to an end now?

Well dearest, will close, heaps and heaps of love and take great care of yourself.

Your loving
Harold

26 June –   Round guns and making out fighting map.

27 June – Zillebeke.
Fine, hot.
Quiet day.
Fine.

☆☆☆☆☆☆☆☆☆☆☆☆☆☆☆

3-7-17

28 June 1917

My own darling Con,
I got 3 of your notitas last night and glad to hear that you are all very fit. Your description of Bindy makes me long to see her and all her little ways, they must be ripping and get more interesting every day, am very sick of missing them, but hope that Nancy will be the same.

Time seems to fly and mail is just off, have not had a minute to myself, but hope to have in a day or two. We expect the Captain back in 3 weeks.

Must close, heaps of love.

Your loving
Harold

28 June – At guns all day, fixing of pits and making plan of position. Quiet day. Fine and dull.

☆☆☆☆☆☆☆☆☆☆☆☆☆☆☆

4-7-17

29 June 1917

My own darling Con,
4.30 a.m., have just finished sending all the men etc. away, and am remaining up here for a few hours to see that everything is straight, so as I do not feel sleepy, will have a wee chat to you, especially as my letters have been very third rate for some days.

We had another nice rain last night which has freshened things up a bit, but still looks and feels like more. We are going back to the wagon lines for a week's rest, which hope will do the men a lot of good, they well deserve it and do not think they have ever had a worse time. But now they will all thoroughly enjoy this and get a bit more rest than if the Major was here.

I wonder if Eric has gone away yet, will try and get over to see him in a day or two. As I have very little to do this morning am going to try and catch a fish. There is a fine lake here, and the only trouble about it is that all the shell that fall into it kill a lot of the fish, which eventually float up to the side of the lake and become rather smelly. But it is a fine sight to see the shell explode in the water; a spray of water goes up for about 100 feet.

Now my servant wants to leave me, and he is quite right too, as he wants to try and better himself and has no chance if he remains a batman, so now he will return to driver and try and work himself up to N.C.O. *(non commissioned officer)*. If he feels that he can gain satisfaction he should most certainly try, as we want good men badly.

I was quite unsuccessful at fishing, and think that the fish must have the wind up and strongly dislike the shells, do not blame them, and if I were them would get into the deepest part of the lake and stay there until we have pushed Bosch away back.

It is very hard to realise that Bindy is nearly a year and 10 months old and we have been married nearly 4 years, in fact getting quite an old couple, but hope to see a little more of you in the near future. When one comes to think of it, since January 1916 we have had jolly little time together, and think it is about time the war ended and let us make up for it.

Must close now, with heaps of love to you and the wee lassies.

      Your loving
      Harold

30/6/17 – Have arrived down safely and hope to have 7 days peace and will very much appreciate it after being up there. Has been raining all morning but as I slept well from 11 p.m. to 11 a.m., and only woke up for breakfast it did not worry me, only decent sleep I have had in the last 6 days, and am now going to have a siesta.

      Your loving
      Harold

29 June – *Round position. Quiet day.*
30 June – *All personnel went down to wagon lines for 7 days rest. Bosch guns very active. Fine hot day.*

Nelson
New Zealand
2017

Dear Harold,

I imagine one of the hardest things about dying for you was the not knowing how your girls turned out, especially Bindy as you knew her so much better than you knew Nancy. She appeared to be the apple of your eye, and you had high hopes for her future. I can tell you that she lived a good life and you would have been proud of her. It must also have been so hard for the girls, as they grew up loving a father they had no memories of. You were a photo on a shelf and a figure in stories told by those who knew you. They had nothing to grasp a hold of in the way my children and grandchildren do – they can reminisce of happy days spent together and laugh at the silly old duffers that Jim and I sometimes are.

The girls' grandfather, Richard John Williams, known to them as Dandan, played a large part in their lives; I know from your letters you held him in high esteem.

John Richard Williams (Dandan) with Bindy and Nancy 1917.

As you already know, both girls attended Hayes Court School as boarders, followed by finishing school in Switzerland. I have a couple of letters that Bindy wrote to her mother from Hayes school; she does not tell us the dates they are written, so I don't know how old she was. The first was written from the sick bay, where she was sent with an earache, she had great fun putting the address on her letter, it took up an entire page: -

Sick Room, Nr Nurse's Room, Nr Isolation Room, Nr Bathroom, Hayes Court School, Hayes, Nr Bromley, Nr London, Nr Kent, Nr Middlesex, England, Nr Ireland, Nr Scotland, Nr Wales, Europe, Northern Hemisphere, Temporal Zone, Nr Arctic Ocean or Equator, the Earth, The World - a planet near the sun.

In a later letter she tells Con, in her childlike way, of a lecture about Hayes and the schoolhouse, telling her it was about 200 years old and goes on to say,

"Sir Vickery Gibbs used to live here and he was very wicked as he walled up a man alive in one of the dormitory walls and his skeleton was found when the lights were being put in".

I'm afraid many years elude me, I met Bindy a year after Jim and I married, we met in Hong Kong and took the opportunity to spend our first year of marriage there. I was young and pregnant with our first baby when I first met Bindy, and I confess that I did not find it easy. It took us quite some time to settle down to each other, but we eventually found our peace and harmony. She was an excellent Granny to all her grandchildren; I know our two children, Laura and Alastair loved to spend time with her, and I am sure that their cousins, Alanda, James and Grace felt the same way. She was able to offer them shelter from their storms.

Bindy joined the Auxiliary Territorial Service (ATS) when Britain was once again at war. She did very well for herself, reaching the rank of Colonel. A very senior member of the ATS was Christian Fraser-Tytler, the wife of your much-admired Captain, I wonder if their paths ever crossed although they would not have known the connection. Bindy inherited your height, no doubt the tallest amongst these marching ladies that she is leading.

Bindy returned to Argentina in 1947 where she met up with the man she had long admired, Noel Kennard of *Estancia Marabu*, perhaps you even met him although he did spend most of his childhood in England. He was ten years senior to Bindy and marriage did not come easily to him. He had lived an adventurous life, serving in the elite Z-Special Force in Australia during the war. However, Bindy got her man and they settled on a farm in El Bolson in Patagonia, growing fruit alongside their family. They had four children, Jim being the eldest, followed by Olivia, Gillian and Angela. Gillian died when a small baby. Jim was christened Conan James Montrose but he grew fed up with people saying his name wrongly, changing his name to Jim when a young man. Our son and two grandsons also carry the middle names of James Montrose. Eventually the desire for better schooling and English rural life drew Bindy back to England although perhaps Noel was a little more reluctant. They eventually settled in South Devon on a 30-acre farm called *Colmer*, where they bred horses, had handfuls of dogs and created a welcoming environment for many people. Argentina was becoming increasingly unstable and has since been through very troubled times, no doubt the family led a safer more stable life in England. Jim has spent most of his working life on the ocean wave. Olivia did not marry, but is an amazing aunt to her nieces and nephews and loves gardening. Angela is a gifted artist and mother to Alanda, James and Grace.

Con did not remarry, she returned to Buenos Aires when her first grandson, Jim, was born, she was able to spend lots of time with the family, and watch your grandchildren grow. Con moved back to England with them in 1963, setting herself up in a very comfortable cottage on the farm, I know it was a

very comfortable home as my wee family spent some time living there. She lived there until her death in 1975.

Noel died in 1983, Bindy had cared for him through his years of declining health. She then moved to a smaller home, enjoying life in Dartmouth, Devon, often entertaining and sharing her home with many visitors. She died in 1997 aged 81, with Jim, Olivia and Angela by her side. As I was collecting Laura from Liverpool University, where she had completed her first year, we were unable to be with them. However, Laura insisted on opening her belated birthday present in the room where Bindy's body lay, the paper rustling as she chatted away to her as she did so, such was her relationship with her Granny. I wonder once again if you were there to meet her, the last of your three girls to join you, your family complete once again in the great beyond.

Con, Bindy and Noel are all buried in North Huish Church yard in South Devon. On the day of her burial, Con's niece Buddy, daughter of her youngest sister Helen, gave Jim a brooch, which had belonged to Con. It was a gold bar with a pearl in the middle and a diamond on either end, apparently Con used to say that you were the pearl and Bindy and Nancy the diamonds. Jim gave it to me for safekeeping and I have since had it made into a ring, the pearl sitting between the diamonds, as I too think of Jim as my pearl and our children Laura and Alastair as my diamonds.

It was not the life you planned for them as you pondered over the future from the battlefields of France, but I am certain that all in all they led a good, comfortable and fulfilling life. You left a hole that could not be filled, but they worked around that hole as best they could. Con had a portrait painted of you on their return to UK, so you were certainly a presence for the family. I have a small copy of it on my wall, your eyes seem to follow me around my room, you are long gone but not forgotten.

With love

Sheila x

July 1917

Harold on ice – date unknown

Only when you drink from the river of silence
shall you sing.
And when you have reached the mountain top,
then you shall begin to climb.
And when the earth shall claim your limbs,
then you shall truly dance.
Kahlil Gibran – *The Prophet*

6-7-17

1 July 1917

My own darling Con,

I got your notita with the two snaps of Bindy. That one of her standing on the lawn in her pyjamas is quite good, and does look cheery and well. One cannot see much of Nancy but what one does looks quite A1, and seems to be in fine condition.

Eric has not gone yet, and I am going to see him this evening, it is rotten luck and hope that there is nothing sticking in his way.

Another Military Cross has been given to one of the officers in this battery, so are getting quite well off for them. He well deserved it. He is the Irish boy named Walker, and in 3 days will be off on leave, so will have something to show for his work, and his people will be very bucked about it.

Had a notita from Lucy, he had just heard of Flurry's death through Mr. Clive, and seems very cut up about it. He hopes to be out in another month and in all probability come somewhere round this district.

Yesterday I had a fine hot bath, the first one for at least 6 weeks and you may bet I thoroughly enjoyed it and had a good old soak. Next Friday we are getting up some sports for the men and also a concert and few barrels of beer and they will enjoy the latter more than anything.

Fancy American troops already in the country, they have been pretty smart about it, and hope they will do a lot of good and prove fine fighters, but this modern warfare will be a new experience to them. The Bosch seems to be going hard at the French, but not getting much for their pain. It is the awful catastrophe that Russia has been so broken to pieces, if they had only put up a really good offensive I believe that the war would have been over this year, and now I have no hopes of it unless we have some extraordinary piece of luck.

Must close up as am just off to tea and then into see Eric, so night night and just tons of love to you all.

Your loving
Harold

1 July –	At wagon lines, dine with Eric at Poperinge. Fine day.
2 July –	At wagon lines. Quiet day.

6-7-17

3 July 1917

Darling Con,

Am just off for 4 days rest and will be very close to Kathleen, so will go and see her. No time for more as we have a cricket match on.

Heaps of love
Harold

3 July – Went to Boulogne with Leith, arrived 4.30 p.m. Fine hot day.

☆☆☆☆☆☆☆☆☆☆☆☆☆☆☆

6-7-17

Hotel De Paris – Boulogne-Sur-Mer
4 July 1917

My own darling Con,

Just a wee notita *(short note)* to say that I have arrived here safely and hope to remain about 3 days, and only wish that you could slip across and keep me company. We arrived about 6 p.m., had dinner and then a stroll on the promenade which was very nice, now it is 11.30 so am going to turn in for a real good sleep.

My teeth are pretty rotten so expect to spend most of my time at the dentist, as I want to get them well fixed up before I go into the line once more. If I get half a chance will run up and see Kathleen, but she is about 13 miles from here and the trains are rotten.

Saw a lot of leave-boats off, and would just have loved to have jumped into them, and seen my little family, never mind, hope it will soon come or the time fly quickly until it does.

The Russians gave me quite a shock, and only hope that they really mean to put up a good fight, as it will make all the difference to the whole show. There are quite a lot of Americans about here and look a smart lot, chiefly doctors and we all know that they are good.

Well I do not expect a notita from you for 4 or 5 days, but keep very fit and just tons and tons of love to you and the wee lassies.

Your loving
Harold

4 July – Shopped morning, went to see Kathleen at Camiere, had a long walk home, 9 miles and then trained it.
Fine.

5 July – Slacked about beach etc.
Grand day, rained evening.

10-7-17

6 July 1917

My own darling Con,

Here I am at the end of my 3 days, and we return to the battery tonight. Anyhow have had a very good time of it and feel all the better for it. Unfortunately they could give me very little attendance on my teeth and only got one stopped, and the others will have to stick it until I come out again.

The day before yesterday I went up to see Kathleen in the afternoon, and was lucky enough to find her off duty, so we went and had tea at a small hotel on the lakeside and spent the best 2 hours I have had for a long time. She is looking very fit and is very cheery as usual, and was in great form. The only thing that she was down hearted about is that the place has been taken over by Americans, and do not think she likes them particularly, and do not blame her. Anyhow she hopes to be shifted soon and get under the British again.

There are some topping places among the sand hills where one could spend a ripping fortnight, and only wish it was us two. I have been stopping in the town the whole time, and today has been the only day warm enough for a bathe, so this morning in we went and had a good 10 minutes of it, but was cold to stop in any longer. Then we had lunch and a good slack on the beach where I carefully fell asleep, and so have turned very sunburnt. I tried to get Kathleen to come down and spend the afternoon with me, but she said that it was quite impossible, sickening rot, and so much red tape about it all. Outside bathing and a stroll there is nothing to do here, and the most annoying part of it all is that every morning when I get up I see old leave-boats steam out, and know very well what it feels like to be on it, but it is rotten to be off it. Anyhow one of these days I will be on it and hurrah for it.

Am just off to have my last little dinner here, all specially ordered, so hope it will not result in indi. When I get back there should be a lot of letters waiting for me, and hope they have got the best of news in it, and all in top-hole.

Heaps and heaps of love to you and the little ones, there were one or two fine kiddies on the sands, and made me long to have Bindy to romp about with.

Your loving
Harold

6 July –   Slacked and bathed.
           Fine day.
7 July –   Returned to wagon lines Ourderdom and went and took over guns on canal bank.
           Fine hot day.

☆☆☆☆☆☆☆☆☆☆☆☆☆☆☆

11-7-17

8 July 1917

My own darling Con,

I got your notita with the photos of the locust. They look quite a healthy fine lot, and *Lucero* must have done them a lot of good, only they might have had the decency of allowing the alfalfa to live. The one of Johnnie is very good, but he has got much greyer, but on the whole looks quite fit on it, but should very much like to see him again.

I got back from my three days leave, which I thoroughly enjoyed, and could well do with another sample of it, and has done me a lot of good although I got a rotten cold, but glad to say it is getting better, and will be quite alright in a few days time.

I also hope to get my Captain's pips very soon, but do not say anything about it, as it may not come off for sometime. Am sorry to say that we are going to lose our old Colonel very shortly, and only hope the next will be as fine a fellow. We have now got a new Major, a very fine fellow and good sort, he stands about 6ft 3ins, and has feet a good deal larger than mine, so you can imagine what they are like. We are not sure whether he is going to remain, but very much hope so.

My boils have quite gone, and only had the two, which did not trouble me much.

We had a great lunch with strawberries and raspberries, the latter were very fine and a grand flavor. If ours at *Lucero* turn out as good am afraid I will make myself ill over them.

Fancy Tommy Wood being engaged, he will be very bucked, and hope she is a fine girl, and when she is expecting I hope he will have a little more consideration for her than he had for Mrs. Lindsell when she was in that way, anyhow he will be a little wiser.

I think that we could have managed the 3 months alright, but probably Mr. King has other ideas. That is a fine price for a bull, and hope Carlos had good luck with it. It is a little fortune and wish we could afford to do a thing like that. What a pity the frost began so early, hope they have not continued, or we will be having another winter like the last one, which will rather knock things on the head.

Yes, by Lucy's note he said that Young's brother had died through a mortal wound, but probably she has not heard, and so as well not to say anything for the present.

You must have enjoyed your day in town, and if I were you would have gone to a theatre, but expect you had a lot to do. By the way how is the bank getting along? Will enclose a cheque for £50 in a couple of weeks time, and also write to L. & Co., as up to date I have not written, but will do so as soon as possible.

So Helen is off to Bethnal Green, wonder how she will like it, isn't it somewhere in London?

I think that you are mistaken about the photo, as I was and am in very fine condition, and weigh kilos. I would like a snap of you, you always send me snaps of the kiddies, but none of your dear self, so buck up and send one along.

Must close, heaps and heaps of love, and a great kiss to each of you.

Your loving
Harold

8 July – Round forward position and looked for new observation post to support line trenches. Fine day.

9 July – At guns all day. Shelled heavily, no damage. Fine.

15-7-17

10 July 1917

My own darling Con,

The weather has turned beautifully cool, and is just right, only one does not want to sit very long in one place. Expect it is the same with you, as there is a north wind on the go. We are now in quite a comfortable place and have good dugouts, which makes all the difference to these pré-história dwelling places.

The new major is a great person and quite the opposite to the last one, which makes all the difference to life, and now will be able to get on very well, the only objection is that he may not remain on.

The Russian offensive seems to have quietened now and hope they will make a really good combined shove, and break through.

Thanks for writing to the Daimler Company, and am sure that you did it very nicely. It will be topping to get into our old bus once more and feel it spinning along those fine Argentine roads, with a nice little purr to help us along.

Yes, I have seen any amount of the Baly show, and thoroughly fed up with it. There must still be plenty of paper in England and plenty of shipping to carry it about so no need for Bosch to think that we will be starved out; and in his own self I do not think that he can believe it. That is, if we can take all precautions, and at the end of this summer will be only too glad to sign peace, and so will everybody else, including myself.

I met Eric's Captain on his way for leave, he seemed very bucked to get away, and will find old England at a really good time, and should have a great time of it.

What is the Perambulator Service, anything to do with babies or what? Never heard of it before, so enlighten me on the matter.

Must close now, just heaps and heaps of love. Keep very fit and well.

Your loving
Harold

10 July –   At guns all day, fired 40 rds. for registration.
Fine day, dull.

16-7-17

11 July 1917

My own darling Con,

Just a wee notitia before the post goes. There is absolutely no news, so will be a very rotten notita.

Bindy seems to be a great person with her visitors, and by your description seems to take very good charge of them, and hope she stands no nonsense and puts her foot down sternly.

More good news of the Russians has come along and they look like keeping up the attack, it will be topping if they do really well, and will end the war this year. There seems to be some trouble in Germany that is political, of course it may be some bluff, but personally I think that they have had enough of it, and if all goes well shortly it will upset them a little more.

No, I have not had any toothache, and hope not to get any more, but will try to get my teeth well seen to whenever I get a chance.

Am afraid that Susan is not very fit and Eric has done his best to get away. Do not say anything about the under mentioned. They are taking officers of under 30 from the A.S.C. *(Army Service Corps)* and putting them into the infantry, and I hear that Eric may possibly go, but I sincerely hope not. So have asked my Colonel to put him into the artillery, but he says he can do very little, but that if he does get in he will endeavor to get him into our little lot, which would be topping. I think that they should consider married men and take all the single ones first, and hope that they do. Do not say a word about this to anybody, as maybe Susan knows nothing about it, and just as well.

Must close with just heaps and heaps of love to you and the wee ones, and bless you all.

       Your loving
       Harold

August 1917

Bindy and Nancy – date unknown.

> Well she spoke with her eyes
> they were filled with despair.
> Generations of sadness
> were burning in there.
> She's a dream I once had
> She's my imaginary girl.
> Hunters and Collectors – *Imaginary Girl*

Nelson
New Zealand
2017

Dear Harold,

This is a letter I wish I were not writing to you, your wounds have taken you out of action, but as to what those wounds were I have no idea. You have moved from the frontline to the 20th General Hospital in Camier, France. You mentioned that Kathleen was nursing there; I hope she was stationed at this hospital, but once again that is a detail I have no answer to. Nursing throughout the war was tough, dangerous and extremely hard work, the facilities were limited and crude but I have no doubt everyone did their absolute best. There were no antibiotics to help tackle infections, and many succumbed to them after enduring surgery. Despite a constant battle to keep the hospitals clean, scabies and lice were a problem. The hospitals treated far more than wounds, they also had to deal with a wide variety of complaints from trench foot to sexually transmitted diseases.

Con was able to visit you, I don't know how long she was able to stay, but I suspect the rules around such visits were pretty strict. The girls stayed with Dandan and their nanny, Alice, at *Westhanger* and I am sure they were well looked after. Con sent the girls a couple of postcards and I know she so wished she was taking you home with her.

6 August 1917

My Darling Bindy,

You are a year and 11 months old. Thank you very much for your nice letter & the lavender you picked for Daddie. He keeps some of it in a little bag beside his bed to smell & Daddie sends Bindy a big kiss for picking it for him. Please kiss Nancy for Daddie & Mummy. I hope she is a good girl. Do you swim in your bath & have cold water in the sponge put down your back now? I hope Dandan gets home from London in time to say goodnight. Give him a kiss from Mummy please & another big one for Bindy.
From her loving
Mummy

I don't have a date for the second card, the one of the smiley little girl with flowers, but the words on it, Bonne Fete, mean Happy Birthday and so I imagine you both sent it to Bindy for her second birthday, although it was unsigned.

> My Darling Bindy,
> Isn't this a nice Baba?
> Mummy has got Daddie in France and is going to try and bring him home very soon to Bindy and Nancy. Daddie sends you and Nancy a big kiss and so does your own Mummy.

And so I leave you in your hospital bed, no doubt on the officer's ward, wondering what is coming next for you. I hope you could close your eyes and dream of *Lucero*, the Southern Cross lighting up the night sky and the silence of your home instead of the banging of guns. I hope your dreams included the paraíso trees getting ready for spring, the horses in the paddocks, and your little girls delighting in their home as you and Con watch them grow up.
With love
Sheila

26 September 1917

In Memory of
Second Lieutenant
Harold Methven Musson
M C
"D" Bty. 149th Bde., Royal Field Artillery who died on 26 September 1917 Age 33

Son of Christopher Joseph and Kate Musson (nee Methven); husband of Constance M. Musson, of 79, Belsize Park Gardens, Hampstead, London.

Remembered with Honour
Etaples Military Cemetery

Commemorated in perpetuity by
the Commonwealth War Graves Commission

Death came, the gallant escort.
He held his hand
And silently walked him to the other side.

Sheila Kennard

Nelson
New Zealand
2017

Dear Harold,

The last great mystery of you eluded me, I don't know how you were wounded or exactly when. I do have the War Diaries of your Brigade from the National Archives, but July 1917 is missing. You are, however, mentioned on the 9th April as having done good work.

Your last letter left me with an abrupt ending, of course that is what many soldiers of all the nations had – one moment here, the next gone. However, the last line of your letter was different to the rest, ending with "bless you all". I wonder if somewhere deep inside you that you realised that your luck was running out and your ladder to the stars was beckoning you.

I am so glad Con was able to spend some time with you, but once again I have no idea how long she was able to spend in France while you were a patient in the *20th General Hospital* in Camiers. In her postcard to Bindy she indicates she hopes to bring you home, but you never did make it back to Blighty. I also have the hospital diaries and they also give me no indication, apart from noting on the 26th September that 1 person died – that must have been you. I guess that you succumbed to an infection that you could not pull yourself out of. You do have a grave, and rest, I hope peacefully in the Étaples Military Cemetery.

Your notice of probate tells me that you left £913 11s 1d to Con. Of course you left so much more in terms of your bloodline family, which has flourished; your children, grandchildren, great grandchildren and great-great grandchildren would fill you with pride. They have all found their way, their paths all very different and yet they arrive at the same place, determined to make the world a more peaceful place.

And so ends my journey with you, not a journey that holds a map, but one we simply navigated together. I am so grateful that I chose to tell your story. One hundred years on from your premature departure we have reached across time and walked the same road, our red thread tangled but not broken.

Until we meet again.

Bless you Harold.
With love
Sheila x

October 1917

As the stars that shall be bright when we are dust,
Moving in marches upon the heavenly plain;
As the stars that are starry in the time of our darkness,
To the end, to the end, they remain.

Laurence Binyon - *For the Fallen*

The Lodge,
New Romney
Kent
10 October 1917

Dear Mrs. Musson,

It is with very deep regret I read in the paper today of the death of your husband, who was in my battery in France.

Your husband was a universal favourite and greatly admired by all of us. He was always so cheerful under the worst of conditions. He never knew what fear was, though severely tested on many occasions. Men such as he are a great loss to the army, and all those who, like myself, had the pleasure of knowing him.

Please accept my heartfelt sympathies in your very great loss.

Yours sincerely

Major Travers Kirkland

Field
11.10.17

Dear Mrs. Musson,

It was with great regret and sorrow that I heard of the great loss you have suffered.

Lt. Musson and I have been together since his transfer from the 150th Brigade in January and it was with great sorrow that I learnt that the life of such a fine character and true gentleman had been cut off in the prime of life. He was loved and respected by all who came into contact with him and was the bravest of men I have had the pleasure of meeting out here.

All the officers and men wish me to convey to you their sincere sympathy in your deep bereavement and I trust that God will comfort you and give you strength in this hour of trial.

Yours sincerely

W.E. Jones – Capt. Rtd.

D/149th Bde RFA

12-10-17

Dear Mrs. Musson,

I am writing to ask if you could spare me a photo of your dear husband?

While he was here at No. 20 General Hospital APO.S/18 BE7 France, I saw so much of him and his beautiful and affectionate character, that I was greatly impressed, and valued him in those short few weeks as a real friend. I should value his likeness immensely.

I often think of you and should be very pleased to hear how you are. Dear Musson was one of those devout men, who leave a lovely record behind them; it was a privilege to have known him. I can only dimly realise what your loss must be; but what a beautiful remembrance he will ever be to you. We can still remember him in Paradise.

I am yours very sincerely
Charles E. Matthews – Senior Chaplain

Harold Methven Musson

Courage is the resistance to fear,
mastery of fear –
not absence of fear.
Mark Twain

Con, Bindy and Nancy – date unknown.

Deep peace of the Running Wave to you.
Deep peace of the Flowing Air to you.
Deep peace of the Quiet Earth to you.
Deep peace of the Shining Stars to you.
Deep peace of the Gentle Night to you.
Deep peace of the Son of Peace to you.
Celtic Blessing.

Acknowledgements

Sky Full of Stars is the result of teamwork, although it is interesting to note that members of the team were long dead when I wrote this book. However, if it were not for them this book would not exist. My gratitude to all the cast of this work is limitless, for all the sacrifice and gifts they offered to future generations.

In the early days I had four student proofreaders who donated their time, Lyn Connor, Kevin Sanderson, Fleur Miller and Rosie Roberts. Thank you for all the corrections and suggestions you made. The final proofing and editing is the work of Odette Singleton-Wards aka Eagle Eye Odey, I owe her a huge thank you for all the help in pulling everything together into this book. Also thanks to Copy Press, Nelson, New Zealand for their work in taking my manuscript and making it into a book.

The cover is the amazing work of Denise Tombs, in my wildest dreams I had not imagined such a beautiful cover, the juxtaposition of Étaples Cemetery and the night sky with the Southern Cross. Thank you for your vision.

My thanks also to the families of Neil Fraser-Tytler, Florence Crimmin, and John Argentine Campbell for opening their doors to me as I searched for their ancestors. To Horace Laffaye and John Daffurn who happily shared information with me.

To all my friends who have cheered me on along the way, you have no idea how much you helped to validate my work, thank you for all the loud and silent cheers that came my way.

Finally, a huge heartfelt thanks to all my family who have helped along the way, Angela and Olivia for the photographs of their grandparents. To my wonderful husband, Jim, who trusted me with these precious letters and let me do as I wished with them. Finally a big thank you to my granddaughter, Isla Beth, who unwittingly gifted me the inspiration to undertake this work.

Bibliography & Resources

Books:
Field Guns in France, Neil Fraser-Tytler; The Naval and Military Press Ltd.
Seeking John Campbell, John Daffurn; Eptex.
Polo In Argentina: A History, Horace Laffaye; McFarland.
Testament Of Youth, Vera Brittain; Virago.
Now It Can Be Told, Philip Gibbs; Garden City Publishing.

Websites:
www.longlongtrail.co.uk
1914-1918.invisionzone.com
www.forces-war-records.co.uk
http://www.planecrashinfo.com
http://shroudsofthesomme.com
http://www.rutlandremembers.org
Wikipedia, the free encyclopedia

Films:
Warhorse, directed by Steven Spielberg; Dreamworks Pictures.
The Crimson Field, a six-part series produced by the BBC.
Anzac Girls, a six-part series produced by Screen Time, Australia.

About the Author

Sky Full of Stars is Sheila's first venture into publishing her work; she has enjoyed the privilege of co-authoring a book with Harold Musson, long gone but with a strong determined voice.

Sheila has a degree in Social Policy from the University of Plymouth and has enjoyed a full and varied career both paid and voluntary, including the Samaritans, nursing premature babies, supporting women in violent relationships, a family mediator in a law firm and a bar girl in Hong Kong. She has a deep interest in all aspects of healing work and has a small complimentary healthcare practice. She considers some of her most important work to have been as a mother and grandmother. She lives in New Zealand with her husband Jim, their labrador and a three-legged cat.

www.sheilakennard.com

sheilakennard6@gmail.com

www.ingramcontent.com/pod-product-compliance
Lightning Source LLC
Chambersburg PA
CBHW061746290426
44108CB00028B/2910